Fin de Siècle Social Theory

Fin de Siècle Social Theory

Relativism, Reduction, and the Problem of Reason

JEFFREY C. ALEXANDER

VERSO

London • New York

First published by Verso 1995
© Verso 1995
All rights reserved

Verso
UK: 6 Meard Street, London W1V 3HR
USA: 180 Varick Street, New York NY 10014–4606

Verso is the imprint of New Left Books

ISBN 1–85984–996–2
ISBN 1–85984–091–4 (pbk)

British Library Cataloguing in Publication Data
A catalogue record for this book is available from the British Library

Library of Congress Cataloging-in-Publication Data
Alexander, Jeffrey C.
Fin de siècle social theory : relativism, reduction, and the
problem of reason / Jeffrey C. Alexander.
    p.   cm.
Includes bibliographical references and index.
ISBN 1–85984–996–2 (hbk.). — ISBN 1–85984–091–4 (pbk.)
1. Sociology—Philosophy. I. Title.
    HM24.A4648   1995
    301—dc20   95–13065   CIP

Typeset by Keystroke, Jacaranda Lodge, Wolverhampton
Printed in Great Britain by Biddles Ltd,
Guildford and King's Lynn

Contents

Acknowledgments

In the background of these papers are the tumultuous historical events of recent years, which have reflected, and reflected upon, the equally great if less historically significant transformations in social theory. If I have been fortunate enough to have been involved in some of these latter developments, it has been in part because of my participation in the Research Committee on Sociological Theory of the International Sociological Association, which I organized with my close Polish colleague, Piotr Sztompka, in the late 1980s. Meetings of this intimate, stimulating, and contentious group of supra-national intellectuals provided the initial occasions for developing the first and second chapters of this book. (The former was published in the *Zeitschrift für Soziologie* [Summer 1994] 23 (2): 165–98), the latter in Alexander and Sztompka, eds, *Rethinking Progress: Movements, Forces, and Ideas at the End of the 20th Century*, Boston: Unwin Hyman, 1990, pp. 15–38.) The occasion for the third chapter was an equally challenging forum organized – or should I say provoked? – by my friend Steven Seidman. (It was published in Seidman and David Wagner, eds, *Postmodernism and General Social Theory*, New York: Blackwell, 1992, pp. 322–68.)

A stay in spring 1992 at the Swedish Center for Advanced Studies in the Social Sciences provided a welcome period of relief from the administrative and teaching responsibilites of American academic life. As I developed the fourth essay in this book (to be published in a reduced form as *La Réduction: Critique de Bourdieu*, Paris: CERF, 1995), and continued to refine the first, I welcomed particularly the collegiality of Bjorn Wittrock, one of the Directors of SCASSS, and two of my Fellows, Hans Joas and (again) Piotr Sztompka.

I have presented portions of the following at various departments and colloquia, and I invariably received criticisms which contributed significantly to the shape of these essays in their final form. I wish to record here my deep gratitude to all those who participated in this routine yet still so important form of collective exchange.

In addition to Piotr Sztompka and Steven Seidman, I would like to acknowledge the continuing importance of conversations with other colleagues and friends: in Sweden, with Ron Eyerman; in England, with Ken Thompson; and in Southern California, with J. Nicholas Entrikin, Roger Friedland, and Ivan Szelenyi.

Over the years I have been challenged and instructed by some very stimulating graduate students at UCLA, with whom I have been having monthly meetings of the 'Culture Club' for ten years. For the essays here I would particularly note the contributions of Philip Smith, Steven Sherwood, Anne Kane, and Eric Rambo.

During the period of the final preparation of these essays, particularly the first and the fourth, I had the good fortune to be spending my sabbatical year in Paris, during which time I was affiliated successively with the Institute des Etudes Politiques (Sciences Po), the Ecole des Hautes Etudes en Sciences Sociales, and the University of Bordeaux. For these opportunities, which simultaneously provided intellectual stimulation and a space for reflection, I would like to thank Alain Touraine and his colleagues at CADIS, particularly François Dubet and Michel Wieviorka. I could not fail to mention, as well, the Parisian collegiality of Daniel Dayan, Laurent Thevenot, Luc Boltanski, Frederic Vandenberghe, Erhard Friedberg, Didier Lapyronnie, François Chazel, Raymond Boudon, and Philip Besnard, all of whom have discussed with me the themes of this book.

While they contributed significantly to the ideas that inform these essays, I cannot, in good faith, hold any of the above-mentioned colleagues responsible for the particular arguments which follow. I should like to thank Simon Prosser, who came up with the title.

Jeffrey C. Alexander
Rue du Val de Grace
July 1994

Introduction

The essays collected here have been provoked by a dilemma. In the course of our century, the preeminence of reason has declined; at the same time, confidence in the ability to be reasonable has become more important than ever before.

It is a mistake to think that reason became central to Western society and social thought only with the development of science, capitalism, and secularism. It was the religious tradition of Judaism and Christianity that established the notion that the world is organized according to God's reason, that the force organizing the world makes abstract demands binding on all human beings, that between our emotions and subjectivities on earth and the objective demands of this universal reasonableness there is an unbridgeable gap generating continuous tension. It was the transcendental leverage of this objectivizing and universalizing religion that fuelled demands for practical perfectionism in this world, and provided, in the critical transition to 'modernity,' a capacity for transformation unprecedented in the other civilizations of the world.

In the sixteenth and seventeenth centuries, with the emergence of modern science and secular social thought, 'reason' was cut off from godly reasonableness and earthly development was understood finally as going its separate way. It remained linear, historical, and ruled by a powerful conception of impersonal and objective force, but it no longer possessed the satisfying and reassuring sense of an ultimate telos, which the transcendental anchorage had provided.

Dreams of salvation became displaced by dreams of reason. Social thinkers came to believe that human beings possessed an innate capacity for transparent and logical thought. They believed that institutions could be developed to express these capacities and that infinite progress and perpetual peace would result. In the early period of 'modernity,' laypeople and sophisticates alike were confident of their abilities to exercise reason. One thinks particularly of the empiricist and rationalist thinkers in the seventeenth and eighteenth centuries, but even the Romantics were enthusiastic. This high confidence coincided with social developments, with the first blush of the theoretical and applied sciences, with the astonishing power of industrial capitalism. It permeated the work of early social thinkers, from Hobbes and Rousseau to Saint-Simon, Comte, and Spencer. In psychology, in art, in economics, and in politics, thinkers advanced perspectives that had a decidedly rationalist form.

This dream of reason foundered in the twentieth century, which had been inaugurated with such hopes for its triumphs. Reason came to ruin in society and in social thought. It was not only the capitalist economies based on applied reason and purportedly rational exchanges that failed, producing conflict and instability on a massive scale. The ethical rationality of Western culture gave way to a ferocious and debilitating upsurge of racism and xenophobia. Within secular culture itself there opened a terrifying chasm of alienation and ennui.

Apparently people were not able to be rational, or at least to continue being so, in the narrow and ultimately impoverishing sense that the initial phases of 'modernity' proposed. This understanding overlooked the unconscious sources of action, of thought, and of social order itself; it failed to thematize the role of intense emotions and of fantasies about love and hate. Most of all, the rationalist perspective overlooked the continuing need that human beings have to make their worlds meaningful, symbolically coherent, patterned, and organized 'as if' the telos provided by the transcendental world still held good in a secularized way.

These needs, these dimensions of life, were denied by the early versions of rationalist thought. As a result, for many of the most creative and sensitive thinkers and artists in the twentieth century, reason came to be experienced as absent, as alienated from itself. Rather than human-made, the world was theorized as nonhuman and oppressive. 'Social forces,' it was said, produced dehumanization, passivity, and a flight from responsibility. Many thinkers and actors came to believe that only sadistic acts of spontaneous, emotionally charged violence could break the 'machine,' could open up a space for new, more authentic forms of humanity and reason to be recognized again. The fateful dichotomy between violence and (degraded) reason – the reason that produced objectification and domination – was for the first time set firmly in place.

When the dream of reason turns into the nightmare of reason there are three possible reactions. The first is to declare the experiment of modernity a failure. The universalism of reason was a pretension, never a real possibility. By creating a fraudulent sense of expansion and scope, in fact, universalism actually was responsible for the vast scale of the disaster that reason created. Relativism and localism are the only standards that can inform a good society. Modernity leads to the Holocaust, postmodernity to tolerance. Objectivity leads to objectification. Only antifoundationalism can create a climate in which, because nothing is demanded, everything is given in return.

This first response to the crisis of reason is not new, but it has been recently revived and carries a certain caché in the postcommunist, postliberal, and postidealist world in which many people conceive of themselves as living today. The second response is at the moment less ideologically compelling but rests at the heart of some of the strongest and most ambitious analytical programs in contemporary social science. It is the response, not of relativism, but of reduction. Reason is not rejected as such, but it is reduced to a method rather than a cultural pattern or a substantive goal. This deracinating social scientific method allows us to see that reason and universal morality do not exist as such; they are merely reflections of social structures in particular forms. Equality is a reflection of bureaucratic levelling and the need for efficient forms of social control; democracy is a product of newly empowered classes in struggle; tolerance is produced by globalization and mobility, individuality by competitive markets and the overlapping networks of social life. There can, in fact, only be claims to reason, claims which function as strategies, as tools to accumulate power. The dream of reason was itself a strategy for domination. Its crisis is not a general problem for society but simply the failure of a specific project. There are other projects now, for which other ideologies are useful. It is pointless to evoke the criterion of universality as such.

In the essays that follow I will try to demonstrate that neither of these responses to the crisis of reason is authentic. First, neither is intellectually coherent. Relativism commits the *epistemological fallacy*, arguing from the presence of subjectivity in reasoning to the absence in reasoning of any universal scope. Reductionism commits the *socio-logical fallacy*, arguing from the social sources of ideas to the absence in ideas of anything other than their social source. Second, neither of these ideas is viable in a social or moral sense. Complex societies can be organized and integrated only if actors and collectivities share some kind of larger sensibility. This sensibility may be anticollective; it may be local and concrete; it may be taken for granted and never thematized in an explicit way. Nonetheless, some sensibility must be widely shared and binding on all concerned. Liberty, tolerance, participation, even multiculturalism depend on socially shared ideas that have a transcendent aim and a universalizing scope. Indeed, we can recognize the authenticity of others – we can positively acknowledge our fellow members of society in a concrete and realistic way – only if we see them as somehow like ourselves, as members of something larger than we are ourselves, as part of a common humanity that creates us as a social group. Reductionism, for its part, undermines the intellectual possibility of such ties just as surely as does relativism. It translates an analytic conception of causality into an attack on the integrity of subjective commitments and the morality of ideas. What would contemporary societies be like if actors and collectivities actually took their moral standards merely as mentalist replications of some 'underlying social structural reality,' the very proposition that reductionism so ardently maintains?

A third response to the crisis of reason is to incorporate relativism and social construction without giving up universalizing intent. It is to see that reason is not an innate capacity and that it must not be impoverished by being understood merely as a calculating tool. Reason is a complex and textured cultural construction, one that can be sustained only by a differentiated and powerful institutional base. Being reasonable, being objective, being tolerant, being inclusive, are symbolic codes and grand narratives which are rooted in traditions, not innate capacities. Despite their constructed quality, however, they can create the sense that the motives of others are transparent and they can induce a sense of responsibility and mutual respect. Reason versus relativism is a false and dangerous dichotomy. Yet the alternative must be something other than treating reason in a crudely reductive way, thus making it relative in a 'social' sense. Reason can constrain certain motives, actions, and social structures and in this sense is not relative to them at all.

It was in the midst of the nineteenth century that the debilitating responses of relativism and reduction first took serious hold. By the end of that century, the first *fin de siècle* period, a genuine crisis of reason was underway. Crystallized by new and persistent tendencies in social theory, its repercussions have been felt in disastrous ways, on the right and on the left, throughout the twentieth century. The founders of contemporary social theory – thinkers like Freud, Weber, Durkheim, and Simmel – participated in this rethinking of rationality but not in its moral or empirical annihilation. They rediscovered the irrational, but they did not give it pride of place. They devoted themselves to explaining irrationality but also to thinking about how it could be transformed and how, as a result, modernity could become a different kind of place.

As the twentieth century draws to a close, we have entered another *fin de siècle* period. For many Western intellectuals at least, recent historic events seem to belie the telos of rational progress. Relativism and reduction once again threaten to displace more reason-centered forms of thought. The ideas of the turn-of-the-century founders of social theory can guide us in formulating an appropriate response, but they must be deepened, more firmly grounded in postpositivism, and pushed beyond the moral and empirical cul-de-sac created by thinking about contemporary history in relation to 'modernization.' The creators of contemporary social theory, not only the first generation but the second generation as well – people like Lévi-Strauss, Parsons, and Keynes – remained fettered by the extraordinary domination that Western society exercised over the world, a domination that has begun to be broken down only in the present day. This fetter created even in the very sophisticated ideas of these thinkers a strong distinction between tradition and modernity, a linear idea of a historical break that suggested that the contemporary period, properly understood, would mark an end-point in history, after which nothing fundamental would ever be able to change.

The world in which we live and write today is a very different one. The forces and ideas that threaten reason and universalism also make it possible to rethink them in a fundamental way. The *assertion* of universality must give way to the *project* of universalism. Rationality must be conceived more as a discourse than an empirical fact. Modernity must be rejected as a developmental category, although 'modernity' can be understood as a linguistic signifier of the greatest import. We cannot be postmodern because we now understand that we never were modern. We cannot be relativists because we now understand that there never were any supra-historical absolutes. We cannot be reductionists because we now understand that the independence and universalism of reason are the very products of a good society itself.

1

Modern, Anti, Post, and Neo:
How Intellectuals Have Coded, Narrated, and Explained the 'New World of Our Time'

History is not a text, not a narrative, master or otherwise. [Yet] as an absent cause, it is inaccessible to us except in textual form, [and] our approach to it and to the Real itself necessarily passes through its prior textualization.

Fredric Jameson

Sometime during the mid-1970s, at the annual meeting of the American Sociological Association, a major debate erupted around modernization theory that crystallized a decade of social and intellectual change. Two speakers were featured, Alex Inkeles and Immanuel Wallerstein. Inkeles reported that his studies of 'modern man' (Inkeles and Smith 1974) had demonstrated that personality shifts toward autonomy and achievement were crucial and predictable results of social modernization, which revolved most centrally around the industrialization of society. The response to Inkeles was appreciative from many of the senior members of the audience, skeptical from the younger. Wallerstein responded to Inkeles in a manner that pleased the younger generation more. 'We do not live in a modernizing world but in a capitalist world,' he proclaimed (1979: 133), asserting that 'what makes this world tick is not the need for achievement but the need for profit.' When Wallerstein went on to lay out 'an agenda of intellectual work for those who are seeking to understand the *world systemic transition from capitalism to socialism in which we are living*' (1979: 135, original italics), he literally brought the younger members of the audience to their feet.[1]

Fifteen years later, the lead article in the *American Sociological*

Review was entitled 'A Theory of Market Transition: From Redistribution to Markets in State Socialism.' The transition referred to in this article was rather different from the one Wallerstein had in mind. Written by Victor Nee, once inclined to Maoism and now a rational choice theorist specializing in China's burgeoning market economy, the article suggested that the only hope for organized socialism was capitalism. In fact, Nee portrayed socialism exactly as Marx had depicted capitalism, and provoked remarkably similar expectations. State socialism, he wrote, was an archaic, outdated mode of production, one whose internal contradictions were leading to capitalism. Employing the class conflict analytic of Marx to the productive system that Marx believed would end such conflict for all time, Nee argued that it is state socialism, not capitalism, that 'appropriates surplus directly from the immediate producers and creates and structures social inequality through the processes of its reallocation' (1989: 665). Such expropriation of surplus – exploitation – can be overcome only if workers are given the opportunity to own and sell their own labor-power. Only with markets, Nee insisted, could workers develop the power to 'withhold their product' and protect their 'labor power' (ibid.: 666). This movement from one mode of production to another would shift power to the formerly oppressed class. 'The transition from redistribution to markets,' he concluded, 'involves a transfer of power favoring direct producers' (ibid.).

A New 'Transition'

In the juxtaposition between these formulations of modernity, socialism, and capitalism there lies a story. They describe not only competing theoretical positions but deep shifts in historical sensibility. We must understand both together, I believe, if either contemporary history or contemporary theory is to be understood at all.

Social scientists and historians have long talked about 'the transition.' A historical phrase, a social struggle, a moral transformation for better or for worse, the term referred, of course, to the movement from feudalism to capitalism. For Marxists, the transition initiated the unequal and contradictory system that produced its antithesis, socialism and equality. For liberals, the transition represented an equally momentous transformation of traditional society but created a set of historical alternatives – democracy, capitalism, contracts, and civil society – that did not have a moral or social counterfactual like socialism ready to hand.

In the last five years, for the first time in the history of social science, 'the transition' has come to mean something that neither of these earlier treatments could have foreseen. It is the transition from communism to capitalism, a phrase that seems oxymoronic even to our chastened ears. The sense of world-historical transformation remains, but the straight line of history seems to be running in reverse.

In this recent period we have witnessed perhaps the most dramatic set of spatially and temporally contiguous social transformations in the history of world. The more contemporary meaning of transition may not entirely eclipse the earlier one, yet there is no doubt that it has already diminished its significance and will arouse significantly more intellectual interest for a long time to come.

This second great transformation, to redirect Polanyi's (1957) famous phrase, has produced an unexpected, and for many an unwelcome, convergence in both history and social thought. It is impossible even for already committed intellectuals to ignore the fact that we are witnessing the death of a major alternative not only in social thought but in society itself.[2] In the foreseeable future, it is unlikely that either citizens or elites will try to structure their primary allocative systems in nonmarket ways.[3]

For their part, social scientists will be far less likely to think of anti-market 'socialist societies' as counterfactual alternatives with which to explain their own. They will be less likely to explain economic stratification by implicitly comparing it with an egalitarian distribution produced by publicly rather than privately held property, a 'plausible world' (Hawthorn 1991) that inevitably seems to suggest that economic inequality is produced by the existence of private property itself. Social scientists will, perhaps, also be less likely to explain status stratification by postulating the counterfactual tendency to communal esteem in a world that is uncorrupted by individualism of a bourgeois rather than socialist kind. Similarly, it will become much more difficult to speak about the emptiness of formal democracy, or to explain its limitations by pointing merely to the existence of a dominant economic class, for these explanations, too, require counterfactuals of a traditionally 'socialist' kind. In brief, it will be much less easy to explain contemporary social problems by pointing to the capitalist nature of the societies of which they are a part.

In this essay, I do not propose a return to 'convergence' or modernization theories of society as such, as some reinvigorated proponents of the early tradition (Inkeles 1991; Lipset 1990) apparently do.[4] I will propose, however, that contemporary social theory must be much more sensitive to the apparent reconvergence of the world's regimes and that, as a result, we must try to incorporate some broad sense of the universal and shared elements of development into a critical, undogmatic, and reflexive theory of social change. Indeed, in the conclusion of this essay I will demonstrate that a growing range of widely diverse contemporary social theorists, from literary radicals and rational choice theorists to postcommunists, are speaking convergence even if (apologies to Molière) they don't believe it is prose, and I will address the challenging question, recently raised so trenchantly by Muller (1992), of whether this emerging conversation can avoid the relatively simplistic and totalizing form that obliterated the complexities of earlier societies and the particularisms of our own.

Despite this new and more sophisticated form, however, what I will later call neo-modern theory will remain as much myth as science (Barbour 1974), as much narrative as explanation (Entrikin 1991). Even if one believes, as I do, that such a broader and more sophisticated theory of social development is now historically compelling, it remains the case that every general theory of social change is rooted not only in cognition but also in existence, that it possesses a surplus of meaning, in Ricoeur's (1977) deeply suggestive phrase. Modernity, after all, has always been a highly relativist term (Bourricaud 1987; Habermas 1981; Pocock 1987). It emerged in the fifth century when newly Christianized Romans wished to distinguish their religiosity from two forms of barbarians, the heathens of antiquity and the unregenerate Jews. In medieval times, modernity was reinvented as a term implying cultivation and learning, which allowed contemporary intellectuals to identify backward, with the classical learning of the Greek and Roman heathens themselves. With the Enlightenment, modernity became identified with rationality, science, and forward progress, a semantically arbitrary relationship that seems to have held steady to this day. Who can doubt that, sooner or later, a new historical period will displace this second 'age of equipoise' (Burn 1974) into which we have so inadvertently but fortuitously slipped. New contradictions will emerge and competing sets of world-historical possibilities will arise, and it is unlikely that they will be viewed in terms of the emerging neo-modernization frame.

It is precisely this sense of the instability, of the imminent transitoriness of the world, that introduces myth into social theory. Despite the fact that we have no idea what our historical possibilities will be, every theory of social change must theorize not only the past but the present and future as well. We can do so only in a nonrational way, in relation not only to what we know but to what we believe, hope, and fear. Every historical period needs a narrative that defines its past in terms of the present, and suggests a future that is fundamentally different, and typically 'even better,' than contemporary time. For this reason, there is always an eschatology, not merely an epistemology, in theorizing about social change.

I proceed now to examine early modernization theory, its contemporary reconstruction, and the vigorous intellectual alternatives that arose in the period between.[5] I will insist throughout on the relation of these theoretical developments to social and cultural history, for only in this way can we understand social theory not only as science but also as an ideology in the sense made famous by Geertz (1973). For unless we recognize the interpenetration of science and ideology in social theory, neither element can be evaluated or clarified in a rational way. With this stricture in mind, I delineate four distinctive theoretical-cum-ideological periods in postwar social thought: modernization theory and romantic liberalism; antimodernization theory and heroic radicalism; postmodern theory and comic detachment; and the emerging phase of neo-modernization or reconvergence theory, which seems to combine the narrative forms of each of its predecessors on the postwar scene.

While I will be engaging in genealogy, locating the historical origins of each phase of postwar theory in an archeological way, it is vital to keep in mind that each one of the theoretical residues of the phases which I examine remains vitally alive today. My archeology, in other words, is an investigation not only of the past but of the present. Because the present is history, this genealogy will help us to understand the theoretical sedimentation within which we live intellectually today.

Modernization: Code, Narrative, and Explanation

Drawing from a centuries-long tradition of evolutionary and Enlightenment-inspired theories of social change, 'modernization' theory as such was born with the publication of Marian Levy's book on Chinese family structure (1949) and died sometime in the mid-1960s, during one of those extraordinarily heated rites of spring that marked student uprisings, antiwar movements, and newly humanist socialist regimes, and which preceded the long hot summers of the race riots and Black Consciousness movement in the United States.

Modernization theory can and certainly should be evaluated as a scientific theory, in the postpositivist, *wissenschaftliche* sense.[6] As an explanatory effort, the modernization model was characterized by the following ideal-typical traits:[7]

1. Societies were conceived as coherently organized systems whose subsystems were closely interdependent.

2. Historical development was parsed into two types of social systems, the traditional and the modern, statuses which were held to determine the character of their societal subsystems in determinate ways.

3. The modern was defined with reference to the social organization and culture of specifically Western societies, which were typified as individualistic, democratic, capitalist, scientific, secular, and stable, and as dividing work from home in gender specifc ways.

4. As a historical process, modernization was held to involve non-revolutionary, incremental change.

5. The historical evolution to modernity – modernization – was viewed as likely to succeed, thus assuring that traditional societies would be provided with the resources for what Parsons (1966) called a general process of adaptive 'upgrading,' including economic take-off to industrialization, democratization via law, and secularization and science via education.

There were important aspects of truth in these models, which were articulated by thinkers of considerable historical and sociological insight. One truth, for example, lay in the insight that there are functional not merely idealistic exigencies that push social systems toward democracy, markets, and the universalization of culture, and that shifts toward 'modernity' in any subsystem create considerable pressures on the others to respond in a complementary way.[8] This understanding made it possible for the more sophisticated among them to make prescient predictions about the eventual instability of state socialist societies, thus avoiding the rational-is-the-real embarrassments encountered by theorists of a more leftist kind. Thus, Parsons (1971: 127) insisted long before perestroika 'that the processes of democratic revolution have not reached an equilibrium in the Soviet Union and that further developments may well run broadly in the direction of Western types of democratic government, with responsibility to an electorate rather than to a self-appointed party.' It should perhaps also be emphasized that, whatever their faults, modernization theorists were not provincials. Despite their ideological intent, the most important of them rarely confused functional interdependence with historical inevitability. Parsons's theorizing, for example (1964: 466, 474), stressed that systemic exigencies actually opened up the possibility of historical choice.

> Underneath the ideological conflicts [between capitalism and communism] that have been so prominent, there has been emerging an important element of very broad consensus at the level of values, centering in the complex we often refer to as 'modernization'. . . . Clearly, definite victory for either side is not the only possible choice. We have another alternative, namely, the eventual integration of both sides – and of uncommitted units as well – in a wider system of order.[9]

Despite these important insights, however, the historical judgment of subsequent social thought has not erred in its evaluation of modernization theory as a failed explanatory scheme. Neither non-Western nor precontemporary societies can be conceptualized as internally homogeneous (cf. Mann 1986). Their subsystems are more loosely coupled (e.g. Alexander and Colomy 1990; Meyer and Rowan 1977) and their cultural codes more independent (e.g. Hall 1985). Nor is there the kind of dichotomized historical development that can justify a single conception of traditional or modern, as Eisenstadt's (e.g. 1964; cf. Alexander 1992a) extensive investigations of 'Axial Age' civilizations make clear. Even the concept 'Western society,' built upon spatial and historical contiguity, fails sufficiently to recognize historical specificity and national variation. Social systems, more-over, are not as internally homogeneous as was supposed, nor are there necessarily grounds for optimism that modernization will succeed. In the first place, universalizing change is neither imminent nor developmental in an idealist sense; it is often abrupt, involving contingent positions of power, and can have murderous results.[10] In the second place, even if one were to accept a linear conceptual scheme, one would have to acknowledge Nietzsche's observation that historical regression is just as possible as progress, indeed, perhaps even more likely. Finally, modernization, even if it does triumph, does not necessarily increase social contentment. It may be that the more highly developed a society, the more it produces, encourages, and relies upon strident and often utopian expressions of alienation and criticism (Durkheim 1937 [1897]).

When we look back on a 'scientifically invalidated' theory that dominated the thinking of an entire intellectual stratum for two decades, those of us who are still committed to the project of a rational and generalizing social science will be inclined to ask ourselves: why was it believed? While we would ignore at our peril the partial truths of modernization theory, we would not be wrong to conclude that there were extra-scientific reasons involved. Social theory (Alexander and Colomy 1995) must be considered not only as a research program but as a generalized discourse, one very important part of which is ideology. It is as a meaning structure, as a form of existential truth, that social scientific theory functions effectively in an extra-scientific way.[11]

To understand modernization theory and its fate, then, we must examine it not only as a scientific theory but as an ideology – not in the mechanistic Marxist or more broadly Enlightenment sense (e.g. Boudon 1986) of 'false consciousness' but in the Geertzian (1973) one. Modernization theory was a symbolic system that functioned not only to explain the world in a rational way, but also to interpret the world in a manner that provided 'meaning and motivation' (Bellah 1970b). It functioned as a metalanguage that instructed people how to live.

Intellectuals must interpret the world, not simply change or even explain it. To do so in a meaningful, reassuring, or inspiring manner means that intellectuals must make distinctions. They must do so especially in regard to phases of history. If intellectuals are to define the 'meaning' of their 'time,' they must identify a time that preceded the present, offer a morally compelling account of why it was superseded, and tell their audiences whether or not such a transformation will be repeated vis-à-vis the world they live in. This is, of course, merely to say that intellectuals produce historical narratives about their own time.[12]

The ideological dimension of modernization theory is further illuminated by thinking of this narrative function in a structuralist, or semiotic, way (Barthes 1977). Because the existential unit of reference is one's own time, the empirical unit of reference must be totalized as one's own society. It must, in other words, be characterized as a whole regardless of the actual nature of its divisions and inconsistencies. Not only one's own time, then, but one's own society must be characterized by a single linguistic term, and the world that preceded the present must be characterized by another single broad term as well. In light of these considerations, the important ideological, or meaning-making, function that modernization theory served seems fairly clear. For Western but especially American and American-educated intellectuals, modernization theory provided a telos for postwar society by making it 'historical.' It did so by providing postwar society with a temporal and spatial identity, an identity that could be formed only in a relation of difference with another, immediately preceding time and place. As Pocock has recently emphasized, 'modernity' must be understood as the 'consciousness rather than the condition of being "modern".' Taking a linguistic model of consciousness, he suggests that such consciousness must be defined as much by difference as identification. The modern is a 'signifier' that functions as an 'excluder' at the same time.

> We call something (perhaps ourselves) modern in order to distance that of which we speak from some antecedent state of affairs. The antecedent is most unlikely to be of neutral effect in defining either what is to be called 'modern' or the 'modernity' attributed to it.
>
> (Pocock 1987: 48)

If I may give to this approach a late Durkheimian turn (Alexander 1989), I would like to suggest that we think of modernity as constructed upon a binary code. This code serves the mythological function of dividing the known world into the sacred and profane, thereby providing a clear and compelling picture of how contemporaries must act to maneuver the space in between.[13] In this sense, the discourse of modernity bears a striking resemblance to metaphysical and religious salvation discourse of diverse kinds (Walzer 1965; Weber 1964 [1922]). It also resembles the more secular dichotomizing discourses that citizens employ to identify themselves with, and to distance themselves from, the diverse individuals, styles, groups, and structures in contemporary societies (Bourdieu 1984; Wagner-Pacifici 1986).

It has been argued, in fact (Alexander 1992b; Alexander and Smith 1993), that a 'discourse of civil society' provides a structured semiotic field for the conflicts of contemporary societies, positing idealized qualities like rationality, individuality, trust, and truth as essential qualities for inclusion in the modern, civil sphere, while identifying qualities such as irrationality, conformity, suspicion, and deceit as traditional traits that demand exclusion and punishment. There is a striking overlap between these ideological constructions and the explanatory categories of modernization theory, for example Parsons's pattern variables. In this sense, modernization theory may be seen as a generalizing and abstracting effort to transform a historically specific categorial scheme into a scientific theory of development applicable to any culture around the entire world.

Because every ideology is carried by an intellectual cadre (Eisenstadt 1986; Konrad and Szelenyi 1979), it is important to ask why the intellectual cadre in a particular time and place articulated and promoted a particular theory. In regard to modernization theory, despite the importance of a small number of influential Europeans like Raymond Aron (c.g. Aron 1962), we are speaking primarily about American and American-educated intellectuals.[14] Following some recent work by Eyerman (1992; cf. Jamison and Eyerman 1994) on the formation of American intellectuals in the 1950s, I would begin by emphasizing the distinctive social characteristics of the postwar period in the United States, particularly the sharpness of the transition to the postwar world. This transition was marked by massive suburbanization and the decline of culturally bounded urban communities, a dramatic reduction in the ethnicity of American life, an extraordinary lessening of labor–capital conflict, and by unprecedented long-term prosperity.

These new social circumstances, coming as they did at the end of two decades of massive national and international upheaval, induced in postwar American intellectuals a sense of a fundamental historical 'break.'[15] On the left, intellectuals like C. Wright Mills and David Riesman issued jeremiads against what they feared was the massification of society. In the liberal center, theorists like Parsons suggested how the same transition had created a more egalitarian, more inclusive, and significantly more differentiated society.[16] On the right, there were cries of alarm about the disappearance of the individual in an authoritarian and bureaucratic welfare state (Buckley 1951; Rand 1957). On every side of the political spectrum, in other words, American intellectuals were motivated by a sense of dramatic and bifurcating social change. This was the social basis for constructing the traditional/modern binary code, an experience of bifurcation that demanded an interpretation of present anxieties, and future possibilities, in relation to the imagined past.

To fully understand the interrelation between history and theory that produced the new intellectuals, however, we must think about narrativity in addition to symbolic structure. In order to do so, we will draw upon the dramaturgical terms of genre theory, which stretches from Aristotle's poetics to the path-setting literary criticism of Northrop Frye (1957), which inspired the more recent 'negative hermeneutics' of historically oriented literary critics like White (1987), Jameson (1980), Brooks (1984), and Fussell (1975).[17]

In such dramaturgical terms we can characterize the historical period that preceded the era of modernization theory as one in which intellectuals 'inflated' the importance of actors and events by emplotting them in a heroic narrative. The 1930s and the war years that followed defined a period of intense social conflict that generated millennial – world-historical – hopes for utopian social transformation, either through communist and fascist revolutions or the construction of an unprecedented kind of 'welfare state.' Postwar American intellectuals, by contrast, experienced the social world in more 'deflationary' terms. With the failure of revolutionary proletarian movements in Europe and the head-long rush to normalization and demobilization in the United States, the heroic 'grand narratives' of collective emancipation seemed less compelling.[18] No longer was the present perceived primarily as a way station to an alternative social order, but, rather, as more or less the only possible system there ever could be.

Such a deflationary acceptance of 'this world' was not necessarily dystopian, fatalistic, or conservative. In Europe and America, for example, there emerged a principled anticommunism that wove together the bare threads of a collective narrative and committed their societies to social democracy. Yet, even for these reformist groups, the deflation of prewar social narratives had strong effects, effects that were very widely shared. Intellectuals as a group became more 'hard-headed' and 'realistic.' Realism diverges radically from the heroic narrative, inspiring a sense of limitation and restraint rather than idealism and sacrifice. Black and white thinking, so important for social mobilization, is replaced by 'ambiguity' and 'complexity,' terms favored by New Critics like Empson (1927) and particularly Trilling (1950), and by 'skepticism,' a position exemplified in Niebuhr's writings (e.g. Niebuhr 1952). The conviction that one has been 'born again' – this time to the *social* sacred – which inspires utopian enthusiasm, is succeeded by the 'thrice-born' chastened soul described by Bell (1962c) and by an acute sense that the social God has failed (Crossman 1950). Indeed, this new realism convinced many that narrative itself – history – had been eclipsed, which produced the representations of this newly 'modern' society as the 'end of ideology' (Bell 1962a) and the portrayal of the postwar world as 'industrial' (Aron 1962; Lipset and Bendix 1960) rather than as capitalistic.

Yet, while realism was a significant mood in the postwar period, it was not the dominant narrative frame through which postwar social science intellectuals charted their times. Romanticism was.[19] Relatively deflated in comparison with heroism, romanticism tells a story that is more positive in its evaluation of the world as it exists today. In the postwar period it allowed intellectuals and their audiences to believe that progress would be more or less continuously achieved, that improvement was likely. This state of grace referred, however, more to individuals than to groups, and to incremental rather than revolutionary change. In the new world that emerged from the ashes of war, it had finally become possible to cultivate one's own garden. This cultivation would be an enlightened, modernist work, regulated by the cultural patterns of achievement and neutrality (Parsons and Shils 1951), culminating in the 'active' (Etzioni 1968) and 'achieving' (McClelland 1953) society.

Romanticism, in other words, allowed America's postwar social science intellectuals, even in a period of relative narrative deflation, to continue to speak the language of progress and universalization. In the United States, what differentiates romantic from heroic narratives is the emphasis on the self and private life. In America's social narratives, heroes are epochal; they lead entire peoples to salvation, as collective representations like the American revolution and the civil rights movement indicate. Romantic evolution, by contrast, is not collective; it is about Tom Sawyer and Huck Finn (Fiedler 1955), about the yeoman farmer (Smith 1950), and Horatio Alger. American intellectuals, then, articulated modernization as a process that freed the self and made society's subsystems responsive to its needs. In this sense modernization theory was behavioral and pragmatic; it focused on real individuals rather than on a collective historical subject like nation, ethnic group, or class.

Existentialism was basic to the romantic American ideology of 'modernism.' American intellectuals, indeed, developed an idiosyncratic, optimistic reading of Sartre. In the milieu saturated with existentialism, 'authenticity' became a central criterion for evaluating individual behavior, an emphasis that was central to Lionel Trilling's (1955) modernist literary criticism but also permeated social theory that ostensibly did not advocate modernization, for example Erving Goffman's (1956) microsociology, with its equation of freedom with role distance and its conception of back-versus-front stage,[20] and David Riesman et al.'s (1950) eulogy for the inner-directed man.

These individualistic romantic narratives stressed the challenge of being modern, and they were complemented by an emphasis on irony, the narrative Frye defines as deflationary vis-à-vis romance but not downright negative in its effects. In the 1950s and early 1960s, the modernist aesthetic in Britain and America stressed irony, introspection, ambiguity. The dominant literary theory, so-called New Criticism, while tracing its origins back to Empson's *The Seven Types of Ambiguity* (1927), came into its own only after the heroic and much more historicist criticism of the 1930s. The key contemporary figure in American letters was Lionel Trilling, who defined the psychological and aesthetic goal of modernity as the expansion of complexity and tolerance for ambiguity. Psychoanalysis was a major critical approach, interpreted as an exercise in introspection and moral control (Rieff 1959). In graphic art, 'modern' was equated with abstraction, the revolt against decoration, and with minimalism, all of which were interpreted as drawing attention away from the surface and providing pathways into the inner self.

It is evidently difficult, at this remove, for contemporary postmodern and post-postmodern intellectuals to recapture the rich and, indeed, often ennobling aspects of this intellectual and aesthetic modernism, almost as difficult as it is for contemporaries to see the beauty and passion of modernist architecture that Pevsner (1949) so effectively captured in his epoch-defining *Pioneers of Modern Design*. The accounts of intellectual-cum-aesthetic modernism proffered by contemporary postmodernists – from Baumann (1989), Seidman (1991b), and Lasch (1985) to Harvey (1989) and Jameson (1988) – is a fundamental misreading. Their construction of it as dehumanizing abstraction, mechanism, fragmentation, linearity, and domination, I will suggest below, says much more about the ideological exigencies that they and other contemporary intellectuals are experiencing today than it does about modernism itself. In culture, in theory, and in art, modernism represented a spareness that devalued artifice not only as decoration but as pretension, and undercut utopianism as a collective delusion that was homologous with neurosis of an individual kind (Fromm 1955, 1956). It was precisely such admirable qualities that Bell (1976) designated as early or 'classical modernity' in his attack on the 1960s in *The Cultural Contradictions of Capitalism*.

This picture was not, of course, an entirely homogeneous one. On the right, engagement in the Cold War provided for some intellectuals a new field for collective heroism, despite the fact that America's most influential modernist thinkers were not as a rule Cold Warriors of the most righteous kind. On the left, both within and outside the US, there were important islands of social criticism that made self-conscious departures from romanticism of both a social democratic and individualist ironic sort.[21] Intellectuals influenced by the Frankfurt School, like Mills and Riesman, and other critics, like Arendt, refused to legitimate the humanism of this individualist turn, criticizing what they called the new mass society as forcing individuals into an amoral, egotistical mode. They inverted modernization theory's binary code, viewing American rationality as instrumental rather than moral and expressive, big science as technocratic rather than inventive. They saw conformity rather than independence; power elites rather than democracy; and deception and disappointment rather than authenticity, responsibility, and romance.

In the 1950s and early 1960s, these social critics did not become highly influential. To do so they would have had to pose a compelling alternative, a new heroic narrative to describe how the sick society could be transformed and a healthy one put in its place.[22] This was impossible to do in the deflationary times. Fromm's *Art of Loving* (1956) followed his denunciation of *The Sane Society* (1955); in the fifties, social solutions often were contained in individual acts of private love. No social program issued from Adorno et al.'s *Authoritarian Personality* (1950). Not only did C. Wright Mills fail to identify any viable social alternatives in his stream of critical studies (see n. 32 below), but he went out of his way to denounce the leaders of the social movements of the thirties and forties as 'the new men of power' (Mills 1948). After nearly twenty years of violence-producing utopian hopes, collective heroics had lost their sheen. The right-wing populism of McCarthy reinforced the withdrawal from public life. Eventually, however, Americans and Western Europeans did catch their breath, with results that must be related, once again, to history and social theory alike.

Antimodernization Theory: The Heroic Revival

Sometime in the later 1960s, between the assassination of President Kennedy and the San Francisco 'summer of love' of 1967, modernization theory died. It died because the emerging younger generation of intellectuals could not believe it was true.

Even if we regard social theory as semiotic system rather than pragmatically inducted generalization, it is a sign system whose signifieds are empirical reality in a rather strictly disciplined sense. So it is important to recognize that during this second postwar period serious 'reality problems' began to intrude on modernization theory in a major way. Despite the existence of capitalist markets, poverty persisted at home (Harrington 1962) and perhaps was even increasing in the third world. Revolutions and wars continually erupted outside of Europe and North America (Johnson 1983), and sometimes even seemed to be produced by modernization itself. Dictatorship, not democracy, was spreading throughout the rest of the world (Moore 1966); postcolonial nations seem to require an authoritarian state (Huntington 1968) and a command economy to be modern, not only in the economy and state but in other spheres as well. New religious movements (Bellah and Glock 1976) emerged in Western countries and in the developing world, with sacralization and ideology gaining ground over secularization, science, and technocracy. These developments strained the central assumptions of modernization theory, although they did not necessarily refute it.[23]

Factual problems, however, are not enough to create scientific revolutions. Broad theories can defend themselves by defining and protecting a set of core propositions, jettisoning entire segments of their perspective as only peripherally important. Indeed, if one looks closely at modernization theory during the middle and late 1960s, and even during the early 1970s, one can see an increasing sophistication as it geared up to meet its critics and to address the reality problems of the day. Dualistic simplifications about tradition and modernity were elaborated – not replaced by – notions that portrayed a continuum of development, as in the later neo-evolutionary theories of Parsons (1964, 1966, 1971), Bellah (1970a), and Eisenstadt (1964). Convergence was reconceptualized to allow parallel but independent pathways to the modern (e.g. Shils [1972] on India, Eisenstadt [1963] on empires, Bendix [1964] on citizenship). Notions like diffusion and functional substitutes were proposed to deal with the modernization of non-Western civilizations in a less ethnocentric manner (Bellah 1957; Cole 1979). The postulate of tight subsystem links was replaced by the notion of leads and lags (Smelser 1968), the insistence on interchange became modified by notions of paradoxes (Schluchter 1979), contradictions (Eisenstadt 1963), and strains (Smelser 1963). Against the metalanguage of evolution, notions about developmentalism (Schluchter and Roth 1979) and globalism (Nettl and Robertson 1968) were suggested. Secularity gave way to ideas about civil religion (Bellah 1970b) and to references to 'the tradition of the modern' (Gusfield 1966).

Against these internal revisions, antagonistic theories of anti-modernization were proposed on the grounds that they were more valid explanations of the reality problems that emerged. Moore (1966) replaced modernization and evolution with revolution and counter-revolution. Thompson (1963) replaced abstractions about evolving patterns of industrial relations with class history and consciousness from the bottom up. Discourse about exploitation and inequality (e.g. Goldthorpe et al. 1969; Mann 1973) contended with, and eventually displaced, discussions of stratification and mobility. Conflict theories (Coser 1956; Dahrendorf 1959; Rex 1961) replaced functional ones; state-centered political theories (Bendix et al. 1968; Collins 1976; Skocpol 1979; Evans et al., 1985) replaced value-centered and multi-dimensional approaches; and conceptions of binding social structures were challenged by microsociologies that emphasized the liquid, unformed, and negotiated character of everyday life.

What pushed modernization theory over the edge, however, were not these scientific alternatives in and of themselves. Indeed, as I have indicated, the revisors of the earlier theory had themselves begun to offer coherent, equally explanatory theories for many of the same phenomena. The decisive fact in modernization theory's defeat, rather, was the destruction of its ideological, discursive, and mythological core. The challenge that finally could not be met was existential. It emerged from new social movements that were increasingly viewed in terms of collective emancipation – peasant revolutions on a world-wide scale, black and Chicano national movements, indigenous people's rebellions, youth culture, hippies, rock music, and women's liberation. Because these movements (e.g. Weiner 1984), profoundly altered the *Zeitgeist* – the experienced tempo of the times – they captured the ideological imaginations of the rising cadre of intellectuals.

In order to represent this shifting empirical and existential environment, intellectuals developed a new explanatory theory. Equally significant, they inverted the binary code of modernization and 'narrated the social' (Sherwood 1994) in a new way. In terms of code, 'modernity' and 'modernization' moved from the sacred to the profane side of historical time, with modernity assuming many of the crucial characteristics that had earlier been associated with traditionalism and backwardness. Rather than democracy and individualization, the contemporary modern period was represented as bureaucratic and repressive. Rather than a free market or contractual society, modern America became 'capitalist,' no longer rational, interdependent, modern, and liberating but backward, greedy, anarchic, and impoverishing.

This inversion of the sign and symbols associated with modernity polluted the movements associated with its name. The death of liberalism (Lowi 1969) was announced, and its reformist origins in the early twentieth century dismissed as a camouflage for extending corporate control (Kolko 1967; Weinstein 1968). Tolerance was associated with fuzzy-mindedness, immorality, and repression (Wolff et al. 1965). The asceticism of Western religion was criticized for its repressive modernity and Eastern and mystical religious were sacralized instead (Brown 1966; cf. Brown 1959). Modernity was equated with the mechanism of the machine (Roszak 1969). For the third world, democracy was defined as a luxury, strong states a necessity. Markets were not luxuries but enemies, for capitalism came to be represented as guaranteeing underdevelopment and backwardness. This inversion of economic ideals carried into the first world as well. Humanistic socialism replaced welfare state capitalism as the ultimate symbol of the good. Capitalist economies were held to produce only great poverty and great wealth (Kolko 1962), and capitalist societies were viewed as sources of ethnic conflict (Bonacich 1972), fragmentation, and alienation (Ollman 1971). Not market society but socialism would provide wealth, equality, and a restored community.

These recodings were accompanied by fundamental shifts in social narratives. Intellectual myths were inflated upwards, becoming stories of collective triumph and heroic transformation. The present was reconceived, not as the denouement of a long struggle but as a pathway to a different, much better world.[24] In this heroic myth, actors and groups in the present society were conceived as being 'in struggle' to build the future. The individualized, introspective narrative of romantic modernism disappeared, along with ambiguity and irony as preferred social values (Gitlin 1987: 377–406). Instead, ethical lines were sharply drawn and political imperatives etched in black and white. In literary theory, the new criticism gave way to the new historicism (e.g. Veeser 1989). In psychology, the moralist Freud was now seen as antirepressive, erotic, and even polymorphously perverse (Brown 1966). The new Marx was sometimes a Leninist and other times a radical communitarian; he was only rarely portrayed as a social democrat or humanist in the earlier, modernist sense.[25]

The historical vignette with which I opened this essay provides an illustration of this shift in sensibility. In his confrontation with Inkeles, Wallerstein portentously announced, 'the time has come to put away childish things, and look reality in the face' (1979: 133). He was not adopting here a realist frame but rather donning a heroic guise. For it was emancipation and revolution that marked the narrative rhetoric of the day, not, as Weber might have said, the hard, dreary task of facing up to workaday demands. To be realistic, Wallerstein suggested, was to realize that 'we are living in the transition' to a 'socialist mode of production, our future world government' (ibid.: 136). The existential question he put to his listeners was, 'How are we relating to it?' He suggested that there were only two alternatives. They could relate to the imminent revolution 'as rational militants contributing to it or as clever obstructors of it (whether of the malicious or cynical variety).' The rhetorical construction of these alternatives demonstrates how the inversion of binary coding (the clear line between good and bad, with modernity being polluted) and the creation of a newly heroic narrative (the militantly millennial orientation to future salvation) were combined.[26] Wallerstein made these remarks, it will be recalled, in a scientific presentation, later published as 'Modernization: *Requiescat in pace.*' He was one of the most influential and original social scientific theorists of the antimodernization theory phase.

The social theories that this new generation of radical intellectuals produced can and must be considered in scientific terms (see, e.g., van den Berg 1980 and Alexander 1987). Their cognitive achievements, indeed, became dominant in the 1970s and have remained hegemonic in contemporary social science long after the ideological totalities in which they were initially imbedded have disappeared.[27] Yet to study the decline of a mode of knowledge, I would insist once again, demands broader, extra-scientific considerations as well. Theories are created by intellectuals in their search for meaning. In response to continuing social change, generational shifts occur that can make the scientific and ideological efforts of earlier intellectual generations seem not only empirically implausible but psychologically shallow, politically irrelevant, and morally obsolete.

By the end of the 1970s, the energy of the radical social movements of the preceding period had dissipated. Some of their demands became institutionalized; others were blocked by massive backlash movements that generated conservative publics and brought right-wing governments to power. The cultural-cum-political shift was so rapid as to seem, once again, to represent some kind of historical-cum-epistemological break.[28] Materialism replaced idealism among political influentials, and surveys reported increasingly conservative views among young people and university students. Marxist ideologues – one thinks of Bernard-Henri Levy (1977) in Paris and David Horowitz (Horowitz and Collier 1989) in the United States – became anticommunist *nouvelles philosophes* and, some of them, neoconservatives. Yippies became yuppies. For many intellectuals who had matured during the radicalism of the 1960s and 1970s, these new developments brought unbearable disappointment. Parallels with the 1950s were evident. The collective and heroic narrative of socialism once again had died, and the end of ideology seemed once again to be at hand.

Postmodernization Theory: Defeat, Resignation, and Comic Detachment

'Postmodernism' can be seen as an explanatory social theory that has produced new middle range models of culture (Foucault 1977; Huyssen 1986; Lyotard 1984), science and epistemology (Rorty 1979), class (Bourdieu 1984), social action (Crespi 1992), gender and family relations (Halpern 1990; Seidman 1991a), and economic life (Harvey 1989; Lasch 1985). In each of these areas, and others, postmodern theories have made original contributions to the understanding of reality.[29] It is not as a theory of the middle range, however, that postmodernism has made its mark. These discussions have become significant only because they are taken to exemplify broad new trends of history, social structure, and moral life. Indeed, it is by intertwining the levels of structure and process, micro and macro, with strong assertions about the past, present, and future of contemporary life that postmodernism has formed a broad and inclusive general theory of society, one which, like the others we have considered here, must be considered in extra-scientific terms, not only as an explanatory source.

If we consider postmodernism as myth – not merely as cognitive descriptions but as their coding and narration into a 'meaningful' frame – we must deal with it as the successor ideology to radical social theory, animated by the failure of reality to unfold in a manner that was consistent with the expectations generated by that antimodernization creed. From this perspective, we can see that while postmodernism seems to be coming to grips with the present and future, its horizon is fixed by the past. Initially (at least) an ideology of intellectual disappointment, Marxist and post-Marxist intellectuals articulated postmodernism in reaction to the fact that the period of heroic and collective radicalism seemed to be slipping away.[30] They redefined this exalted collective present, which had been held to presage an even more heroic imminent future, as a period that was now passed. They declared that it had been superseded not for reasons of political defeat but because of the structure of history itself.[31] The defeat of utopia had threatened a mythically incoherent possibility, namely that of historical retrogression. It threatened to undermine the meaning structures of intellectual life. With postmodern theory, this imminent defeat could be transformed into an immanent one, a necessity of historical development itself. The heroic 'grand narratives' of the left had merely been made irrelevant by history; they were not actually defeated. Myth could still function. Meaning was preserved.

The most influential early attributions of postmodernism were filled with frank revelations of theoretical perplexity, testimonies to dramatic shifts in reality, and expressions of existential despair.[32] Fredric Jameson (1988: 25), for example, identified a 'new and virtually unimaginable quantum leap in technological alienation.' Despite his methodological commitments, Jameson resists the impulse to fall back on the neo-Marxist certainties of the earlier age. Asserting that shifts in the productive base of society had created the superstructural confusions of a transitional time, he bemoaned 'the incapacity of our minds, at least at present, to map the great global multinational and decentered communication network in which we find ourselves caught as individual subjects' (ibid.: 15). Referring to the traditional role of art as a vehicle for gaining cultural clarity, Jameson complained that this meaning-making reflex had been blocked: we are 'unable to focus our own present, as though we have become incapable of achieving aesthetic representations of our own current experience' (ibid.: 20).[33]

Yet, the intellectual meaning-making triumph of mature post-modernism is already visible in Jameson's depiction of this new order as privatized, fragmented, and commercial. With these terms, the perplexities and blockages of rationality which Jameson succeeded in articulating can be explained not as personal failure but as historical necessities based on reason itself. What threatened meaninglessness now becomes the very basis for meaning; what has been constructed is a new present and a new past. No wonder that Jameson described (ibid.: 15) postmodernism as first and foremost a 'periodizing concept,' suggesting that the term was created so that intellectuals and their audiences could make sense of these new times: 'The new postmodernism expresses the inner truth of that newly emergent social order of late capitalism' (ibid.).

Postmodern theory, then, may be seen, in rather precise terms, as an attempt to redress the problem of meaning created by the experienced failure of 'the sixties.' Only in this way can we understand why the very dichotomy between modern and postmodern was announced, and why the contents of these new historical categories are described in the ways they are. From the perspective developed here, the answers seem clear enough. Continuity with the earlier period of antimodern radicalism is maintained by the fact that postmodernism, too, takes 'the modern' as its explicit foe. In the binary coding of this intellectual ideology, modernity remains on the polluted side, representing 'the other' in postmodernism's narrative tales.

Yet, in this third phase of postwar social theory, the contents of the modern are completely changed. Radical intellectuals had emphasized the privacy and particularism of modern capitalism, its provinciality, and the fatalism and resignation it produced. The postmodernization alternative they posited was, not postmodern, but public, heroic, collective, and universal. It is precisely these latter qualities, of course, that postmodernization theory has condemned as the very embodiment of modernity itself. In contrast, they have coded privacy, diminished expectations, subjectivism, individuality, particularity, and localism as the embodiments of the good. As for narrative, the major historical propositions of postmodernism – the decline of the grand narrative and the return to the local (Lyotard 1984), the rise of the empty symbol, or simulacrum (Baudrillard 1983), the end of socialism (Gorz 1982), the emphasis on plurality and difference (Seidman 1991b, 1992) – are transparent representations of a deflationary narrative frame. They are responses to the decline of 'progressive' ideologies and their utopian beliefs.

The resemblances to radical antimodernism, then, are superficial and misleading. In fact, there is a much more significant connection between postmodernism and the period that preceded radicalism, that is, modernization theory itself. Modernization theory, we recall, was itself a deflationary ideology following an earlier heroic period of radical quest. It, too, contained emphases on the private, the personal, and the local.

While these similarities reveal how misleading the intellectual self-representations of intellectual ideologies can be, it is obviously true that the two approaches differ in fundamental ways. These differences emerge from their positions in concrete historical time. The postwar liberalism that inspired modernization theory followed upon a radical movement that understood transcendence within a progressivist frame, one which, while aiming to radicalize modernism, hardly rejected it. Thus, while the romantic and ironic dimensions of postwar liberalism deflated heroic modernism, its movement away from radicalism made central aspects of modernism even more accessible.

Postmodernism, by contrast, followed upon a radical intellectual generation which had condemned not only liberal modernism but also key tenets of the very notion of modernization as such. The New Left rejected the Old Left in part because it was wedded to the modernization project; they preferred the Frankfurt School (e.g. Jay 1973), whose roots in German Romanticism coincided more neatly with its own, antimodernist tone. While postmodernism, then, is indeed a deflationary narrative vis-à-vis heroic radicalism, the specificity of its historical position means that it must place both heroic (radical) and romantic (liberal) versions of the modern onto the same negative side. Successor intellectuals tend to invert the binary code of the previously hegemonic theory. For postmodernism, the new code, modernism: postmodernism, implied a larger break with 'universalist' Western values than did the traditionalism:modernism of the immediate postwar period or the capitalist modernism:socialist antimodernization dichotomy that succeeded it.[34]

In narrative terms as well there are much greater deflationary shifts. Although there remains, to be sure, a romantic tenor in some strands of postmodernist thought, and even collectivist arguments for heroic liberation, these 'constructive' versions (Rosenau 1992; Thompson

1992) focus on the personal and the intimate and tend to be offshoots of social movements of the 1960s, for example gay and lesbian 'struggles,' the women's 'movement,' and the ecology activists like Greens. Insofar as they do engage public policy, such movements articulate their demands much more in the language of difference and particularism (e.g. Seidman 1991b and 1992) than in the universalistic terms of the collective good. The principal, and certainly the most distinctive, thrust of the postmodern narrative, moreover, is strikingly different. Rejecting not only heroism but romanticism as well, it tends to be more fatalistic, critical, and resigned, in short more comically agnostic, than these more political movements of uplift and reform suggest. Rather than upholding the authenticity of the individual, postmodernism announced, via Foucault and Derrida, the death of the subject. In Jameson's (1988: 15) words, 'the concep tion of a unique self and private identity is a thing of the past.' Another departure from the earlier, more romantic version of modernism is the singular absence of irony. Rorty's political philosophy is a case in point. Because he espouses irony and complexity (e.g. Rorty 1985, 1989), he maintains a political if not an epistemological liberalism, and because of these commitments he must distance himself from the postmodernist frame.

Instead of romance and irony, what has emerged full blown in postmodernism is the comic frame. Frye calls comedy the ultimate equalizer. Because good and evil cannot be parsed, the actors – protagonists and antagonists – are on the same moral level, and the audience, rather than being normatively or emotionally involved, can sit back and be amused. Baudrillard (1983) is the master of satire and ridicule, as the entire Western world becomes Disneyland at large. In the postmodern comedy, indeed, the very notion of actors is eschewed. With tongue in cheek but a new theoretical system in his mind, Foucault announced the death of the subject, a theme that Jameson canonized with his announcement that 'the conception of a unique self and private identity is a thing of the past.' Postmodernism is the play within the play, a historical drama designed to convince its audiences that drama is dead and that history no longer exists. What remains is nostalgia for a symbolized past.

Perhaps we may end this discussion with a snapshot of Daniel Bell, the intellectual whose career neatly embodies each of the scientific-cum-mythical phases of history I have thus far described. Bell came to intellectual self-consciousness as a Trotskyist in the 1930s. For a time after the Second World War he remained in the heroic anticapitalist mode of figures like C. Wright Mills, whom he welcomed as a colleague at Columbia University. His famous essay on the assembly line and deskilled labor (1962b [1956, 1947]) demonstrated continuity with prewar leftist work. By insisting on the concept of alienation, Bell committed himself to 'capitalism' rather than 'industrialism,' thus championing epochal transformation and resisting the postwar modernization line. Soon, however, Bell made the transition to realism, advocating modernism in a more romantically individualist than radical socialist way. Although *The Coming of Post-Industrial Society* appeared only in 1973, Bell had introduced the concept as an extension of Aron's industrialization thesis nearly two decades before. Post-industrial was a periodization that supported progress, modernization, and reason while undermining the possibilities for heroic transcendence and class conflict. Appearing in the midst of antimodernist rebellion, *The Coming of Post-Industrial Society* was reviewed with perplexity and disdain by many intellectuals on the antimodernist left, although its oblique relationship with theories of postscarcity society were sometimes noted as well.

What is so striking about this phase of Bell's career, however, is how rapidly the modernist notion of postindustrial society gave way to postmodernism, in content if not explicit form. For Bell, of course, it was not disappointed radicalism that produced this shift but his disappointments with what he came to call late modernism. When Bell turned away from this degenerate modernism in *The Cultural Contradictions of Capitalism* (1976), his story had changed. Post-industrial society, once the epitome of modernism, now produced, not reason and progress, but emotionalism and irrationalism, categories alarmingly embodied in sixties youth culture. Bell's solution to this imminent self-destruction of Western society was to advocate the return of the sacred (1977), a solution that exhibited the nostalgia for the past that Jameson would later diagnose as a certain sign of the coming of the postmodern age.

The comparison of Bell's postindustrial argument with Harvey's post-Fordism (1989) is revealing in this regard. Harvey takes similar developments in the productive arrangements of high-information capitalism but draws a far different conclusion about their effects on the consciousness of the age. Bell's anti-Marxism – his (1978) emphasis on the asynchronicity of systems – allows him to posit rebellion in the form of youth culture and to posit cultural salvation in the ideal of 'the sacred return' (cf. Eliade 1954). Harvey's continued commitment to orthodox base–superstructure reasoning, by contrast, leads him to postulate fragmentation and privatization as inevitable, and unstoppable, results of the post-Fordist productive mode. Bell's conservative attack on modernism embraces nostalgia; Harvey's radical attack on postmodernism posits defeat.

Postmodern theory is still, of course, very much in the making. As I have already mentioned, its middle-range formulations contain significant truths. Evaluating the importance of its general theorizing, by contrast, depends upon whether one places poststructuralism under its wing.[35] Certainly theorists of the strong linguistic turn – thinkers like Foucault, Bourdieu, Geertz, and Rorty – began to outline their understandings long before postmodernism appeared on the scene. Nevertheless, their emphasis on relativism and constructivism, their principled antagonism to an identification with the subject, and their skepticism regarding the possibility of totalizing change make their contributions more compatible with postmodernism than either modernism or radical antimodernization. Indeed, these theorists wrote in response to their disappointment with modernism (Geertz and Rorty vis à vis Parsons and Quine), on the one hand, and heroic antimodernism (Foucault and Bourdieu vis-à-vis Althusser and Sartre), on the other. Nonetheless, Geertz and Bourdieu can scarcely be called postmodern theorists, and strong culturalist theories cannot be identified with the broad ideological sentiments that the term post-modernism implies.

I would maintain here, as I have earlier in this essay, that scientific considerations are insufficient to account for shifts either toward or away from an intellectual position. If, as I believe to be the case, the departure from postmodernism has already begun, we must look closely, once again, at extra-scientific considerations, at recent events and social changes that seem to demand yet another new 'world-historical frame.'

Neo-modernism: Dramatic Inflation and Universal Categories

In postmodern theory intellectuals have represented to themselves and to society at large their response to the defeat of the heroic utopias of radical social movements, a response that, while recognizing defeat, did not give up the cognitive reference to that utopic world. Every idea in postmodern thought is a reflection upon the categories and false aspirations of the traditional collectivist narrative, and for most post-modernists the dystopia of the contemporary world is the semantic result. Yet, while the hopes of left intellectuals were dashed by the late 1970s, the intellectual imagination of others was rekindled. For when the left lost, the right won and won big. In the 1960s and 1970s, the right was a backlash, reactive movement. By 1980 it had become triumphant and began to initiate far-reaching changes in Western societies. A fact that has been conveniently overlooked by each of the three intellectual generations we have considered thus far – and most grievously by the postmodernist movement that was historically co-terminous with it – is that the victory of the neo-liberal right had, and continues to have, massive political, economic, and ideological repercussions around the globe.

The most striking 'success' for the right was, indeed, the defeat of communism, which was not only a political, military, and economic victory but, as I suggested in the introduction to this essay, also a triumph on the level of the historical imagination itself. Certainly there were objective economic elements in the bankruptcy of the Soviet Union, including growing technological deficiencies, sinking export proceeds, and the impossibility of finding desperately needed capital funds by switching to a strategy of internal growth (Muller 1992: 139). Yet the final economic breakdown had a political cause, for it was the computer-based military expansion of America and its NATO allies, when combined with the right-wing-inspired technology boycott, that brought the Soviet party dictatorship to its economic and political knees. While the lack of access to documents makes any definitive judgment decidedly premature, there seems no doubt that these policies were, in fact, among the principal strategic goals of the Reagan and Thatcher governments, and that they were achieved with signal effect.[36]

This extraordinary, and almost completely unexpected, triumph over what once seemed not only a socially but an intellectually plausible alternative world (see p. 8, above) has had the same kind of destabilizing, de-ontologizing effects on many intellectuals as the other massive historical 'breaks' I have discussed above. It has created, as well, the same sense of imminence and the conviction that the 'new world' in the making (cf. Kumar 1992) demands a new and very different kind of social theory.[37]

This negative triumph over state socialism has been reinforced, moreover, by the dramatic series of 'positive successes' during the 1980s for aggressively capitalist market economies. This has been most often remarked upon (most recently by Kennedy 1993) in connection with the NICs, the newly industrialized, extraordinarily dynamic Asian economies which have arisen in what was once called the third world. It is important not to underestimate the ideological effects of this world-historical fact: high-level, sustainable transformations of backward economies were achieved not by socialist command economies but by zealously capitalist states.

What has often been overlooked, however, is that during this same timeframe the capitalist market was also reinvigorated, both symbolically and objectively, in the capitalist West. This transpired not only in Thatcherite Britain and Reaganite America, but perhaps even more dramatically in the more 'progressive' and interventionist regimes like France and, subsequently, in countries like Italy, Spain, and, even more recently, in Scandinavia itself. Not only was there, in other words, the obvious and ideologically portentous bankruptcy of most of the world's communist economies, but there was the marked privatization of nationalized capitalist economies in both authoritarian-corporatist and socialist-democratic states. The world-wide recession that followed the longest period of sustained growth in capitalist history does not seem to have dampened the revival of market commitments, as the recent triumph of Clinton's neoliberalism in the United States demonstrates very well. In the late 1960s and 1970s, the intellectual successors to modernization theory, neo-Marxists like Baran and Sweezy (1966) and Mandel (1968), announced the imminent stagnation of capitalist economies and an inevitably declining rate of profit.[38] History has proved them wrong, with far-reaching ideological results (Chirot 1990).

'Rightward' developments on the more specifically political plane have been as far-reaching as those on the economic. As I mentioned earlier, during the late 1960s and 1970s it had become ideologically fashionable, and empirically justifiable, to accept political authoritarianism as the price of economic development. In the last decade, however, events on the ground seem to have challenged this view, and a radical reversal of conventional wisdom is now underway. It is not only communist tyrannies that have opened up since the mid-1980s, but the very Latin American dictatorships that seemed so 'objectively necessary' only an intellectual generation before. Even African dictatorships have recently begun to show signs of vulnerability to this shift in political discourse from authoritarianism to democracy.

These developments have created social conditions – and mass public sentiment – that would seem to belie the postmodern intellectuals' coding of contemporary (and future) society as fatalistic, private, particularistic, fragmented, and local. They also would appear to undermine the deflated narrative frame of postmodernism, which has insisted either on the romance of difference or, more fundamentally, on the idea that contemporary life can only be interpreted in a comic way. And, indeed, if we look closely at recent intellectual discourse, we can observe, in fact, a return to many earlier, modernist themes.

Because the recent revivals of market and democracy have occurred on a world-wide scale, and because they are categorically abstract and generalizing ideas, universalism has once again become a viable source for social theory. Notions of commonality and institutional convergence have reemerged, and with them the possibilities for intellectuals to provide meaning in a utopian way.[39] It seems, in fact, that we are witnessing the birth of a fourth postwar version of myothopoeic social thought. 'Neo-modernism' (cf. Tiryakian 1991) will serve as a rough-and-ready characterization of this phase of postmodernization theory until a term appears that represents the new spirit of the times in a more imaginative way.

In response to economic developments, different groupings of contemporary intellectuals have reinflated the emancipatory narrative of the market, in which they inscribe a new past (antimarket society) and a new present/future (market transition, full-blown capitalism) that makes liberation dependent upon privatization, contracts, monetary inequality, and competition. On one side, a much enlarged and more activist breed of intellectual conservatives has emerged. Although their policy and political concerns have not, as yet, greatly affected the discourse of general social theory, there are exceptions that indicate the potential is there. James Coleman's massive *Foundations of Social Theory* (1990), for example, has a self-consciously heroic cast; it aims to make neo-market, rational choice the basis not only for future theoretical work but for the re-creation of a more responsive, law-abiding, and less degraded social life.[40]

Much more significant is the fact that within liberal intellectual life, among the older generation of disillusioned utopians and the younger intellectual groups as well, a new and positive social theory of markets has reappeared. For many politically engaged intellectuals, too, this has taken the theoretical form of the individualistic, quasi-romantic frame of rational choice. Employed initially to deal with the disappointing failures of working-class consciousness (e.g. Pzeworski 1985 and Wright 1985; cf. Elster 1989), it has increasingly served to explain how state communism, and capitalist corporatism, can be transformed into a market-oriented system that is liberating or, at least, substantively rational (Moene and Wallerstein 1992; Nee 1989; Pzeworski 1991). While other politically engaged intellectuals have appropriated market ideas in less restrictive and more collectivist ways (e.g. Blackburn 1991b; Friedland and Robertson 1990; Szelenyi 1988), their writings, too, betray an enthusiasm for market processes that is markedly different from the left-leaning intellectuals of earlier times. Among the intellectual advocates of 'market socialism,' there has been a similar change. Kornai (1990), for example, has expressed distinctly fewer reservations about free markets in his more recent writings than in the path-breaking works of the 1970s and 1980s that brought him to fame.

This neo-modern revival of market theory is also manifest in the rebirth and redefinition of economic sociology. In terms of research program, Granovetter's (1974) earlier celebration of the strengths of the market's 'weak ties' has become a dominant paradigm for studying economic networks (e.g. Powell 1991), one that implicitly rejects postmodern and antimodern pleas for strong ties and local communities. His later argument for the 'imbeddedness' (1985) of economic action has transformed (e.g. Granovetter and Swedberg 1992) the image of the market into a social and interactional relationship that has little resemblance to the deracinated, capitalist exploiter of the past. Similar transformations can be seen in more generalized discourse. Adam Smith has been undergoing an intellectual rehabilitation (Boltanski 1993: 38–98; Boltanski and Thevenot 1991: 60–84; Hall 1985; Heilbroner 1986). Schumpeter's 'market realism' has been revived; the individualism of Weber's marginalist economics has been celebrated (Holton and Turner 1986); so has the market-acceptance that permeates Parsons's theoretical work (Holton 1992 and Holton and Turner 1986).

In the political realm, neo-modernism has emerged in an even more powerful way, as a result, no doubt, of the fact that it has been the political revolutions of the last decade that have reintroduced narrative in a truly heroic form (contra Kumar 1992: 316) and challenged the postmodern deflation in the most direct way. The movements away from dictatorship, motivated in practice by the most variegated of concerns, have been articulated mythically as a vast, unfolding 'drama of democracy' (Sherwood 1994), literally as an opening up of the spirit of humanity. The melodrama of social good triumphing, or almost triumphing, over social evil – which Peter Brooks (1984) so brilliantly discovered to be the root of the nineteenth-century narrative form – has populated the symbolic canvas of the late twentieth-century West with heroes and conquests of truly world-historical scope. This drama started with the epochal struggle of Lech Walesa, and what seemed to be virtually the entire Polish nation (Tiryakian 1988) against Poland's coercive party-state. The day-to-day dramaturgy that captured the public imagination ended initially in Solidarity's inexplicable defeat. Eventually, however, good did triumph over evil, and the dramatic symmetry of the heroic narrative was complete. Mikhail Gorbachev began his long march through the Western dramatic imagination in 1984. His increasingly loyal world-wide audience fiercely followed his epochal struggles in what eventually became the longest running public drama in the postwar period. This grand narrative – which might be entitled 'The Making, Unmaking, and Resurrection of an American Hero: Gorbachev and the Discourse of the Good' (Alexander and Sherwood 1994) – produced cathartic reactions in its audience, which the press called 'Gorbymania' and Durkheim would have labelled the collective effervescence that only symbols of the sacred inspire. This drama was reprised in what the mass publics, media, and elites of Western countries construed as the equally heroic achievements of Nelson Mandela and Václav Havel, and later of Boris Yeltsin, the tank-stopping hero who succeeded Gorbachev in Russia's post-communist phase (Alexander and Sherwood 1992). Similar experiences of exaltation and renewed faith in the moral efficacy of democratic revolution were produced by the social drama that took place in 1989 in Tiananmen Square, with its strong ritualistic overtones (Chan 1994) and its classically tragic denouement.

It would be astonishing if this reinflation of mass political drama did not manifest itelf in equally marked shifts in intellectual theorizing about politics. In fact, in a manner that parallels the rise of the 'market,' there has been the powerful reemergence of theorizing about democracy. Liberal ideas about political life, which emerged in the eighteenth and nineteenth centuries and which were displaced by the 'social question' of the great industrial transformation, seem like contemporary ideas again. Dismissed as historically anachronistic in the anti- and postmodern decades, they have become quite suddenly à la mode (cf. Alexander 1991).

This reemergence has taken the form of the revival of the concept of 'civil society,' the informal, non-state, and non-economic realm of public and personal life that Tocqueville, for example, defined as vital to the maintenance of the democratic state. Rising initially from within the intellectual debates that helped spark the social struggles against authoritarianism in Eastern Europe (cf. Cohen and Arato 1992) and Latin American (Stepan 1985), the term was 'secularized' and given more abstract and more universal meaning by American and European intellectuals who were connected with these movements, like Cohen and Arato (1992) and Keane (1988a, 1988b). Subsequently, they utilized the concept to begin theorizing in a manner that sharply demarcated their own 'left' theorizing from the antimodernization, antiformal democracy writings of an earlier day.

Stimulated by these writers and also by the English translation (1989 [1962]) of Habermas's early book on the bourgeois public sphere, debates about pluralism, fragmentation, differentiation, and participation have become the new order of the day. Frankfurt theorists, Marxist social historians, and even some postmodernists have become democratic theorists under the sign of the 'public sphere' (see, e.g., the essays by Postpone, Ryan, and Eley in Calhoun 1993 and the more recent writings of Held, e.g. 1987).[41] Communitarian and internalist political philosophers, like Walzer (1992a, b), have taken up the concept to clarify the universalist yet non-abstract dimensions in their theorizing about the good. For conservative social theorists (e.g. Banfield 1991; Shils 1991a, b; Wilson 1991), civil society is a concept that implies civility and harmony. For neo-functionalists (e.g. Mayhew 1992; Sciulli 1992; and Alexander 1992b), it is an idea that denotes the possibility of theorizing conflicts over equality and inclusion in a less anticapitalist way. For old functionalists (e.g. Inkeles 1991), it is an idea that suggests that formal democracy has been a requisite for modernization all along.

But whatever the particular perspective that has framed this new political idea, its neo-modern status is plain to see. Theorizing in this manner suggests that contemporary societies either possess, or must aspire to, not only an economic market but a distinctive political zone, an institutional field of universal if contested domain (Touraine 1994). It provides a common empirical point of reference, which implies a familiar coding of citizen and enemy, and allows history to be narrated, once again, in a teleological manner that gives the drama of democracy full force.

Neo-modernism and Social Evil: Nationalism as Polluted Representation

This problem of the demarcation of civil as opposed to uncivil society points to issues that go beyond the narrating and explanatory frameworks of neo-modern theory that I have described thus far. Romantic and heroic narratives that describe the triumph, or possible triumph, of markets and democracies have a reassuringly familiar form. When we turn to the binary coding of this emerging historical period, however, certain problems arise. Given the resurgence of universalism, of course, one can be confident that what is involved is a specification of the master code, described earlier as the discourse of civil society. Yet, while this almost archetypical symbolization of the requisites and

antonyms of democracy establishes general categories, historically specific 'social representations' (Moscovici 1984) must also be developed
to articulate the concrete categories of good and evil in a particular time
and place. In regard to these secondary elaborations, what strikes one
is how difficult it has been to develop a set of binary categories that is
semantically and socially compelling, a black-versus-white contrast
that can function as a successor code to postmodern:modern or, for
that matter, to the socialist:capitalist and modern:traditional symbolic
sets that were established by earlier intellectual generations, and which
by no means have entirely lost their efficacy today.[42]

To be sure, the symbolization of the good does not present a real
problem. Democracy and universalism are key terms, and their more
substantive embodiments are free market, individualism, and human
rights. The problem comes in establishing the profane side. The abstract
qualities that pollution must embody are obvious enough. Because
they are produced by the principle of difference, they closely resemble
the qualities that were opposed to modernization in the postwar
period, qualities that identified the pollution of 'traditional' life. But
despite the logical similarities, earlier ideological formulations cannot
simply be taken up again. Even if they effectuate themselves only
through differences in second-order representations, the differences
between present-day society and the immediate postwar period are
enormous. Faced with the rapid onrush of 'markets' and 'democracy,'
and the rapid collapse of their opposites, it has proven difficult
to formulate equally universal and far-reaching representations of
the profane. The question is this: Is there an oppositional movement
or geo-political force that is a convincingly and fundamentally
dangerous, that is a 'world-historical,' threat to the 'good'? The once
powerful enemies of universalism seemed to be historical relics, out
of sight and out of mind, laid low by a historical drama that seems
unlikely soon to be reversed. It was for this semantic reason that,
in the interim period after '1989', many intellectuals, and certainly
broad sections of Western publics, experienced a strange combination
of optimism and self-satisfaction, energetic commitment and moral
disrepair.

In comparison with the modernization theory of the postwar years,
neo-modern theory involves fundamental shifts in both symbolic time
and symbolic space. In neo-modern theory, the profane can neither be
represented by an evolutionarily preceding period of traditionalism
nor identified with the world outside of North America and Europe.
In contrast with the postwar modernization wave, the current one is
global and international rather than regional and imperial, a difference

articulated in social science by the contrast between early theories of dependency (Frank 1966) and more contemporary theories of globalization (Robertson 1992). The social and economic reasons for this change center on the rise of Japan, which this time around has gained power not as one of Spencer's military societies – a category that could be labelled backward in an evolutionary sense – but as a civilized commercial society.

Thus, for the first time in 500 years (see Kennedy 1987), it has become impossible for the West to dominate Asia, either economically or culturally. When this objective factor is combined with the pervasive de-Christianization of Western intellectuals, we can understand the remarkable fact that 'orientalism' – the symbolic pollution of Eastern civilization that Said (1978) articulated so tellingly scarcely more than a decade ago – seems no longer to be a forceful spatial or temporal representation in Western ideology or social theory, although it has by no means entirely disappeared.[43] A social scientific translation of this ideological fact, which points the way to a post-postmodern, or neo-modern, code is Eisenstadt's (1987: vii) call for 'a far-reaching reformulation of the vision of modernization, and of modern civilizations.' While continuing to code modern in a thoroughly positive way, this conceptualization explains it not as the end of an evolutionary sequence, but as a highly successfully globalizing movement.

> Instead of perceiving modernization as the final stage in the fulfillment of the evolutionary potential common to all societies – of which the European experience was the most important and succinct manifestation and paradigm – modernization (or modernity) should be viewed as one specific civilization or phenomenon. Originating in Europe, it has spread in its economic, political and ideological aspects all over the world. ... The crystallization of this new type of civilization was not unlike the spread of the great religions, or the great imperial expansions, but because modernization almost always combined economic, political, and ideological aspects and forces, its impact was by far the greatest.
>
> (ibid.)

Original modernization theory transformed Weber's overtly Western-centric theory of world religions into a universal account of global change that still culminated in the social structure and culture of the postwar Western world. Eisenstadt proposes to make modernization itself the historical equivalent of a world religion, which relativizes it, on the one hand, and suggests the possibility of selective indigenous appropriation (Hannerz 1987, 1989), on the other.

The other side of this decline of orientalism among Western theorists

is what seems to be the virtual disappearance of 'third world-ism' –
what might be called occidentalism – from the vocabulary of intellectuals
who speak from within, or on behalf of, developing countries. A
remarkable indication of this discursive shift can be found in an
opinion piece that Edward Said published in the *New York Times*
protesting the imminent Allied air war against Iraq in early 1991. While
reiterating the familiar characterization of American policy toward
Iraq as the result of an 'imperialist ideology,' Said justified his opposition not by pointing to the distinctive worth of national or political
ideology but by upholding universality: 'A new world order has to be
based on authentically general principles, not on the selectively applied
might of one country' (Said 1991). More significantly, Said denounced
Iraqi President Saddam Hussein and the 'Arab world,' representing
them in particularizing categories that polluted them as the enemies of
universalism itself.

> The traditional discourse of Arab nationalism, to say nothing of the quite
> decrepit state system, is inexact, unresponsive, anomalous, even comic. . . .
> Today's Arab media are a disgrace. It is difficult to speak the plain truth
> in the Arab world. . . . Rarely does one find rational analysis – reliable
> statistics, concrete and undoctored descriptions of the Arab world today
> with its . . . crushing mediocrity in science and many cultural fields.
> Allegory, complicated symbolism and innuendo substitute for common
> sense.
>
>   (ibid.)

When Said concludes that there appears to be a 'remorseless Arab
propensity to violence and extremism,' the end of occidentalism
seems complete.

Because the contemporary recoding of the antithesis of universalism can be geographically represented neither as non-Western nor
as temporally located in an earlier time, the social sacred of neo-
modernism cannot, paradoxically, be represented as 'modernization.'
In the ideological discourse of contemporary intellectuals, it would
seem almost as difficult to employ this term as it is to identify the
good with 'socialism.' Not modernization but democratization, not
the modern but the market – these are the terms that the new social
movements of the neo-modern period employ. These difficulties in
representation help to explain the new saliency of non-national,
international organizations (Thomas and Lauderdale 1988), a salience
that points, in turn, to elements of what the long-term representation
of a viable ideological antinomy might be. For European and
American intellectuals, and for those from outside of the West as well,

the United Nations and European Community have taken on new legitimacy and reference, providing institutional manifestations of the new universalism that transcend earlier great divides.

The logic of these telling institutional and cultural shifts is that 'nationalism' – not traditionalism, communism, or the 'East' – is coming to represent the principal challenge to the newly universalized discourse of the good. Nationalism is the name intellectuals and publics are now increasingly giving to the negative antinomies of civil society. The categories of the 'irrational,' 'conspiratorial,' and 'repressive' are taken to be synonymous with forceful expressions of nationality, and equated with primordiality and uncivilized social forms. That civil societies have always themselves taken a national form is being conveniently neglected, along with the continuing nationalism of many democratic movements themselves.[44] It is true, of course, that in the geo-political world that has so suddenly been re-formed, it is the social movements and armed rebellions for national self-determination that trigger military conflicts that can engender large-scale wars.

Is it any wonder, then, that nationalism is now routinely portrayed as the successor of communism, not only in the semantic but in the organizational sense? This equation is made by high intellectuals, not only in the popular press. 'Far from extinguishing nationalism,' Liah Greenfeld (1992) wrote recently in *The New Republic*, 'communism perpetuated and reinforced the old nationalist values. And the intelligentsia committed to these values is now turning on the democratic regime it inadvertently helped to create.'

> The democratic intelligentsia, which took shape in opposition to the Communist state, is, in fact, much more motivated by nationalist than by democratic concerns. . . . To accomplish a transition from communism to democracy, Russia needs to renounce the traditions that made communism possible: the anti-democratic values of its nationalism.
>
> (ibid.)

It does not seem surprising that some of the most promising younger generation of American social theorists have shifted from concerns with modernization, critical theory, and citizenship to issues of identity and nationalism. In addition to Greenfeld, one might note the new work of Rogers Brubaker, whose studies of central European and Russian nationalism (e.g. Brubaker 1994) make similar links between Soviet communism and contemporary nationalism, although from a less culturalist, more neo-institutional perspective. One might note also some of the recent writings of Craig Calhoun (e.g. 1992).

It is the failure to confirm such a semantic and organizational analogy with communism that has prevented religious fundamentalism from occupying a similar categorially polluting role. It has been unable to do so despite the currency of fundamentalism-versus-modernity in everyday speech (e.g. Barber 1992) and the myriad examples of its very real dangers to democracy, markets, and social differentiation that are ready to hand.[45] On the one hand, because intellectuals in democratic nations are continually criticizing the renewal of fundamentalist forms of religiosity in their democratic countries, it is difficult for them to equate secular with democratic or to place fundamentalist religiosity completely outside the pale of democratic life. On the other hand, postcommunist nations are not particularly fundamentalist; nor has fundamentalism posed the same kind of *realpolitik* basis for the renewal of large-scale conflict as the militant assertion of national rights.

In Winter 1994, *Theory and Society*, a bellweather of intellectual currents in Western social theory, devoted a special issue to nationalism. In their introduction to the symposium, John Comaroff and Paul Stern make particularly vivid the link between nationalism-as-pollution and nationalism-as-object-of-social-science.

> Nowhere have the signs of the quickening of contemporary history, of our misunderstanding and misprediction of the present, been more clearly expressed than in the . . . assertive renaissance of nationalisms. . . . World events over the past few years have thrown a particularly sharp light on the darker, more dangerous sides of nationalism and claims to sovereign identity. And, in so doing, they have revealed how tenuous is our grasp of the phenomenon. Not only have these events confounded the unsuspecting world of scholarship. They have also shown a long heritage of social theory and prognostication to be flatly wrong.
>
> (Comaroff and Stern 1994: 35)

While these theorists do not, of course, deconstruct their empirical argument by explicitly relating it to the rise of a new phase of myth and science, it is noteworthy that they do insist on linking the new understanding of nationalism to the rejection of Marxism, modernization theory, and postmodern thought (ibid.: 35–7). In their own contribution to this special revival issue, Greenfeld and Chirot insist on the fundamental antithesis between democracy and nationalism in the strongest terms. After discussing Russia, Germany, Romania, Syria, Iraq, and the Cambodian Khmer Rouge, they write:

> The cases we discuss here show that the association between certain types of nationalism and aggressive, brutal behavior is neither coincidental nor

inexplicable. Nationalism remains the world's most powerful, general, and primordial basis of cultural and political identity. Its range is still growing, not diminishing, throughout the world. And in most places, it does not take an individualistic or civic form.

(Greenfeld and Chirot 1994: 123)

The new social representation of nationalism and pollution, based upon the symbolic analogy with communism, has also permeated the popular press. Serbia's expansionist military adventures have provided a crucial field of collective representation. See, for example, the categorial relationships that are established in the following editorial from the *New York Times*:

> Communism can pass easily into nationalism. The two creeds have much in common. Each offers a simple key to tangled problems. One exalts class, the other ethnic kinship. Each blames real grievances on imagined enemies. As a Russian informant shrewdly remarked to David Shipler in *The New Yorker*: 'They are both ideologies that liberate people from personal responsibility. They are united around some sacred [read profane] goal.' In varying degrees and with different results, old Bolsheviks have become new nationalists in Serbia and many former Soviet republics.

The *Times* editorial writer further codes the historical actors by analogizing the current break-up of Czechoslovakia to the nationalism that preceded it, and which ultimately issued from the First World War:

> And now the same phenomenon has surfaced in Czechoslovakia. . . . There is a . . . moral danger, described long ago by Thomas Masaryk, the founding president of Czechoslovakia, whose own nationalism was joined inseparably to belief in democracy. 'Chauvinism is nowhere justified,' he wrote in 1927, 'least of all in our country. . . . To a positive nationalism, one that seeks to raise a nation by intensive work, none can demur. Chauvinism, racial or national intolerance, not love of one's own people, is the foe of nations and of humanity.' Masaryk's words are a good standard for judging tolerance on both sides.
> (June 16, 1992; reprinted in the *International Herald Tribune*)

The analogy between nationalism and communism, and their pollution as threats to the new internationalism, is even made by government officials of formerly communist states. For example, in late September 1992, Andrei Kozyrev, Russia's Foreign Minister, appealed to the United Nations to consider setting up international trusteeships to oversee the move to independence by former Soviet non-Slavic republics. Only a UN connection, he argued, could prevent the newly independent states from discriminating against national minorities. The symbolic crux of his argument is the analogy between two categories of pollution. 'Previously, victims of totalitarian regimes and ideologies needed protection,' Kozyrev told the UN General Assembly. 'Today, ever more often one needs to counter aggressive nationalism that emerges as a new global threat.'[46]

Modernization Redux? The Hubris of Linearity and the Dangers of Theoretical Amnesia

In 1982, when Anthony Giddens confidently asserted that 'modernization theory is based upon false premises' (p. 144), he was merely reiterating the common social scientific sense of the day, or at least his generation's version of it. When he added that the theory had 'served . . . as an ideological defence of the dominance of Western capitalism over the rest of the world,' he reproduced the common understanding of why this false theory had once been believed. Today both these sentiments seem anachronistic. Modernization theory (e.g. Parsons 1964) stipulated that the great civilizations of the world would converge towards the institutional and cultural configurations of Western society. Certainly we are witnessing something very much like this process today, and the enthusiasm it has generated is hardly imposed by Western domination.

The sweeping ideological and objective transformations described in the preceding section have begun to have their theoretical effect, and the theoretical gauntlet that the various strands of neo-modernism have thrown at the feet of postmodern theory are plain to see. Shifting historical conditions have created fertile ground for such post-post-modern theorizing, and intellectuals have responded to these conditions by revising their earlier theories in creative and often far-reaching ways. Certainly, it would be premature to call neo-modernism a 'successor theory' to postmodernism. It has only recently become crystallized as an intellectual alternative, much less emerged as the victor in this ideological-cum-theoretical fight. It is unclear, further, whether the movement is nourished by a new generation of intellectuals or by fragments of currently competing generations who have found in neo-modernism a unifying vehicle to dispute the postmodern hegemony over the contemporary field. Despite these qualifications, however, it must be acknowledged that a new and very different current of social theorizing has emerged on the scene.

With this success, however, there comes the grave danger of theoretical amnesia about the problems of the past. Retrospective verifications of modernization theory have begun in earnest. One of the most acute reappraisals was written by Muller (1992), who offered fulsome praise for the once disgraced perspective even while suggesting that any current version must be fundamentally revised (cf. Muller 94). 'With an apparently more acute sense of reality,' Muller (1992: 111) writes, 'the sociological theory of modernity had recorded the long-term developments within the Eastern European area, currently taking place in a more condensed form, long before they were empirically verifiable.' Muller adds, for good measure, that 'the *grand theory* constantly accused of lacking contact with reality seemingly proves to possess predictive capacity – the classical sociological modernization theory of Talcott Parsons' (ibid., original italics). Another sign of this reappraisal can be found in the return to modernization theory made by distinguished theorists who were once neo-Marxist critics of capitalist society. Bryan Turner (1986), for example, now defends Western citizenship against radical egalitarianism and lauds (Holton and Turner 1986) Parsons for his 'anti-nostalgic' acceptance of the basic structures of modern life. While Giddens's (1990, 1991, 1992) position is more ambiguous, his recent work, too, reveals an unacknowledged yet decisive departure from the conspicuously anti-modernization stance that marked his earlier ideas. A portentious tone of crisis frames this new work, which Giddens conspicuously anchors in the abrupt emergence of social developments that in his view could not have been foreseen.

> In the social sciences today, as in the social world itself, we face a new agenda. We live, as everyone knows, at a time of endings ... *Fin de siècle* has become widely identified with feelings of disorientation and malaise ... We are in a period of evident transition – and the 'we' here refers not only to the West but to the world as a whole.
>   (Giddens 1994a: 56; cf. Beck 1994: 1 and Lash 1994: 110)

The new and historically unprecedented world that Giddens discovers, however, turns out to be nothing other than modernity itself (see below). Even among former communist apparatchiks themselves, there is growing evidence (i.e. Borko cited in Muller 1992: 112) that similar 'retro-dictions' about the convergence of capitalist and communist societies are well underway, tendencies that have caused a growing number of 'revisits' to Schumpeter as well.

The theoretical danger here is that this enthusiastic and long over-due reappreciation of some of the central thrusts of postwar social science might actually lead to the revival of convergence and modernization theories in their earlier forms. In his reflections on the recent transitions in Eastern Europe, Habermas (1990: 4) employs such evolutionary phrases as 'rewinding the reel' and 'rectifying revolution.' Inkeles's (1991) recent tractatus to American policy agencies is replete with such convergence homilies as a political 'party should not seek to advance its objectives by extra-political means.' Sprinkled with advice about 'the importance of locating . . . the distinctive point where additional resources can provide greatest leverage,' the article displays the kind of over-confidence in controlled social change that marked the hubris of postwar modernization thought. When Lipset (1990) claims the lesson of the second great transition as the failure of the 'middle way' between capitalism and socialism, he is no doubt correct in an important sense, but the formulation runs the danger of reinforcing the tendentious, either/or dichotomies of earlier thinking in a manner that could justify not only narrow self-congratulation but unjustified optimism about imminent social change. Jeffrey Sachs and other *simpliste* expositors of the 'big bang' approach to transition seem to be advocating a rerun of Rostow's earlier 'take-off' theory. Like that earlier species of modernization idea, this new monetarist modernism throws concerns of social solidarity and citizenship, let alone any sense of historical specificity, utterly to the winds (see Leijonhofvud 1993 and the perceptive comments by Muller 1994: 17–27).

Giddens's enthusiastic return to the theory of modernity provides the most elaborate case in point. Despite the qualifying adjectives he employs to differentiate his new approach from the theories he once rejected – he speaks at different points of 'high,' 'late,' and 'reflexive' modernity – his model rests upon the same *simpliste* set of binary oppositions as did earlier modernization theory in its most banal forms. In his most recent formulation, for example, Giddens (1994a: 63–5, 79, 84, 104–5) insists upon a clear-cut and decisive polarity between traditional and modern life. 'Traditional order,' he claims, rests upon 'formulaic notions of truth,' which conflate 'moral and emotional' elements, and upon 'ritual practices,' organized by 'guardians' with unchallengeable power. These beliefs and practices, he declares, create a 'status' based, 'insider/outsider' society. By contrast, in the period of 'reflexive modernity' everything is different. Ritual is displaced by 'real' and 'pragmatic' action, formulaic ideas by 'propositional' ones, guardians by 'skeptical' experts, and status by 'competence.'

From this familiar conceptual binarism there follows the equally familiar empirical conclusion; tradition, Giddens discovers, has been completely 'evacuated' from the contemporary phase of social life. To provide some distance from earlier postwar theory, Giddens suggests that these earlier versions were naive; they had not realized that their own period, which they took to be thoroughly modern, actually remained firmly rooted in the past – 'for most of its history, modernity has rebuilt tradition as it has dissolved' (ibid.: 56; cf. Beck 1994: 2). What Giddens has really done, however, is to historicize the present by invoking the alternatives of modernization theory in an even more arbitrary way. Indeed, his renewal of the tradition/modern divide is much more reductive than the complex and nuanced, if ultimately contradictory arguments that emerged from within classical modernization theory in its terminal phase, arguments about which Giddens seems completely unaware. Nor does Giddens appear to have learned anything from the debates that so successfully persuaded postmodernization intellectuals to abandon the historically arbitrary, Western-centered, and theoretically tendentious approach to tradition he now takes up. Only by ignoring the implications of the linguistic turn, for example, can he conceive modernity in such an individualistic and pragmatic way (cf. Lash's [1994] similar criticism). Finally, Giddens's version of neomodernism is impoverished in an ideological and moral sense. The problem is not only that he fails to provide a compelling alternative vision of social life – a failure rooted in the forced choice nature of the binary categories themselves – but also that his arguments give credence to the 'end of ideology' argument in a new way. In the face of the changes wrought by reflexive modernization, Giddens suggests (1994b), the very difference between reformism and conservatism has become passé. Contemporary empirical developments demonstrate not only that politics must go beyond the traditional alternatives of capitalism and socialism but beyond the very notions of 'left' and 'right.' Such is the intellectual amnesia that the new historical disjuncture has produced and upon which its continued misunderstanding depends.

While many of the recent social scientific formulations of market and democracy discussed above avoid the most egregious distortions of the kind I have just described, the universalism of their categories, the heroism of their *Zeitgeist,* and the dichotomous strictures of their codes make the underlying problems difficult to avoid. Theories of market transition, even in the careful hands of a scholar as conscientious as Victor Nee, sometimes suggest a linearity and rationality that historical experience belies. Civil society theory, despite the extraordinary self-consciousness of philosophers like Cohen and Walzer, seems unable to theorize empirically the demonic, anti-civil forces of cultural life that it normatively proscribes (cf. Alexander 1994 and Sztompka 1991).

If there is to be a new and more successful effort at constructing a social theory about the fundamentally shared structures of contemporary societies (cf. Sztompka 1993: 136–41), it will have to avoid these regressive tendencies, which resurrect modernization ideas in their most simplistic forms. Institutional structures like democracy, law, and market are functional requisites if certain social competencies are to be achieved and certain resources to be acquired; they are not, however, either historical inevitabilities or linear outcomes, nor are they social panaceas for the problems of non-economic subsystems or groups (see, e.g., Rueschemeyer 1993). Social and cultural differentiation may be an ideal-typical pattern that can be analytically reconstructed over time; however, whether or not any particular differentiation occurs – market, state, law, or science – depends on the normative aspirations (e.g. Sztompka 1991), strategic position, history, and powers of particular social groups. No matter how socially progressive in itself, moreover, differentiation displaces as much as it resolves, and can create social upheaval on an enormous scale. Social systems may well be pluralistic and the causes of change multidimensional; at any given time and in any given place, however, a particular subsystem and the group that directs it – economic, political, scientific, or religious – may successfully dominate and submerge the others in its name. Globalization is, indeed, a dialectic of indigenization and cosmopolitanism, but cultural and political asymmetries remain between more and less developed regions, even if they are not inherent contradictions of some imperialistic fact. While the analytic concept of civil society must by all means be recovered from the heroic age of democratic revolutions, it should be de-idealized so that 'anti-civil society' – the countervailing processes of decivilization, polarization, and violence – can be seen also as typically 'modern' results. Finally, these new theories must be pushed to maintain a decentered, self-conscious reflexivity about their ideological dimensions even while they continue in their efforts to create a new explanatory scientific theory. For only if they become aware of themselves as moral constructions – as codes and as narratives – will they be able to avoid the totalizing conceit that gave early modernizing theory such a bad name. In this sense, 'neo-' must incorporate the linguistic turn associated with 'post-'modern theory, even while it challenges its ideological and more broadly theoretical thrust.

In one of his last and most profound theoretical meditations, François Bourricaud (1987: 19–21) suggested that 'one way of defining modernity is the way in which we define solidarity.' The notion of modernity can be defended, Bourricaud believed, if, rather than 'identify[ing] solidarity with equivalence,' we understand that the "general spirit" is both universal and particular.' Within a group, a generalizing spirit 'is universal, since it regulates the intercourse among members of the group.' Yet, if one thinks of the relations between nations, this spirit 'is also particular, since it helps distinguish one group from all others.' In this way, it might be said that 'the "general spirit of a nation" assures the solidarity of individuals, without necessarily abolishing all their differences, and even establishing the full legitimacy of some of them.' What of the concept of universalism? Perhaps, Bourricaud suggested, 'modern societies are characterized less by what they have in common or by their structure with regard to well-defined universal exigencies, than by the fact of their involvement in the *issue* of universalization' as such (italics added).

Perhaps it is wise to acknowledge that it is a renewed sense of involvement in the project of universalism, rather than some lipid sense of its concrete forms, that marks the character of the new age in which we live. Beneath this new layer of the social top soil, moreover, lie the tangled roots and richly marbled subsoil of earlier intellectual generations, whose ideologies and theories have not ceased to be alive. The struggles between these interlocutors can be intimidating and confusing, not only because of the intrinsic difficulty of their message but because each presents itself not as form but as essence, not as the only language in which the world makes sense but as the only real sense of the world. Each of these worlds does make sense, but only in a historically bounded way. Recently, a new social world has come into being. We must try to make sense of it. For the task of intellectuals is not only to explain the world; they must interpret it as well.

Notes

1. As I remember the event, and it was certainly an event, the entire audience became rather heated up. One leading leftist sociologist of development offered the sarcastic intervention that modernization theory had actually produced world-wide poverty, and made the pointed suggestion that Inkeles try selling his tired modernization line somewhere else. At this point, shouts arose from various quarters of the audience and this distinguished social scientist had to be physically restrained from underscoring his theoretical point in a decidedly nonintellectual manner. The article from which I am quoting, written by Wallerstein and published in a collection in 1979, clearly was drawn from the ASA talk referred to above, although my references to the talk are drawn from memory. Tiryakian (1991) places Wallerstein's article in a similar historical perspective and provides an analysis of the fate of modernization theory that bears a marked similarity to the one I undertake here.

2. This impossibility is strikingly expressed in the cri de coeur issued by Shoji Ishitsuka, one of Japan's leading Lukács scholars and 'critical theorists':

The whole history of Social Enlightenment, which was so great for its realization of the idea of equality, as well as so tragic for its enforcement of dictatorship, has ended. . . . The crisis of the human sciences [which has resulted] can be described as a crisis of recognition. The progress-oriented historical viewpoint has totally disappeared because the historical movement is now toward capitalism from socialism. The crisis also finds its expression in the whole decline of stage-oriented historical theory in general. (Ishitsuka 1994)

Cf. Hobsbawm (1991: 17): 'All this is now over. . . . We are seeing not the crisis of a type of movement, regime, of economy, but its end. Those of us who believed that the October Revolution was the gate to the future of world history have been shown to be wrong.' Or Bobbio (1991: 3): 'In a seemingly irreversible way, the great political utopia . . . has been completely upturned into its exact opposite.'

3. 'We should henceforth conclude that the future of socialism, if it has one, can only lie within capitalism,' writes Steven Lukes (1990: 574) in an effort to come to grips with the new transitions. For an intelligent, often anguished, and revealing intra-left debate on the ideological and empirical implications of these events, see the debate to which Lukes's essay forms a part: Goldfarb (1990), Katznelson (1990), Heilbroner (1990) and Campeanu (1990). See also the important and revealing collection *After the Fall* (Blackburn 1991a).

4. For some contentious and revealing formulations of these issues, see the debate between Nikolai Genov, Piotr Sztompka, Franco Crespi, Hans Joas, myself, and other theorists in the 1991 and 1992 issues of *Theory*, the newsletter of the Research Committee on Sociological Theory of the International Sociological Association. Those exchanges, which reproduced many of the old lines of modernization versus anti-modernization debate, demonstrated how difficult it is to step outside of binary thinking on the convergence issue, for reasons that the following analysis of codes will make clear.

5. Paul Colomy and I (1995) have introduced the term 'reconstruction' to indicate a path of scientific cumulation that is more radical vis-à-vis the originating tradition than the kinds of efforts at specification, elaboration, or revision that more typically mark the efforts of social scientists who wish to keep their theoretical tradition alive in response to intellectual challenge and the loss of scientific prestige. Reconstruction suggests that fundamental elements of the founder's 'classical' work are changed, often by incorporating elements from its challengers, even while the tradition as such is defended, e.g. Habermas's effort to 'reconstruct historical materialism' in the mid-1970s. Reconstruction should also be distinguished from 'theory creation,' in which a fundamentally different theoretical tradition is created, e.g. Habermas's later effort to create the theory of communicative action.

6. By scientific, I do not evoke the principles of empiricism. I do mean to refer, however, to the explanatory ambition and propositions of a theory, which must be evaluated in their own terms. These can be interpretive and cultural, eschew narrative or statistical causality and, indeed, the natural scientific form. By extra-scientific, I mean to refer to a theory's mythical or ideological function.

7. I draw here from a broad range of writings that appeared in the 1950s and early 1960s by such figures as Daniel Lerner, Marion Levy, Alex Inkeles, Talcott Parsons, David Apter, Robert Bellah, S.N. Eisenstadt, Walt Rostow, and Clark Kerr. None of these authors accepted each of these propositions as such, and some of them, as we will see, 'sophisticated' them in significant ways. Nonetheless, these propositions can be accepted as forming the common denominator upon which the great part of the tradition's explanatory structure was based. For an excellent overview of this traditon that, while more detailed, agrees in fundamental respects with the approach taken here, see Sztompka (1993: 129–36).

8. Probably the most sophisticated formulation of this truth is Smelser's elaboration (e.g. 1968), during the final days of modernization theory, of how modernization produced leads and lags between subsystems, a process which, borrowing from Trotsky, he called uneven and combined development. Like virtually every other important younger theorist of the period, Smelser eventually gave up on the modernization model,

in his case for a 'process' model (Smelser 1991) that delineated no particular epochal characteristics and which allowed subsystems to interact in a highly open-ended way.

9. I am grateful to Muller (1992: 118) for recalling this passage. Muller notes the 'acute sense of reality' (ibid.: 111) displayed in modernization theory's 'amazing hypotheses' (ibid.: 112) about the eventual demise of state socialism. He insists, quite correctly in my view, that 'it was not the [neo-Marxist] critique of capitalism in the 1970s which correctly read the secular trends of the late twentieth century – it was Parsons' theory' (ibid.).

10. 'Seen historically, "modernization" has always been a process propelled by inter-cultural exchange, military conflicts and economic competition among states and power blocks – as, likewise, Western postwar modernization took place within a newly created world order' (Muller 1992: 138). See also the critiques of classical differentiation theory in Alexander (1988) and Alexander and Colomy (1990).

11. This existential or mythical dimension of social scientific theory is generally ignored in interpretations of social scientific thought, except for those occasions when it is glossed as political ideology (e.g. Gouldner 1970). Simmel acknowledged a genre of speculative work in social science, which he called 'philosophical sociology,' but he carefully differentiated it from the empirical disciplines or parts thereof. For example, he wrote in his *Philosophy of Money* that a philosophical sociology was necessary because there exist questions 'that we have so far been unable either to answer or to discuss' (quoted in Levine 1991: 99, italics added). As I see it, however, questions that are essentially unanswerable lie at the heart of all social scientific theories of change. This means that one cannot neatly separate the empirical from the nonempirical. In terms I employ below, even theorists in the social sciences are intellectuals, even if most intellectuals are not social scientific theorists.

12. 'We can comprehend the appeal of historical discourse by recognizing the extent to which it makes the real desirable, makes the real into an object of desire, and does so by its imposition, upon events that are represented as real, of the formal coherency that stories possess. ... The reality that is represented in the historical narrative, in "speaking itself," speaks *to* us ... and displays to us a formal coherency that we our-selves lack. The historical narrative, as against the chronicle, reveals to us a world that is putatively "finished," done with, over, and yet not dissolved, not falling apart. In this world, reality wears the mask of a meaning, the completeness and fullness of which we can only *imagine*, never experience. Insofar as historical stories can be completed, can be given narrative closure, can be shown to have had a *plot* all along, they give to reality the odor of the *ideal*.' (White 1980: 20, original italics)

13. Of course, as Caillois (1959) pointed out, and as Durkheim's original work obscured, there are actually three terms that so classify the world, for there is also the 'mundane.' Myth disdains the very existence of the mundane, moving between the highly charged poles of negative repulsion and positive attraction.

14. The retrospective account by Lerner, one of the architects of modernization theory, indicates the pivotal nature of the American reference:

[After] World War II, which witnessed the constriction of European empires and the diffusion of American presence ... one spoke, often resentfully, of the Americanization of Europe. But when one spoke of the rest of the world, the term was 'Westernization.' The postwar years soon made clear, however, that even this larger term was too parochial. ... A global referent [was needed]. In response to this need, the new term 'modernization' evolved.
(Lerner 1968: 386)

An interesting topic of investigation would be the contrast between European theorists of modernization and American ones. The most distinguished European and the most original, Raymond Aron, had a decidedly less optimistic view of convergence than his American counterparts, as he demonstrated, e.g., in his *Progress and Disillusion* (1968), which forms an extremely interesting counterpart to his convergence argument in *Eighteen Lectures on Industrial Society* (1962). While there seems little doubt that

Aron's version of convergence theory also represented a response to the cataclysm of the Second World War, it was more a fatalistic and resolute reaction than an optimistic and pragmatic one. See the account in his *Memoirs* (Aron 1990).

15. 'The Forties was a decade when the speed with which one's own events occurred seemed as rapid as the history of the battlefields, and for the mass of people in America a forced march into a new jungle of emotion was the result. The surprises, the failures, and the dangers of that life must have terrified some nerve of awareness in the power and the mass, for, as if stricken ... the retreat to a more conservative existence was disorderly, the fear of communism spread like an irrational hail of boils. To anyone who could see, the excessive hysteria of the Red wave was no preparation to face an enemy, but rather a terror of the national self' (Mailer 1987 [1960]: 14).

16. In terms of the break induced in American intellectuals by the postwar period, it is revealing to compare this later change theory of Parsons with his earlier one. In the essays on social change he composed in the decade after 1937, Parsons consistently took Germany as his model, emphasizing the destablilizing, polarizing, and antidemocratic implications of social differentiation and rationalization. When he referred to modernization in this period, and he rarely did, he employed the term to refer to a pathological, over-rationalizing process, one that produced the symptomatic reaction of 'traditionalism.' After 1947, Parsons took the United States as the type case for his studies of social change, relegating Nazi Germany to the status of deviant case. Modernization and traditionalism were now viewed as structural processes rather than as ideologies, symptoms, or social actions.

17. It is ironic that one of the best recent explications of, and justifications for, Frye's version of generic history can be found in the Marxist criticism of Jameson, which purports to refute its bourgeois form yet makes heavy use of its substantive content. Jameson (1980: 130) calls Frye's method a 'positive hermeneutic' because 'his identification of mythic patterns in modern texts aims at reinforcing our sense of the affinity between the cultural present of capitalism and the distant mythical past of tribal societies, and at awakening a sense of the continuity between our psychic life and that of primitive peoples.' He offers his 'negative hermeneutic' as an alternative, asserting that it uses 'the narrative raw material shared by myth and "historical" literatures to sharpen our sense of historical difference, and to stimulate an increasingly vivid apprehension of what happens when plot falls into history ... and enters the force fields of the modern societies' (ibid.)

Despite the fact that Jameson is wedded to a reflection theory of ideology, he produces, in fact, an excellent rationale for the use of genre analysis in understanding historical conflicts. He argues that an influential social 'text' must be understood as 'a socially symbolic act, as the ideological – but formal and immanent – response to a historical dilemma' (ibid.: 139). Because of the strains in the social environment that call texts forth, 'it would seem to follow that, properly used, genre theory must always in one way or another project a model of the coexistence or tension between several generic modes or strands.' With this 'methodological axiom,' Jameson suggests, 'the typologizing abuses of traditional genre theory criticism are definitely laid to rest' (ibid.: 141).

For the relevance of generic theory to the analysis of social rather than literary texts, see the historical writings of Slotkin (1973), the sociological studies of Wagner-Pacifici (1986) and Gibson (1991), and more recently the work of Margaret R. Somers (e.g. 1992).

For the particularities of my own approach to social genre and its relation to cultural codes, I am indebted to conversations with Philip Smith (1991, 1993) and Steven Sherwood (1994), whose own writings are important theoretical statements in their own right.

18. By using the postmodern term 'grand narrative' (Lyotard 1984), I am committing anachronism, but I am doing so in order to demonstrate the lack of historical perspective implied by the postmodernist slogan 'the end of the grand narrative.' Grand narratives, in fact, are subjected to periodic historical deflation and inflation, and there are always other, less inflated generic constructions 'waiting' to take their place. I will point out below,

indeed, that there are important similarities between the postwar period of narrative deflation and the 1980s, which produced a broadly similar inturning that postmodernism characterized to such great effect as a historically unprecedented social fact.

19. Romanticism is used here in the technical, genre sense suggested by Frye (1957), rather than in the broad historical sense that would refer to post-classical music, art, and literature, which in the terms employed here was more 'heroic' in its narrative implications.

20. When I arrived at the University of California, Berkeley, for graduate school in Sociology in 1969, some of the Department's Chicago school sociologists, influenced by Goffman and Sartre, announced an informal faculty-student seminar on 'authenticity.' This represented an existentialism-inspired response to the alienation emphasis of the sixties. As such, it was historically out of phase. Nobody attended the seminar.

21. The present account does not, in other words, assume complete intellectual consensus during the phases described. Counter-trends existed, and they should be noted. There is also the very real possibility (see n. 27, below) that intellectuals and their audiences had access to more than one code/narrative at any given point in historical time, an access that Wagner-Pacifici (personal communication) calls discursive hybridity. My account does suggest, however, that each of these phases was marked, indeed was in part constructed by, the hegemony of one intellectual framework over others. Narratives are constructed upon binary codes, and it is the polarity of binary oppositions that allows historicizing intellectuals to make sense of their time. 'Binarism' is less an esoteric theoretical construct than an existential fact of life.

22. This points to one quibble I have with Jamison and Eyerman's *Seeds of the Sixties* (1994), their brilliant account of these fifties critical intellectuals. Jamison and Eyerman argue that they failed to exert influence at the time primarily because of the conservatism of the dominant society. It seems important to add, however, that their own ideology was partly responsible, for it was insufficiently historical in the future-oriented, narrative sense. A more important disagreement would be that Jamison and Eyerman seem to accept 'mass society' as an actual empirical description of both social structural and cultural modernization in the fifties. In so doing, they may be mistaking an intellectual account for a social reality. These vestiges of a realist epistemology – in what is otherwise an acutely cultural and constructivist approach – makes impossible to appreciate the compelling humanism that informed so much of the work of the very fifties intellectuals whom these critics often attacked.

23. A publication that in retrospect takes on the appearance of a representative, and representational, turning point between these historical phases, and between modernization theory and what succeeded it, is David Apter's edited book *Ideology and Discontent* (1964). Among the contributors were leading modernization social scientists, who grappled with the increasingly visible anomalies of this theory, particularly the continuing role of utopian and revolutionary ideology in the third world, which inspired revolutions, and, more generally, with the failure of 'progressive' modernizing development. Geertz's 'Ideology as a Cultural System' (1973 [1964]), so central to developments in postmodernization theories, appeared first in this volume. Apter himself, incidentally, demonstrated a personal theoretical evolution paralleling the broader shifts documented here, moving from an enthusiastic embrace, and explication, of third world modernization, which concentrated on universal categories of culture and social structure (see, e.g., Apter 1963), to a postmodern skepticism about 'liberating' change and an emphasis on cultural particularity. This latter position is indicated by the self-consciously antimodernist and antirevolutionary themes in the striking deconstruction of Maoism that Apter (1987) published in the late 1980s. The intellectual careers of Robert Bellah and Michael Walzer (cf. my discussion of Smelser's shifting concerns in n. 8, above) reveal similar though not identical contours.

These examples and others (see n. 20, above) raise the intriguing question that Mills described as the relationship between history and biography. How did individual intellectuals deal with the historical succession of code/narrative frames, which pushed them into interstitial positions vis-à-vis the 'new world of our time'? Some remained committed to their earlier frameworks and became, as a result, either permanently or temporarily 'obsolete.' Others changed their frameworks and became contemporary, not necessarily for opportunistic reasons but because of personal encounters with profoundly jarring historical experiences, which sometimes gave them a keen appreciation for 'the new.'

24. See, for example, the millennial tone of the contemporary articles collected in *Smiling through the Apocalypse: Esquire's History of the Sixties* (Esquire editors 1987).

25. An illustrative case study of one dimension of this evolution would be the British *New Left Review*. Created initially as a forum for disseminating humanistic Marxism – oriented toward existentialism and consciousness – vis-à-vis the mechanistic perspective of the Old Left, in the late 1960s it was an important forum for publishing Sartre, Gramsci, Lefebvre, Gorz, and the early Lukács. By 1970, it had turned into a forum for Leninism and Althusserianism. The cover of its Fall 1969 issue was emblazoned with the slogan, 'Militancy.'

26. In order to forestall misunderstanding in regard to the kind of argument I am making here, I should emphasize that this and other correlations I am positing between code, narrative, and theory constitute what Weber, drawing on Goethe, called 'elective affinities' rather than historically, sociologically, or semiotically causal relations. Commitment to these theories could, in principle, be induced by other kinds of ideological formulations, and have been, in earlier times and other national milieux. Nor need these particular versions of code and narrative always be combined. Nonetheless, in the historical periods I consider here, the positions did mesh in complementary ways.

27. This brief aside about the 'lag' in generational production is important to emphasize. It is primarily new generations coming to political and cultural self-consciousness that produces new intellectual ideologies and theories, and, as Mannheim first emphasized, generational identities tend to remain constant despite shifts in historical time. The result is that, at any given point, the 'intellectual milieu' considered as a totality will contain a number of competing ideological formulations produced by historically generated archeological formations. Insofar as there remain authoritative intellectual figures within each generation, furthermore, earlier intellectual ideologies will continue to socialize some members of succeeding generations. Authoritative socialization, in other words, exacerbates the lag effect, which is further increased by the fact that access to the organizational infrastructures of socialization – e.g. control of graduate training programs in major universities, editorships of leading journals – may be attained by the authoritative members of generations whose ideology/theory may already be 'refuted' by developments that are occurring among younger generations. These considerations produce layering effects that make it difficult to recognize intellectual successions until long after they are crystallized.

These inertial effects of generational formations suggest that new ideologies/theories may have to respond not only to the immediately preceding formation – which is their primary reference point – but in a secondary way to all the formations that remain in the social milieu at the time of their formation. For example, while postmodernism will be portrayed here as a response primarily to antimodernization theories of revolutionary intent, it is also marked by the need to posit the inadequacy of postwar modernism and, indeed, of prewar Marxism. As I indicate below, however, postmodernism's responses to the latter movements are mediated by their primary response to the ideology/theory immediately preceding it. Indeed, it only understands the earlier movements as they have been screened by the sixties generation.

28. This sense of imminent, apocalyptic transformation was exemplified in the 1980s by the post-Marxist and postmodern British magazine *Marxism Today*, which hailed, in millennial language, the arrival of 'New Times':

> Unless the Left can come to terms with those New Times, it must live on the sidelines. . . . Our world is being remade. . . . In the process our own identities, our sense of self, our own subjectivities are being transformed. We are in transition to a new era.
>
> (*Marxism Today*, October 1988; quoted in Thompson 1992: 238)

29. A compendium of postmodernism's middle-level innovations in social scientific knowledge has been compiled by Crook, Pakulski, and Waters (1992). For a cogent critique of the socio-economic propositions such middle-range theories of the post-modern age either advance or assume, see Herpin (1993). For other critiques, Alexander (1991, 1992), Archer (1987), and Giddens (1991).

30. In December 1986, the *Guardian*, a leading independent British newspaper broadly on the left, ran a three-day-long major series, 'Modernism and Post-Modernism.' In his introductory article, Richard Gott announced, by way of explanation, that 'the revolutionary impulses that had once galvanized politics and culture had clearly become sclerotic' (quoted in Thompson 1992: 222). Thompson's own analysis of this event is particularly sensitive to the central role played in it by the historical deflation of the heroic revolutionary myth:

> Clearly this newspaper thought the subject of an alleged cultural shift from modernism to post-modernism sufficiently important for it to devote many pages and several issues to the subject. The reason it was considered important is indicated by the sub-heading: 'Why did the revolutionary movement that lit up the early decades of the century fizzle out. In a major series, *Guardian* critics analyse late twentieth-century malaise'. . . . The subsequent articles made it even clearer that the cultural 'malaise' represented by the shift from modernism was regarded as symptomatic of a deeper social and political malaise.
>
> (ibid.)

The stretching of revolutionary fervor, and the very term 'modernism,' to virtually the entirety of the pre-postmodernism twentieth century – sometimes, indeed, to the entire post-Enlightenment era – is a tendency common to postmodernist theory. A natural reflection of its binary and narrative functions, such broad claims play a vital role in situating the 'postmodern' age vis-à-vis the future and the past.

31. 'La révolution qu'anticipaient les avant-gardes et les partis d'extrême gauche et que dénonçaient les penseurs et les organisations de droit ne s'est pas produite. Mais les sociétés avancés n'en ont pas moins subi une transformation radicale. Tel est le constat commun que font les sociologues . . . qui ont fait de la postmodernité le thème de leurs analyses' (Herpin 1993: 295).

32. It is these sentiments precisely that characterize C. Wright Mills's early musings about what he called the 'Fourth Epoch,' in a 1959 radio interview that, to my knowledge, marked the first time that the term 'postmodern' in its contemporary sense ever appeared.

> We are at the end of what is called The Modern Age. Just as Antiquity was followed by several centuries of Oriental ascendancy which Westerners provincially call The Dark Ages, so now The Modern Age is being succeeded by a post-modern period. Perhaps we call it: The Fourth Epoch.
>
> The ending of one epoch and the beginning of another is, to be sure, a matter of definition. But definitions, like everything social, are historically specific. And now *our basic definitions of society and of self are being overtaken by new realities*. I do not mean merely that we feel *we are in an epochal kind of transition*, I mean that too many of our explanations are derived from the great historical transition from the Medieval to the Modern Age; and that when they are generalized for use today, they become unwieldly, irrelevant, not convincing. And I mean also that *our major orientations – liberalism and socialism – have virtually collapsed as adequate explanations of the world and of ourselves*.
>
> (Mills 1963: 236, italics added; quoted in Thompson, forthcoming)

As an anticapitalist critical theorist who experienced deep disappointment with the heroic utopianism of class-oriented communism and social movements, Mills's personal situation anticipated the 'transition experience' that compelled the postmodernist movement twenty years hence. In 1959, however, the time of high modernist hegemony, Mills's efforts at historical sense-making could hardly have had the ring of truth. Liberalism was yet to have its greatest days, and the heroic radicalism of the 1960s was scarcely foreseen. This shows, once again, that while in any historical period there exist contending mythical constructions, those that are out of phase will be ignored; they will be seen as failing to 'explain' the 'new world of our times.'

33. This mood of pessimism should be compared to the distinctly more optimistic tone of Jameson's 'Preface' to *The Political Unconscious*, his collection of essays written during the 1970s, in which he seeks to 'anticipate . . . those new forms of collective thinking and collective culture which lie beyond the boundaries of our own world,' describing them as the 'yet unrealized, collective, and decentered cultural production of the future, beyond realism and modernism alike' (1980: 11). Scarcely a decade later, what Jameson found to be beyond modernism turned out to be quite different from the collective and liberating culture he had sought.

34. Postmodern theorists are fond of tracing their antimodern roots to Romanticism, to anti-Enlightenment figures like Nietzsche, to Simmel, and to themes articulated by the early Frankfurt School. Yet the earlier, more traditionally Marxist rebellion against modernization theory often traced its lineage in similar ways. As Seidman (1983) demonstrated before his postmodern turn, Romanticism itself had significant universalizing strains, and between Nietzsche and Simmel there exists a fundamental disagreement over the evaluation of modernity itself.

35. It depends upon a number of other contingent decisions as well, for example upon ignoring postmodernism's own claim that it does not have or advocate a general theory. (See, e.g., my exchange with Seidman [Alexander 1991 and Seidman 1991b].) There is, in addition, the much more general problem of whether postmodernism can even be spoken of as a single point of view. I have taken the position here that it can be so discussed, even while I have acknowledged the diversity of points of view within it. There is no doubt, indeed, that each of the four theories I examine here only exists, as such, via an act of hermeneutical reconstruction. Such an ideal-type methodology is, I would argue, not only philosophically justifiable (e.g. Gadamer 1975) but intellectually unavoidable, in the sense that the hermeneutics of common sense continually refers to 'postmodernism' as such. Nonetheless, these considerations should not obscure the fact that a typification and idealization is being made. In more empirical and concrete terms, each historical period and each social theory under review contained diverse patterns and parts.

36. The link between glasnost and perestroika and President Ronald Reagan's military build-up – particularly his Star Wars project – has been frequently stressed by former Soviet officials who participated in the transition that began in 1985. For example:

> Former top soviet officials said Friday that the implications of then-President Reagan's 'Star Wars' proposal and the Chernobyl accident combined to change Soviet arms policy and help end the Cold War. Speaking at Princeton University during a conference on the end of the Cold War, the officials said . . . Soviet President Mikhail Gorbachev was convinced that any attempt to match Reagan's Strategic Defense Initiative of 1983 . . . could do irreparable harm to the Soviet economy.
>
> (Reuters News Service. February 27, 1993)

37. This sense of fundamental, boundary-destroying break is clearly exhibted in the recent work of Kenneth Jowitt, which searches for biblical imagery to communicate a sense of how widespread and threatening is the contemporary genuine intellectual disorientation:

> For nearly half a century, the boundaries of international politics and the identities of its national participants have been directly shaped by the presence of a Leninist regime world centered in the Soviet Union. The Leninist extinction of 1989 poses a fundamental challenge to these boundaries and identities. . . . Boundaries are an essential component of a recognizable and coherent identity. . . . The attenuation of or dissolution of boundaries is more often than not a traumatic event – all the more so when boundaries have been organized and understood in highly categorical terms. . . . The Cold War was a 'Joshua' period, one of dogmatically centralized boundaries and identities. In contrast to the biblical sequence, the

Leninist extinction of 1989 has moved the world from a Joshua to a Genesis environment: from one centrally organized, rigidly bounded, and hysterically concerned with impenetrable boundaries to one in which territorial, ideological, and issue boundaries are attenuated, unclear, and confusing. We now inhabit a world that, while not 'without form and void,' is one in which the major imperatives are the same as in Genesis, 'naming and bounding.'

(Jowitt 1992: 306–7)

Jowitt compares the world-reshaping impact of the events of 1989 with those of the Battle of Hastings in 1066.

38. One of the little-noticed battle-grounds of intellectual ideology over the last thirty years has been the 'shopping center,' a.k.a. 'the mall.' Making its appearance after the Second World War in the United States, it came to represent for many conservative liberals the continuing vitality – contrary to the dire predictions of Marxist thought in the 1930s – of 'small business' and the 'petit bourgeoisie.' Later, neo-Marxists like Mandel devoted a great deal of space to the shopping centers, suggesting that this new form of organization had staved off capitalism's ultimate economic stagnation, describing it as the organizational equivalent of advertising's 'artificial creation' of 'false needs.' In the 1980s, these same sprawling congeries of mass capitalism, now transformed into upscale but equally plebeian malls, became the object of attack from postmodernists, who saw them not as wily stop-gaps to stagnation but as perfect representations of the fragmentation, commercialism, privatism, and retreatism that marked the end of utopian hope (and possibly of history itself). The most famous example of the latter is Jameson (e.g. 1988) on the Los Angeles Bonaventure Hotel.

39. For example, in his recent plea to fellow members of the academic left – many if not most of whom are now postmodern in their promotion of difference and particularism – Todd Gitlin argues not only that a renewal of the project of universalism is necessary to preserve a viable critical intellectual politics but also that such a movement has already begun:

If there is to be a Left in more than a sentimental sense, its position ought to be: This desire for human unity is indispensable. The ways, means, basis, and costs are a subject for disciplined conversation. . . . Now, alongside the indisputable premise that knowledge of many kinds is specific to time, place, and interpretive community, thoughtful critics are placing the equally important premise that there are unities in the human condition and that, indeed, the existence of common understandings is the basis of all communication (= making common) across boundaries of language and history and experience. Today, some of the most exciting scholarship entails efforts to incorporate new and old knowledge together in unified narratives. Otherwise there is no escape from solipsism, whose political expression cannot be the base of liberalism or radicalism.

(Gitlin 1993: 36–7)

40. The massive negative response among contemporary social theorists to Coleman's tome – the review symposium in *Theory and Society* (e.g. Alexander 1991) is not an untypical example – is less an indication that rational choice theory is being massively rejected than an expression of the fact that neo-modernism is not, at this time, sympathetic to a conservative political tilt. This may not be true in the future.

41. There is clear evidence that this transformation is world-wide in scope. In Quebec, for example, Arnaud Sales, who worked earlier in a strongly Marxist tradition, now insists on a universal relatedness among conflict groups and incorporates the language of 'public' and 'civil society.'

If, in their multiplicity, associations, unions, corporations, and movements have always defended and represented very diversified opinions, it is probable that, despite the power of economic and statist systems, the proliferation of groups founded on a tradition, a way of life, an opinion or a protest has probably never been so broad and so diversified as it is at the end of the twentieth century.

(Sales 1991: 308)

42. See my earlier remarks (n. 27, above) on the inertial effects of intellectual ideologies and on the social conditions that exacerbate them.

43. This would seem, at first glance, to confirm Said's quasi-Marxist insistence that it was the rise of the West's actual power in the world – imperialism – that allowed the ideology of orientalism to proceed. What Said does not recognize, however, is that there is a more general code of sacred and profane categories of which the 'social representations' of orientalism is a historically specific subset. The discourse of civil society is an ideological formation that preceded imperialism and that informed the pollution of diverse categories of historically encountered others – Jews, women, slaves, proletarians, homosexuals, and more generally enemies – in quite similar terms.

44. Exceptions to this amnesia can, however, be found in the current debate, particularly among those French social theorists who remain strongly influenced by the Republican tradition. See, for example, Michel Wieviorka's (1993: 23–70) lucid argument for a contested and double-sided understanding of nationalism and Dominique Schnapper's (1994) powerful defense of the national character of the democratic state. For another good recent statement of this more balanced position, see Hall (1993).

45. Most recently, see Khosrokhavar's (1993) illumating discussion of how the negative utopia of Shi'ite religion undermined the more universalistic strains in the Iranian revolution.

46. In a telling observation on the paradoxical relationship of nationalism to recent events, Wittrock (1991) notes that when West Germany pressed for reunification, it both affirmed the abstract universalism of notions like freedom, law, and markets and, at the same time, the ideology of nationalism in its most particularistic, ethnic, and linguistic sense, the notion that the 'German people' could not be divided.

References

Adorno, T., E. Frankel-Brunswick, D.J. Levinson, and N. Sanford (1950) *The Authoritarian Personality*. New York: Harpers.

Alexander, J.C. (1987) *Twenty Lectures: Sociological Theory since World War II*. New York: Columbia University Press.

Alexander, J.C. (1988) *Action and Its Environments*. New York: Columbia University Press.

Alexander, J.C., ed. (1989) *Durkheimian Sociology: Cultural Studies*. New York: Cambridge University Press.

Alexander, J.C. (1991) 'Sociological Theory and the Claim to Reason: Why the End is Not in Sight. Reply to Seidman.' *Sociological Theory* 9 (2): 147–53.

Alexander, J.C. (1992a) 'The Fragility of Progress: An Interpretation of the Turn Toward Meaning in Eisenstadt's Later Work.' *Acta Sociologica* 35: 85–94.

Alexander, J.C. (1992b) 'Citizen and Enemy as Symbolic Classification: On the Polarizing Discourse of Civil Society,' pp. 289–308 in M. Fournier and M. Lamont, eds, *Cultivating Differences*. Chicago: University of Chicago Press.

Alexander, J.C. (1992) 'General Theory in the Postpositivist Mode: The "Epistemological Dilemma" and the Case for Present Reason,' pp. 322–68 in S. Seidman and D. Wagner, eds, *Postmodernism and Social Theory*. New York: Basil Blackwell.

Alexander, J.C. (1994) 'The Return to Civil Society.' *Contemporary Sociology* 23: 797–803.

Alexander, J.C., and P. Colomy, eds (1990) *Differentiation Theory and Social Change*. New York: Columbia University Press.

Alexander, J.C., and P. Colomy (1995) 'Traditions and Competition: Preface to a Postpositivist Approach to Knowledge Accumulation,' in Alexander, *Neofunctionalism and Beyond*. New York and Oxford: Blackwell.

Alexander, J.C., and S. Sherwood (1992) 'Why Yeltsin Can't Get No Respect in America.' *Los Angeles Times*, February 2: Section M, p. 2.

Alexander, J.C., and S. Sherwood (1994) 'The Making, Unmaking, and Resurrection of an American Hero: Gorbachev and the Discourse of the Good.' Unpublished ms.
Alexander, J.C., and P. Smith (1993) 'The Discourse of American Civil Society: A New Proposal for Cultural Studies.' *Theory and Society* 22: 151–207.
Apter, D. (1963) *Ghana in Transition*. New York: Atheneum.
Apter, D., ed. (1964) *Ideology and Discontent*. London: Free Press.
Apter, D. (1987) 'Mao's Republic.' *Social Research* 54 (4): 691–729.
Archer, M. (1987) 'Revisiting the Revival of Relativism.' *International Sociology* 2 (3): 235–50.
Aron, R. (1962) *Eighteen Lectures on Industrial Society*. New York: Free Press.
Aron, R. (1968) *Progress and Disillusionment: The Dialectics of Modern Society*. New York: Praeger.
Aron, R. (1990) *Memoirs: Fifty Years of Political Reflection*. New York and London: Holmes Meier.
Banfield, E.C., ed. (1991) *Civility and Citizenship*. New York: Paragon.
Baran, P.A., and M. Sweezy (1966) *Monopoly Capital*. New York: Monthly Review Press.
Barber, B. (1992) 'Jihad vs. McWorld.' *The Atlantic Monthly*, March: 53–65.
Barbour, I. (1974) *Myths, Models, and Paradigms: The Nature of Scientific and Religious Language*. London: SCM Press.
Barthes, R. (1977) 'Introduction to the Structural Analysis of Narratives,' pp. 79–124 in Barthes, *Image–Music–Text*. London: Fontana.
Baudrillard, J. (1983) *In the Shadow of the Silent Majority – Or the End of the Social*. New York: Semiotext(e).
Baumann, Z. (1989) *Modernity and the Holocaust*. Ithaca: Cornell University Press.
Beck, U. (1994) 'The Reinvention of Politics: Towards a Theory of Reflexive Modernization,' pp. 1–55 in Beck, A. Giddens, and S. Lash, *Reflexive Modernization: Politics, Tradition and Aesthetics in the Modern Social Order*. Cambridge: Polity
Bell, D. (1962a) *The End of Ideology: On the Exhaustion of Political Ideas in the Fifties*. New York: Free Press.
Bell, D. (1962b) 'Work and Its Discontents,' pp. 227–72 in Bell, *The End of Ideology: On the Exhaustion of Political Ideas in the Fifties*. New York: Free Press.
Bell, D. (1962c) 'The Mood of Three Generations,' pp. 299–314 in Bell, *The End of Ideology: On the Exhaustion of Political Ideas in the Fifties*. New York: Free Press.
Bell, D. (1973) *The Coming of Post-Industrial Society*. New York: Basic Books.
Bell, D. (1976) *The Cultural Contradictions of Capitalism*. New York: Basic Books.
Bell, D. (1977) 'The Return of the Sacred?' *British Journal of Sociology* 27 (4): 419–49.
Bell, D. (1978) 'The Disjuncture of Realms.' Unpublished ms.
Bellah, R.N. (1957) *Tokugawa Religion*. Boston: Beacon.
Bellah, R.N. (1970a) 'Religious Evolution,' pp. 20–50 in Bellah, *Beyond Belief*. New York: Harper & Row.
Bellah, R.N. (1970b) 'The Sociology of Religion,' pp. 3–19 in Bellah, *Beyond Belief*. New York: Harper & Row.
Bellah, R.N. (1970c) 'Civil Religion in America,' pp. 168–89 in Bellah, *Beyond Belief*. New York: Harper & Row.
Bellah, R.N., and C. Glock, eds (1976) *The New Religious Consciousness*. Berkeley and Los Angeles: University of California Press.
Bendix, R. (1964) *Nation-Building and Citizenship*. New York: Doubleday.
Bendix, R., et al., eds (1968) *State and Society*. Berkeley and Los Angeles: University of California Press.
Blackburn, R. (1991a) *After the Fall: The Failure of Communism and the Future of Socialism*. London: Verso.
Blackburn, R. (1991b) 'Fin-de-Siècle: Socialism after the Crash,' pp. 173–249 in Blackburn, ed., *After the Fall: The Failure of Communism and the Future of Socialism*. London: Verso.
Bobbio, N. (1991) 'The Upturned Utopia,' pp. 3–5 in Blackburn, ed., *After the Fall*:

The Failure of Communism and the Future of Socialism. London: Verso.

Boltanksi, L. (1993) *La Souffrance à distance*. Paris: Editions Metailie.

Boltanski, L., and L. Thevenot (1991) *De la justification*. Paris: Gallimard.

Bonacich, E. (1972) 'A Theory of Ethnic Antagonism: The Split Labor Market.' *American Sociological Review* 37: 547–59.

Boudon, R. (1984) *L'Ideologie*. Paris: Fayard.

Bourdieu, P. (1984) *Distinction: A Social Critique of the Judgement of Taste*. Cambridge, Mass.: Harvard University Press.

Bourricaud, F. (1987) '"Universal Reference" and the Process of Modernization,' pp. 12–21 in S.N. Eisenstadt, ed., *Patterns of Modernity, Vol. I*: London: Frances Pinter.

Brooks, P. (1984) *The Melodramatic Imagination*. New York: Columbia University Press.

Brown, N.O. (1959) *Life against Death*. Middletown, Conn.: Wesleyan University Press.

Brown, N.O. (1966) *Love's Body*. New York: Vintage.

Brubaker, R. (1994) 'Nationhood and the National Question in the Soviet Union and Post-Soviet Eurasia: An Institutional Account.' *Theory and Society* 23 (1): 47–78.

Buckley, W. (1951) *God and Man at Yale*. Chicago: Regnery.

Burn, W.L. (1974) *The Age of Equipoise*. London: George Allen and Unwin.

Caillois, R. (1959) *Man and the Sacred*. New York: Free Press.

Calhoun, C. (1993) 'Nationalism and Civil Society: Democracy, Identity and Self-Determination.' *International Sociology* 8 (4): 387–411.

Campeanu, P. (1990) 'Transition in Europe.' *Social Research* 57 (3): 587–90.

Chan, E. (1994) 'Tian-Anmen and the Crisis of Chinese Society: A Cultural Analysis of Ritual Process.' Unpublished Ph.D. thesis, UCLA, Los Angeles, California.

Chirot, D. (1990) 'After Socialism, What? Ideological Implications of the Events of 1989 in Eastern Europe for the Rest of the World.' Manuscript.

Cohen, J., and A. Arato (1992) *Civil Society and Political Theory*. Boston: MIT Press.

Cole, R.E. (1979) *Work, Mobility, and Participation: A Comparative Study of the American and Japanese Automobile Industry*. Berkeley and Los Angeles: University of California Press.

Coleman, J. (1990) *Foundations of Social Theory*. Cambridge, Mass.: Harvard University Press.

Collins, R. (1976) *Conflict Sociology*. New York: Academic Press.

Comaroff, J.L., and P.C. Stern (1994) 'New Perspectives on Nationalism and War.' *Theory and Society* 23 (1): 35–46.

Coser, L. (1956) *The Functions of Social Conflict*. New York: Free Press.

Crespi, F. (1992) *Power and Action*. Oxford: Blackwell.

Crook, S., J. Pakulski, and M. Waters (1992) *Postmodernization: Change in Advanced Society*. London: Sage.

Crossman, R., ed. (1950) *The God That Failed*. New York: Harper & Row.

Dahrendorf, R. (1959) *Class and Class Conflict in Industrial Society*. Stanford: Stanford University Press.

Durkheim, E. (1937 [1897]) *Suicide*. New York: Free Press.

Eisenstadt, S.N. (1963) *The Political System of Empires*. New York: Free Press.

Eisenstadt, S.N. (1964) 'Social Change, Differentiation, and Evolution.' *American Sociological Review* 29: 235–47.

Eisenstadt, S.N., ed. (1986) *The Origins and Diversity of Axial Age Civilizations*. Albany: SUNY Press.

Eisenstadt, S.N. (1987) 'Preface,' pp. vii–ix in Eisenstadt, ed., *Patterns of Modernity, Vol. I: The West*. London: Frances Pinter.

Eliade, M. (1954) *The Myth of the Eternal Return*. Princeton: Princeton University Press.

Elster, J. (1989) *The Cement of Society: A Study of Social Order*. New York: Cambridge University Press.

Empson, W. (1935) *Seven Types of Ambiguity*. London: Chatto & Windus.

Entrikin, N. (1991) *The Betweenness of Place*. Baltimore: Johns Hopkins University Press.

Esquire editors (1987) *Smiling through the Apocalypse: Esquire's History of the Sixties*. New York: Esquire.

Etzioni, A. (1968) *The Active Society*. New York: Free Press.

Evans, P., D. Rueschemeyer, and T. Skocpol, eds (1985) *Bringing the State Back In*. New York: Cambridge University Press.

Eyerman, R. (1992) 'Intellectuals: A Framework for Analysis, with Special Reference to the United States and Sweden.' *Acta Sociologica* 35: 33–46.

Fiedler, L. (1955) *An End to Innocence*. Boston: Beacon.

Foucault, M. (1977) *Discipline and Punish: The Birth of the Prison*. New York: Pantheon.

Frank, A.G. (1966) 'The Development of Underdevelopment.' *Monthly Reivew* 18 (4): 17–31.

Friedland, R. and A.F. Robertson, eds. (1990) *Beyond the Marketplace: Rethinking Economy and Society*. New York: Aldine de Gruyter.

Fromm, E. (1955) *The Sane Society*. New York: Reinhard.

Fromm, E. (1956) *The Art of Loving*. New York: Harper & Row.

Frye, N. (1957) *Anatomy of Criticism*. Princeton: Princeton University Press.

Fussell, P. (1975) *The Great War and Modern Memory*. Oxford: Oxford University Press.

Gadamer, G. (1975) *Truth and Method*. New York: Seabury.

Geertz, C. (1973) 'Ideology as a Cultural System,' pp. 193–233 in Geertz, *The Interpretation of Cultures*. New York: Basic Books.

Gibson, W.J. (1991) 'The Return of Rambo: War and Culture in the Post-Vietnam Era,' pp. 376–95 in A. Wolfe, ed., *America at Century's End*. Berkeley and Los Angeles: University of California Press.

Giddens, A. (1982) *Sociology: A Brief but Critical Introduction*. London: Macmillan.

Giddens, A. (1990) *The Consequences of Modernity*. Cambridge: Polity.

Giddens, A. (1991) *Modernity and Self-Identity: Self and Identity in the Late Modern Age*. Cambridge: Polity.

Giddens, A. (1992) *The Transformation of Intimacy*. Cambridge: Polity.

Giddens, A. (1994a) 'Living in Post-Traditional Society,' pp. 56–109 in U. Beck, Giddens, and S. Lash, *Reflexive Modernization: Politics, Tradition and Aesthetics in the Modern Social Order*. Cambridge: Polity.

Giddens, A. (1994b) *Beyond Left and Right*. Cambridge: Polity.

Gitlin, T. (1987) *The Sixties*. New York: Bantam

Gitlin, T. (1993) 'From Universality to Difference: Notes on the Fragmentation of the Idea of the Left.' *Contention* 2 (2): 15–40.

Goffman, E. (1956) *The Presentation of Self in Everyday Life*. New York: Anchor Doubleday.

Goldfarb, J.C. (1990) 'Post-Totalitarian Politics: Ideology Ends Again.' *Social Research* 57 (3): 533–56.

Goldthorpe, J., D. Lockwood, F. Beckhofer, and J. Platt, eds (1969) *The Affluent Worker and the Class Structure*. Cambridge: Cambridge University Press.

Gorz, A. (1982) *Farewell to the Working Class*. London: Pluto.

Gouldner, A. (1970) *The Coming Crisis of Western Sociology*. New York: Equinox.

Granovetter, M. (1974) *Getting a Job: A Study of Contracts and Careers*. Cambridge, Mass.: Harvard University Press.

Granovetter, M. (1985) 'Economic Action and Social Structure: A Theory of Embeddedness.' *American Journal of Sociology* 91 (3): 481–510.

Granovetter, M., and R. Swedberg, eds (1992) *The Sociology of Economic Life*. Boulder, Col.: Westview Press.

Greenfeld, L. (1992) 'Kitchen Debate: Russia's Nationalist Intelligentsia.' *The New Republic*, September 21: 22–5.

Greenfield, L., and C. Chirot (1994) 'Nationalism and Aggression.' *Theory and Society* 23 (1): 79–130.

Gusfield, J. (1966) 'Tradition and Modernity: Misplaced Polarities in the Study of Social Change.' *American Journal of Sociology* 72: 351–62.

Habermas, J. (1981) 'Modernity versus Postmodernity.' *New German Critique* 22: 3–14.

Habermas, J. (1989 [1962]) *The Structural Transformation of the Public Sphere.* Boston: Beacon.

Habermas, J. (1990) 'What Does Socialism Mean Today? The Rectifying Revolution and the Need for New Thinking on the Left.' *New Left Review* 183: 3–21.

Hall, J. (1985) *Powers and Liberties: Causes and Consequences of the Rise of the West.* Oxford: Oxford University Press.

Hall, J. (1993) 'Nationalisms: Classified and Explained.' *Daedalus* 122 (3): 1–28.

Halpern, D. (1990) *100 Years of Homosexuality and Other Essays on Greek Love.* New York: Routledge.

Hannerz, U. (1987) 'The World in Creolization.' *Africa* 57 (4): 546–59.

Hannerz, U. (1989) 'Notes on the Global Ecumene.' *Public Culture* 1 (2): 66–75.

Harrington, M. (1962) *The Other America.* New York: Macmillan.

Harvey, D. (1989) *The Conditions of Post-Modernity.* Oxford: Blackwell.

Hawthorn, G. (1991) *Plausible Worlds: Possibility and Understanding in History and the Social Sciences.* Cambridge: Cambridge University Press.

Heilbroner, R., ed. (1986) *The Essential Adam Smith.* New York: Norton.

Heilbroner, R. (1990) 'Rethinking the Past, Rehoping [sic] the Future.' *Social Research* 57 (3): 579–86.

Held, D. (1987) *Models of Democracy.* Stanford: Stanford University Press.

Herpin, N. (1993) 'Au-delà de la consommation de mass? Une discussion critique des sociologues de la post-modernité.' *L'anneé Sociologique* 43: 294–315.

Hobsbawm, E.(1991) 'Goodbye to All That,' pp. 115–25 in R. Blackburn, ed., *After the Fall: The Failure of Communism and the Future of Socialism.* London: Verso.

Holton, R. (1992) *Economy and Society.* London: Routledge.

Holton, R., and B. Turner (1986) *Talcott Parsons on Economy and Society.* London: Routledge & Kegan Paul.

Horowitz, D., and P. Collier (1989) *Destructive Generation: Second Thoughts about the 60s.* New York: Summit.

Huntington, S.P. (1968) *Political Order in Changing Societies.* New Haven: Yale University Press.

Huyssen, A. (1986) 'Mapping the Postmodern,' pp. 178–240 in Huyssen, *After the Great Divide.* Bloomington: Indiana University Press.

Inkeles, A. (1991) 'Transitions to Democracy.' *Society* 28 (4): 67–72.

Inkeles, A., and D.H. Smith (1974) *Becoming Modern: Industrial Change in Six Developing Countries.* Cambridge, Mass.: Harvard University Press.

Ishitsuka, S. (1994) 'The Fall of Real Socialism and the Crisis in Human Sciences.' *Social Justice* 27 (3).

Jameson, F. (1980) *The Political Unconscious: Narrative as a Socially Symbolic Act.* Ithaca: Cornell University Press.

Jameson, F. (1988) 'Postmodernism and Consumer Society,' pp. 13–29 in E.A. Kaplan, ed., *Postmodernism and Its Discontents.* London: Verso.

Jamison, A. and R. Eyerman (1994) *Seeds of the Sixties.* Berkeley and Los Angeles: University of California Press.

Jay, M. (1973) *The Dialectical Imagination.* Boston: Beacon.

Jowitt, K. (1992) *New World Disorder: The Leninist Extinction.* Berkeley and Los Angeles: University of California Press.

Johnson, P. (1983) *Modern Times: The World from the Twenties to the Eighties.* New York: Harper & Row.

Katznelson, I. (1990) 'Does the End of Totalitarianism Signify the End of Ideology?' *Social Research* 57 (3): 557–70.

Keane, J. (1988a) *Democracy and Civil Society*. London: Verso.

Keane, J., ed. (1988b) *Civil Society and the State*. London: Verso.

Kennedy, P. (1987) *The Rise and Fall of Great Powers: Economic Change and Military Conflict 1500–2000*. New York: Vintage.

Kennedy, P. (1993) *Preparing for the Twenty-First Century*. New York: Random House.

Khosrokhavar, F. (1993) *L'Utopie sacrifiée: Sociologie de la révolution iranienne*. Paris: Presses de la Fondation Nationale des Sciences Politiques.

Kolko, G. (1962) *Wealth and Power in America*. London: Thames & Hudson.

Kolko, G. (1967) *Triumph of Conservatism: Reinterpreting American History 1900–1916*. New York: Free Press.

Konrad, G., and I. Szelenyi (1979) *The Intellectuals on the Road to Class Power*. New York: Harcourt Brace.

Kornai, J. (1990) *The Road to a Free Economy. Shifting from a Socialist System: The Example of Hungary*. New York: Norton.

Kumar, K. (1992) 'The Revolutions of 1989: Socialism, Capitalism, and Democracy.' *Theory and Society*. 21: 309–56.

Lash, S. (1985) 'Postmodernity and Desire.' *Theory and Society* 14 (7): 1–31.

Lash, S. (1990) *Sociology of Postmodernism*. London: Routledge.

Lash, S. (1994) 'Reflexivity and its Doubles: Structure, Aesthetics, Community,' pp. 110–73 in U. Beck, A. Giddens, and Lash, *Reflexive Modernization: Politics, Tradition and Aesthetics in the Modern Social Order*. Cambridge: Polity.

Leijonhofvud, A. (1993) *The Nature of the Depression in the Former Soviet Union*. Unpublished ms, Department of Economics, UCLA, Los Angeles.

Lerner, D. (1968) 'Modernization. Social Aspects,' *International Encyclopedia of Social Science* 10: 386–95.

Levine, D.N. (1991) 'Simmel as Educator: On Individuality and Modern Culture.' *Theory, Culture and Society* 8: 99–117.

Levy, B.-H. (1977) *Barbarism with a Human Face*. New York: Harper & Row.

Levy, M. (1949) *The Family Revolution in Modern China*. Cambridge, Mass.: Harvard University Press.

Lipset, S.M. (1990) 'The Death of the Third Way.' *The National Interest* (Summer): 25–37.

Lipset, S.M., and R. Bendix (1960) *Social Mobility in Industrial Society*. Berkeley and Los Angeles: University of California Press.

Lowi, T. (1969) *The End of Liberalism*. New York: Norton.

Lukes, S. (1990) 'Socialism and Capitalism, Left and Right.' *Social Research* 57 (3): 571–7.

Lyotard, J.-F. (1984) *The Postmodern Condition: A Report on Knowledge*. Minneapolis: University of Minnesota Press.

McClelland, D. (1953) *The Achievement Motive*. New York: Appleton-Century-Crofts.

Mailer, N. (1987 [1960]) 'Superman Comes to the Supermarket: Jack Kennedy as a Presidential Candidate,' pp. 3–30 in Esquire editors, *Smiling through the Apocalypse: Esquire's History of the Sixties*. New York: Esquire.

Mandel, E. (1968) *Marxist Economic Theory*. 2 vols. New York: Monthly Review.

Mann, M. (1973) *Workers on the Move*. Cambridge: Cambridge University Press.

Mann, M. (1986) *The Sources of Social Power, Vol. 1*. New York: Cambridge University Press.

Mayhew, L. (1990) 'The Differentiation of the Solidary Public,' pp. 295–322 in J.C. Alexander and P. Colomy, eds, *Differentiation Theory and Social Change*. New York: Columbia University Press.

Meyer, J., and B. Rowan (1977) 'Institutionalized Organizations: Formal Structure as Myth and Ceremony.' *American Journal of Sociology* 83: 340–63.

Mills, C.W. (1948) *The New Men of Power: America's Labor Leaders*. New York: Harcourt Brace.

Mills, C.W. (1963) 'Culture and Politics: The Fourth Epoch,' in *The Listener*, March 12, 1959; reprinted in Mills, *Power, Politics, People*. New York: Ballantine.

Moene, K.O., and M. Wallerstein (1992) *The Decline of Social Democracy*. Working Paper Series: 225. Institute of Industrial Relations, UCLA, Los Angeles, California.

Moore, B. (1966) *The Social Origins of Dictatorship and Democracy*. Boston: Beacon.

Moscovici, S. (1984) 'The Phenomenon of Social Representations,' pp. 3–70 in R.M. Farr, and S. Moscovici, eds, *Social Representations*. Cambridge: Cambridge University Press.

Muller, K. (1992) '"Modernizing" Eastern Europe: Theoretical Problems and Political Dilemmas.' *European Journal of Sociology* 33: 109–50.

Muller, K. (1994) 'From Post-Communism to Post-Modernity? Economy and Society in the Eastern European Transformations,' in B. Grancelli, ed., *Social Change and Modernization: Lessons from Eastern Europe*. New York: De Gruyter.

Nee, V. (1989) 'A Theory of Market Transition: From Redistribution to Markets in State Socialism.' *American Sociological Review* 54: 663–81.

Nettl, J.P., and R. Robertson (1968) *International Systems and the Modernization of Societies*. New York: Basic Books.

Niebuhr, R. (1952) *The Irony of American History*. New York: Scribners.

Ollman, B. (1971) *Alienation: Marx's Concept of Man in Modern Society*. Cambridge: Cambridge University Press.

Parsons, T. (1964) 'Evolutionary Universals in Society.' *American Sociological Review* 29 (3): 339–57.

Parsons, T. (1966) *Societies: Evolutionary and Comparative Perspectives*. Englewood Cliffs, New Jersey: Prentice Hall.

Parsons, T. (1971) *The System of Modern Societies*. Englewood Cliffs, New Jersey: Prentice Hall.

Parsons, T., and E. Shils (1951) 'Values, Motives, and Systems of Action,' pp. 47–243 in Parsons and Shils, eds, *Towards a General Theory of Action*. Cambridge, Mass.: Harvard University Press.

Pevsner, N. (1949) *Pioneers of Modern Design from William Morris to Walter Gropius*. New York: Museum of Modern Art.

Pocock, J.G.A. (1987) 'Modernity and Anti-modernity in the Anglophone Political Traditions,' pp. 44–59 in S.N. Eisenstadt, ed., *Patterns of Modernity, Vol. I: The West*. London: Frances Pinter.

Polanyi, K. (1957) *The Great Transformation: The Political and Economic Origins of Our Time*. Boston: Beacon.

Powell, W.N. (1991) 'Neither Market nor Hierarchy: Network Forms of Organization,' in B.M. Shaw and L.L. Cummings, eds, *Research in Organizational Behavior*, vol. 12. New York: JAI Press.

Przeworski, A. (1985) *Capitalism and Social Democracy*. New York: Cambridge University Press.

Przeworski, A. (1991) *Democracy and the Market: Political and Economic Reforms in Eastern Europe and Latin America*. New York: Cambridge University Press.

Rand, A. (1957) *Atlas Shrugged*. New York: Random House.

Reisman, D., N. Glazer and P. Denny (1950) *The Lonely Crowd*. New Haven: Yale University Press.

Rex, J. (1961) *Key Problems in Sociological Theory*. London: Routledge and Kegan Paul.

Rieff, P. (1959) *Freud: Mind of the Moralist*. New York: Anchor Doubleday.

Ricoeur, P. (1977) *The Rule of Metaphor*. Toronto: Toronto University Press.

Robertson, R. (1992) *Globalization: Social Theory and Global Culture*. London: Sage.

Rorty, R. (1979) *Philosophy and the Mirror of Nature*. Princeton: Princeton University Press.

Rorty, R. (1985) 'Postmodern Bourgeois Liberalism,' pp. 214–21 in R. Hollinger, ed., *Hermeneutics and Praxis*. Notre Dame, Ind.: Notre Dame University Press.

Rorty, R. (1989) *Contingency, Irony, Solidarity*. New York: Cambridge University Press.

Rosenau, P.M. (1992) *Postmodernism and the Social Sciences*. Princeton: Princeton University Press.

Roszak, T. (1969) *The Making of a Counter-Culture: Reflections on the Technocratic Society and Its Youthful Opposition*. New York: Doubleday.

Rueschemeyer, D. (1993) 'The Development of Civil Society after Authoritarian Rule.' Unpublished ms, Department of Sociology, Brown University, Providence, Rhode Island.

Said, E. (1978) *Orientalism*. New York: Pantheon.

Said, E. (1991) 'A Tragic Convergence.' *New York Times*, January 11: Section 1, p. 29.

Sales, A. (1991) 'The Private, the Public, and Civil Society: Social Realms and Power Structures.' *International Political Science Review* 12 (4): 295–312.

Schluchter, W. (1979) 'The Paradox of Rationalization,' pp. 11–64 in Schluchter and G. Roth, eds, *Max Weber's Vision of History*. Berkeley and Los Angeles: University of California Press.

Schluchter, W., and G. Roth, eds, (1979) *Max Weber's Vision of History*. Berkeley and Los Angeles: University of California Press.

Schnapper, D. (1994) *La Communauté des citoyens: Sur l'idee moderne de nation*. Paris: Gallimard.

Sciulli, D. (1990) 'Differéntiation and Collegial Formations: Implications of Societal Constitutionalism,' pp. 367–405 in J.C. Alexander and P. Colomy, eds, *Differentiation Theory and Social Change*. New York: Columbia University Press.

Seidman, S. (1983) *Liberalism and the Origins of European Social Theory*. Berkeley and Los Angeles: University of California Press.

Seidman, S. (1991a) *Romantic Longings: Love in America, 1830–1980*. New York: Routledge.

Seidman, S. (1991b) 'The End of Sociological Theory: The Postmodern Hope.' *Sociological Theory* 9 (2): 131–46.

Seidman, S. (1992) 'Postmodern Social Theory as Narrative with a Moral Intent,' pp. 47–81 in S. Seidman and D.G. Wagner, eds, *Postmodernism and Social Theory*. New York: Blackwell.

Sherwood, S.J. (1994) 'Narrating the Social: Postmodernism and the Drama of Democracy,' *Journal of Narrative and Life History* 4 (1/2): 69–88.

Shils, E. (1972) *Intellectuals and the Powers*. Chicago: Chicago University Press.

Shils, E. (1991a) 'The Virtue of Civil Society.' *Government and Opposition* 26: 3–20.

Shils, E. (1991b) 'Civility and Civil Society,' in E.C. Banfield, ed., *Civility and Citizenship*. New York: Paragon.

Skocpol, T. (1979) *States and Social Revolutions*. New York: Cambridge University Press.

Slotkin, R. (1973) *Regeneration through Violence: The Mythology of the American Frontier, 1600–1860*. Middletown, Conn.: Wesleyan University Press.

Smelser, N. (1963) *Theory of Collective Behavior*. New York: Free Press.

Smelser, N. (1968) 'Toward a Theory of Modernization,' pp. 125–46 in Smelser, *Essays in Sociological Explanation*. Engelwood Cliffs, New Jersey: Prentice Hall.

Smelser, N. (1991) *Social Paralysis and Social Change: British Working-Class Education in the Nineteenth Century*. Berkeley and Los Angeles: University of California Press.

Smith, H.N. (1950) *Virgin Land*. Cambridge, Mass.: Harvard University Press.

Smith, P. (1991) 'Codes and Conflict: Towards a Theory of War as Ritual.' *Theory and Society* 20: 103–38.

Smith, P. (1993) 'The Culture of War.' Unpublished Ph.D. dissertation, UCLA, Los Angeles, California.

Somers, M.R. (1992) 'Narrativity, Narrative Identity, and Social Action: Rethinking English Workng-Class Formation.' *Social Science History* 16 (4): 591–630.

Stepan, A. (1985) 'State Power and the Strength of Civil Society in the Southern Cone of Latin America,' pp. 317–43 in P. Evans, D. Rueschemeyer, and T. Skocpol, eds, *Bringing the State Back In*. New York: Cambridge University Press.

Szelenyi, I. (1988) *Socialist Embourgeoisement in Rural Hungary*. Madison, Wis.: University of Wisconsin Press.

Sztompka, P. (1991) 'The Intangibles and Imponderables of the Transition to Democracy.' *Studies in Comparative Communism* 34: 295–311.

Sztompka, P. (1993) *The Sociology of Social Change*. Oxford: Blackwell.

Thomas, G.M. and P. Lauderdale (1988) 'State Authority and National Welfare Programs in World System Context.' *Sociological Forum* 3 (3): 383–99.

Thompson, E.P. (1963) *The Making of the English Working Class*. New York: Pantheon.

Thompson, K. (1992) 'Social Pluralism and Post-Modernity,' pp. 222–71 in Thompson et al., eds, *Modernity and Its Futures*. Oxford: Blackwell.

Thompson, K. (forthcoming) *Essential Quotations in Sociology*. London: Routledge.

Tiryakian, E. (1988) 'From Durkheim to Managua: Revolutions as Religious Revivals,' pp. 44–65 in J.C. Alexander, ed., *Durkheimian Sociology: Cultural Studies*. New York: Cambridge University Press.

Tiryakian, E. (1991) 'Modernization: *Exhumetur in pace*.' *International Sociology* 6 (2): 165–80.

Touraine, A. (1994) *Qu'est-ce que la démocratie?* Paris: Fayard

Trilling, L. (1950) *The Liberal Imagination*. New York: Harcourt Brace Jovanovich.

Trilling, L. (1955) *The Opposing Self: Nine Essays in Criticism*. London: Secker & Warburg.

Turner, B.S. (1986) *Citizenship and Capitalism*. London: Allen & Unwin.

van den Berg, A. (1980) 'Critical Theory: Is There Still Hope?' *American Journal of Sociology* 86 (3): 449–79.

Veeser, H.A., ed. (1989) *The New Historicism*. New York: Routledge.

Wagner-Pacifici, R. (1986) *The Moro Morality Play: Terrorism as Social Drama*. Chicago: University of Chicago Press.

Wallerstein, E. (1979) 'Modernization: *Requiescat in pace*,' pp. 132–7 in Wallerstein, *The Capitalist World-Economy*. New York: Cambridge University Press.

Walzer, M. (1965) *Revolution of the Saints*. Cambridge, Mass.: Harvard University Press.

Walzer, M. (1992a) 'The Civil Society Argument,' pp. 89–107 in C.Mouffe, ed., *Dimensions of Radical Democracy: Pluralism, Citizenship, Community*. London: Verso.

Walzer, M. (1992b) 'Constitutional Rights and the Shape of Civil Society,' pp. 113–26 in R.E. Calvert, ed., *The Constitution of the People: Reflections on Citizens and Civil Society*. Lawrence: University Press of Kansas.

Weber, M. (1964 [1922]) *The Sociology of Religion*. Boston: Beacon.

Weiner, J. (1984) *Come Together: John Lennon in His Times*. New York: Random House.

Weinstein, J. (1968) *Corporate Ideology in the Liberal State, 1900–1918*. Westport, Conn.: Greenwood Press.

White, H. (1980) 'The Value of Narrativity in the Representation of Reality,' pp. 1–25 in W.J.T. Mitchell, ed., *On Narrative*. Chicago: University of Chicago Press.

White, H. (1987) *The Content of Form: Narrative Discourse and Historical Representation*. Baltimore: Johns Hopkins University Press.

Wieviorka, M. (1993) *La Démocratie a l'épreuve: Nationalisme, populisme, ethnicité*. Paris: Editions La Découverte.

Wilson, J.Q. (1991) 'Incivility and Crime,' in E.C. Banfield, ed., *Civility and Citizenship*. New York: Paragon.

Wittrock, B. (1991) 'Cultural Identity and Nationhood: The Reconstitution of Germany – Or the Open Answer to an Almost Closed Question,' pp. 76–87 in M. Trow and T. Nybom, eds, *University and Society: Essays on the Social Role of Research and Higher Education*. London: Jessica Kingsley.

Wolff, R.P., H. Marcuse, and B. Moore, Jr. (1965) *A Critique of Pure Tolerance*. Boston: Beacon.

Wright, E.O. (1985) *Classes*. London: Verso.

2

Between Progress and Apocalypse:
Social Theory and the Dream of Reason in the Twentieth Century

Social theory is a mental reconstruction of its time, not a reflection but a self-reflection. Art is self-reflection in an iconic and expressive form. Theoretical self-reflection is intellectual and abstract. It leads not to experience and epiphany but to analysis and thought. Social theory cannot induce catharsis, but it can transform understanding. We need social theory if we are going to understand our world. As this great and terrible century draws to a close, this need has never been more important.

The thesis of this essay is that the twentieth century is a unique construction, a historically demarcated world, and that twentieth-century theory is differentiated from earlier theorizing in much the same way. This may be an illusion for future historians to correct. Certainly, neither theory nor history can hope to break out of the self-conceptions of its own time. At this point, however, the historical uniqueness of our century seems to be an empirical fact. It is certainly a social one, for in this uniqueness most of the participants in this century have fervently believed.

To comprehend the underlying motifs of our century, and eventually its social theory, we must clarify what initially marked the West off from other civilizations, the modern West from earlier periods in its history, and the twentieth century from earlier Western modern societies. This distinguishing notion is 'progress' and the possibility of perfection it implies.

All complex societies, of course, have had myths about the Golden Age. Only in the West, however, did people seriously begin to think that such a new age might occur in this rather than some extraterrestrial or fantastical world. This-worldly conceptions were formulated in Judaism three or four thousand years ago. If the Jews kept their covenant with God, the Bible promised, God would establish his reign of perfection on earth – what came to be called the millennium. Because Jews were the chosen people, God promised to eventually redeem them. Christianity believed that Christ had been sent to renew this redemptive promise. We have lived in what might be called a millennial civilization ever since.

Yet Christianity still placed the millennium far off in the distant future. It would certainly not happen in our lifetimes. The lot of human beings on earth, at any given point in time, could hardly be changed. This dualism began to shift with the Reformation, which was much more emphatically this-worldly. Protestants, and especially Calvinists and Puritans, worked hard in this world, with the hope of bringing about the kingdom of God on earth. This initial belief in the possibility of worldly perfection was reinforced and greatly extended by Renaissance humanism, with its earthiness and optimism about improving nature and society. The Enlightenment translated this growing perfectionism into the vocabulary of secular progress. As Becker (1932) suggested in *The Heavenly City of the Eighteenth-Century Philosophers*, the philosophers believed in the imminent possibility of a secular golden age.

Perfectionism is the belief that the human world can become the mirror of the divine. This possibility has defined the essence of modernity. To be modern is to believe that the masterful transformation of the world is possible, indeed that it is likely.[1] In the course of modernity, this pledge to worldly transformation has been renewed time and time again. No matter what the disaster, the hope and belief in imminent perfection never disappears. The faith in perfection has informed all the great experiments of the modern world, big and small, good and bad, the incessant reformism and the revolutions launched from the left and from the right.[2]

With the Enlightenment and the growth of secular, scientific thought, the ethos of perfectionism became inseparable from the claims of reason.[3] Reason is the self-conscious application of the mind to social and natural phenomena. Through reason, people came to believe, we can master the world. Through this mastery, we can become free and happy. The world can be made a reasonable place. It can be reconstructed. Marx and Hegel produced their own versions of such perfectionism; neither believed in it less fervently than the other.[4]

In the twentieth century this fundamental tenet of modernity has been challenged and ultimately changed. The faith in progress has often been severely disappointed and the sense that there is the real possibility for perfection has diminished. This dimunition has not occurred in every place and at every moment, of course; in the end, however, it has so permeated modern life that it has deeply affected its core. Modern became postmodern long before the contemporary period. The experience of this century has been a tragic one. The originality of its social theory lies in coming to grips with this experience. This, at least, is the thesis I will seek to advance here.

The Rational Line: Progress

I do not want to advance this thesis in a polemical or one-sided way. If one does so, the argument becomes myth and caricature, and loses its force. Our understanding of the twentieth century must be more subtle and more complex. To recognize its tragic proportions does not mean to ignore the hopes that it has inspired and the real progress it has achieved.

From the point of view of the present day, it is possible to look back on this century as a time of wondrous achievement. It is especially possible, and likely, for Americans to do so, but it is by no means impossible for Europeans.[5] Doing so reflects the particular historical vantage point of the present day; it also reflects the continuing intensity of the progressivist faith. History can, after all, certainly be reconstructed in different ways.

If we look back at the beginning of this century, we can see great hopes. In Germany and in the Austro-Hungarian Empire, large social democratic parties existed, and their progress appeared to many as inexorable. By pledging themselves to control the market and by demanding full voting rights, these parties promised to incorporate the working classes into industrial economies and to democratize the state.[6]

Similar progressive forces seemed to be expanding in other industrialized nations. In England, radical utilitarians and Fabian socialists had increasing access to power, and Marxian socialism itself was becoming a stronger and more militant force. In environments less hospitable to socialism, liberalism was developing a social program of its own. French 'solidarism' and American 'progressivism' were seen as prime examples of the successful mitigation of capitalism's harshest face.

The progressive view of our century can be sustained by drawing a straight line from these promising developments to the condition of industrial societies today. One can argue that Marxism, liberalism, social democracy, and even democratic conservatism have succeeded in transforming and, indeed, in perfecting modern life.

This rational line can be justified by pointing, for example, to the extraordinary increase in material wealth. Through the rationality of capitalism and industrial production, this affluence has ameliorated the conditions of everyday life throughout the class structure of advanced societies. These conditions are not limited, moreover, to consumption in a narrow sense. It is primarily as a result of this material transformation (Hart 1985: 29–49) that deaths in childbirth (for both infants and mothers) have been virtually eliminated and that such deadly diseases as tuberculosis have passed from the scene. One may point to the achievements of modern science, both pure and applied, which have contributed to such life-giving disciplines as modern medicine. The series of technological revolutions that has increased material productivity hundreds of times over make Marx's predictions about the exhaustion of capitalism seem not just antique but almost reactionary. We are in the midst of what has been called the fourth industrial revolution, the transformation of information capacity that began with the transistor and miniaturization and, with the computer chip and super-computerization, has continued on an unprecedented scale.

The rational line can be further sustained by pointing to the expansion of human rights. T.H. Marshall (1964) drew an evolutionary model of the progress from civil to political to social rights. Over the last forty years, civil and political rights have been extended to religious and racial groups that had been excluded from Western societies for hundreds and sometimes even thousands of years. Social rights have been expanded to groups who were considered to be deserving of their unfortunate fates only a century ago – like the physically and mentally handicapped. For the first time since the neolithic revolution ten thousand years ago, women are beginning to have substantial access to the institutional and cultural centers of society.

These advances may rightly be considered to be evidence of the advance of reason, and they are being applied to civilizations which did not initially share in the benefits of this-worldly millennial religion. Decolonization has extended 'European' progress while allowing national aspirations to be freely expressed. Revolution, which has often been the vehicle for this decolonization, has been the primary trigger that has allowed modernization in the backward, unrationalized areas of the world. It, too, can be considered a successful example of the extension of world mastery which has helped to perfect life in the modern world.

On these grounds it may be argued that the twentieth century has been a time of progress, that this is not only a plausible view but also a valid one. Not only Americans and Europeans argue this view today, but articulate leaders in India, China, Brazil, and Japan as well. The twentieth century is a good and sensible world. Yes, evil and irrationality still exist, but their origins are outside of us. They stem from traditionalism and antimodernity, with religious fanatics in Iran, with tribal hostilities in Africa, with nationalist antagonism in Israel. Closer to home, they arise in impoverished groups who have not had the access to modernity that education and material comfort can provide. When we walk through our modern lives, organizing our lifeworlds with good sense and a modicum of comfort, it seems only reasonable to think that reason has prevailed.

The Dream of Reason

The reality of this vision of the twentieth century is underscored by the fact that it has produced a line of intellectual reasoning, a line of social theory, that goes along with it. I will call this the dream of reason. It is the image of this rationally perfected life in thought, but not of course a reflection of 'real,' material life alone. Because life is itself filled with ideas, the perfected life is filled with ideas about perfection. The reasonable life of today can be traced back to the dream of a this-worldly millennium that began thousands of years ago. Of course, while the millennial dream is religious, the dream of reason is post-religious. Still, the dream of reason operates with the metaphysical props of faith that were exemplified in Hegel's work a century ago.

We can see the dream of reason most distinctly by pointing to four spheres of modern thought: philosophy, psychology, art, and social engineering.

The most characteristic school of twentieth-century philosophy must surely be logical positivism, which believed that any thought worth thinking could be reduced to rational and eventually mathematical propositions. Philosophy from this perspective would be little more than a truth language, a code that would state the conditions for knowing. In this form, philosophy would allow language and thought to transparently reflect the external world. Words are induced from things that actually exist (Wittgenstein 1922). Thought is a rational induction from this reality. Philosophy must hone the relationship between words and things. Metaphysics will be abolished forthwith.

We should not be so blinded by the surreal dimension of modern art that we fail to see that much of aesthetic modernism is consistent with this rationalizing view. There is a clear movement in modernity which argues that art should be sparse, minimal, flat, rational, and 'true.' It should not be fictive but direct, not personal but objective. The great exemplifications of this are architecture and prose. The origins of modern architecture are the aesthetic dictum that form is to follow function. Those who created this style (Pevsner 1977) actually believed that their buildings represented no fictive design but only followed inevitably from the shape of engineering and efficient rational design. While this self-understanding may be false – engineering and efficiency do not have an implicit design – the International Style that resulted was of a decidedly rationalist bent – straight lines, angles, and flat surfaces.

A similar demand for directness, simplicity, objectivity, and efficiency characterizes twentieth-century prose. In the model of science, modern prose language aims to be transparent vis-à-vis its subject matter and denuded of 'style' as such, as that notion was exemplified, for example, in Renaissance speech and writing (Lanham 1976). Connotation and ambiguity are pruned from articles and books. In the English language it was Hemingway who blazed this trail, with his short, flat, journalistic sentences. It was *Time* magazine that made this style the mass language of the day.

In psychology two contradictory movements reflect this sense of the ultimate reasonableness of the world. In Piaget's (1972) developmental psychology, adult persons have developed the capacity for universalistic cognition and rule-oriented morality. These capacities develop from processes that are inherent in the life process. Individuals become rational because of realistic experiences. Faced with the growing complexity of reality, they act pragmatically and develop new modes of reasoning through trial and error. Behaviorism also sees individuals as acting in straightforward rational ways. Pavlov, Watson, and Skinner argued that people are formed not by subjective fantasy but by their environments, that they are molded into whatever they are pushed into being. Like pigeons and well-trained dogs, human beings are rational in a narrow and efficient sense. If we know their past conditioning, we can make predictions about how they will act in the future.

Theories about the possibility of rational planning have been reinforced by developmental and behavioristic psychology, but they also constitute an intellectual movement in their own right. This thought originates in the nineteenth century as a species of secular perfectionism, with people like Saint-Simon, Bentham, and Marx. It has become dominant in the twentieth century, elaborated by democratic socialist theorists of the welfare state like Marshall and Mannheim (1940) and by technocratic communist thought as well. The belief is that the world can be subjected to rational control, that the whole ball of wax can be molded by reason into a desirable shape. Rawls (1971) is the greatest English-speaking proponent of this faith in perfection through reason. Habermas (1984) elaborates rationalism in a continental, anti-utilitarian romantic idiom.

The Alternative Vision of Decline: The Prophecy of Georges Sorel

With a very few exceptions, these rationalist streams of thought, no matter how brilliant and enlightening, have not represented the greatest and most original achievements of twentieth-century social theory. One reason is that they do not represent something that is really new; they are extensions of the perfectionist thinking of earlier days. But there is another, much more important reason as well. In its rationalist form, twentieth-century social theory cannot fulfill its self-reflective task. It does not tell us the absolutely essential things we must know about the new kind of society in which we have lived.

A straight line between the hopes of the turn-of-the-century period and the achievements of the present day cannot be drawn. There is, rather, a tortuous path. If the newly dawning century embodied fulsome hopes for social reform, it was also known as the *fin de siècle* and the 'age of anxiety.' The dream of reason has continued to inspire the thought of our time, but it is the nightmare of reason that has captured the most profound theoretical imaginations of the age.

As an entrée into this darker side of modernity, we might look briefly at the thought of Georges Sorel, the French revolutionary syndicalist who published his original and disturbing *Reflections on Violence* in 1908. Earlier I referred to the large socialist workers' parties that were carriers for the ideas, forces, and often the reality of progress in that turn-of-the-century period. Sorel conceived of himself as speaking for a very different segment of the community of dispossessed. He insists (1950 [1908]: 66) that there remained large groups of workers, small employers of labor, and farmers – as well, one might add, as working-class leaders and intellectuals like himself – who bitterly opposed modernity and saw little hope for social progress within its rationalizing frame. These groups provided a constituency for a much more extreme left, one cut off from the progressive and ameliorating groups of the socialist center. As Sorel explains, 'Parliamentary Socialism does not mingle with the main body of the parties of the extreme left' (ibid.: 67).

These parties are the revolutionaries. In one sense, of course, their ideal is not all that dissimilar from the reformers'. They, too, want a perfect society ordered by reason. They are certain, however, that such a society cannot be institutionalized in the 'present phase' of social life. Reason has become an other-worldly ideal that can be realized only through violent world transformation. What has happened until now has not been progressive. Sorel denigrates 'the trash of Parliamentary literature.' He despises progressives and has no patience for democratic politics. Such appeals to reason, he writes, are 'confused'; they serve only 'to hide the terrible fear' that marks the inevitable tension between social classes. If socialism is to succeed it must become revolutionary. Rather than appealing to the rationality of the middle and upper classes, socialists must try to make them afraid: 'The workers have no money but they have at their disposal a much more efficacious means of action: they can inspire fear.' If the bourgeoisie are afraid, Sorel argues, they will engage in selfish behavior and eventually, repression. This is all to the good. It unmasks the real, antiprogressive face of society, and it will inspire the proletariat to be revolutionary in turn.

Sorel believes that socialism must turn away from social and political reform toward the program of the general strike. As a collective act of deliberate violence, the general strike will inspire fear and usher in a cataclysmic revolution. This violence is associated by Sorel with the very group that according to the rational line embodies reason, the proletariat. Sorel has posed the fateful dichotomy of twentieth-century life. He has opposed violence and reason and equated progress with violence and force. Fifty years later Sartre (1976) takes up violence in much the same way, promulgating it as a means of liberating debourgeoisification; from Sartre, Fanon (1965) took violence as the model for anticolonial revolt.[7] In important respects, however, Sorel's opposition of violence to reason was more sophisticated; it was certainly more disturbing and more revealing.

Sorel's opposition is unusually revealing because he relativized this threat of revolutionary violence by calling it a myth. Whether there could or, in strategic terms, should be a violent strike was not Sorel's concern. Violent revolution was a myth in which workers had to believe in order to maintain their esprit de corps and to inspire repressive reactions in the ruling classes. Myth is necessary because people are irrational. They are moved by impulses, not by 'observation of contemporary facts [or by] a rational interpretation of the present' (ibid.: 99). 'Infinitely simpler mental processes' are involved. Only by promoting the myth of violence can the socialists reawaken the spirit of alienation and hatred that creates the desire to destroy bourgeois society.

Sorel's theory is an apologia for left-wing terrorism.[8] It is also a prophecy of the irrationality to come.[9] Finally, it is a brilliant and representative invention of social theory in the twentieth century. Faced with the disappointment of his socialist hopes for progress, Sorel theorizes that individuals are not as rational as progressive theory had thought. Moving against the rational line, he establishes a commonality between modern actors and the myth-worshipers of traditional societies. It is not surprising that Sorel himself wavers between revolutionary left and right. For he has abandoned rationality not just as an explanation of human action but as a normative stance. He advocates irrationality in its most violent form. This, in fact, is where Sorel's thought differs from the more important twentieth-century social theory we will examine below. For while Sorel understood the pathologies of modernity, he could think of no way to overcome them.

The Degenerate Line: Irrationality

Before we can get to this theory, we need to examine the life upon which they reflect. It can be argued that in twentieth-century life there has been a real declension, a decline that for many has made progress seem like a dream, or even a myth.

Since we have been thinking about Sorel, let us begin with socialism. Marxists and utopians alike have considered socialism (via revolution or reform) to be the very embodiment of reason. For Marx, communalization would overcome the alienation of reason and subjectivity upon which capitalism is based. As the twentieth century has unfolded, however, it has become increasingly clear that revolutionary movements of the left often intensify the 'alienation of reason' in drastic ways.[10] This counter-intuitive fact should not be understood in essentialist terms. It has nothing to do with some inherent perversity of revolutionary action but with the sociological conditions under which revolutions typically emerge. Revolutionaries represent groups who have been subject to quite terrible oppression and strains. Typically, they have been excluded from the legitimate centers of their societies and often from their very societies themselves; they have been denied access to universities, subjected to despicable prejudices, impoverished, often jailed, sometimes tortured and murdered.

None of this mitigates what Marx himself would surely have regarded as the savage degradation of the revolutionary tradition in the twentieth century. In their alienation, revolutionaries, in and out of power, have not only advocated distorted and caricatured thought and speech but often acted barbarously, engaging in systematic force and fraud. For several decades after the outbreak of the Russian Revolution, not only socialists but also a wide range of thoughtful people regarded communism as a legitimate carrier of reason. The true nature of Russian communism was masked by its claims to reason and scientific accuracy. Wealth, technology, literacy, high culture, hygiene, and class inclusion have been the perfectionist references for official communist rhetoric (Koch 1993).

It eventually became clear to many, however, that almost right from the beginning this revolutionary society has made of the hopes for perfection a bitter joke. Lenin initiated, and Stalin established (Johnson 1983: 49–103), a system that suppressed the very exercise of reason. Mao, Castro, and Eastern European puppet rulers followed in their wake. Twentieth-century communism has been more like the medieval church than a model for rationality and progress (Aron 1957). Ruled by an ideological pope and directed by a clerisy of party faithful, official communism spreads the dogma of the proletarian messiah, whose message and needs remain to be interpreted in appropriate ways. Reason is monopolized by this communist church; it is impossible for private individuals to possess it. For the masses, coercion and violence are the only recourse. Russian communism subjected first counterrevolutionaries, then conservatives, kulaks, Jews, Christians, and 'other' nationalities to unprecedented repression. Once in power, communist parties – these purported vanguards of reason and progress – have institutionalized vocabularies of double-think and systems of thought control that have come to symbolize the nightmares of reason in our time.[11]

Murder and massive political repression in China; genocidal barbarity in revolutionary Cambodia and dreary failure in its occupiers, Vietnam; the overwhelming inadequacies of centrally planned state economies – intellectuals who hope for human progress might well ask: what is left of the revolutionary dream of reason today? It may be that the communist version of this dream has become exhausted

only two centuries after it began. Certainly intellectual disillusionment with the progressive promises of socialism and communism is
one of the most distinctive developments of the late twentieth century
(Alexander 1988).[12]

I have not begun with communism because it is the unique embodiment of bad faith and irrationality. This is the line of the conservative
right in America and elsewhere, and it is a cop-out intellectually and
morally. One must acknowledge that antiprogress and antireason
occurred throughout Western societies, in capitalist and democratic
countries as well.

The rational line describes the twentieth century as involving gradual
democratization, the extension of rights and privileges to the lower
classes, the opening up of ghettos, and the persistent spreading of
secular rationality throughout society. In point of fact, even before
the twentieth century truly began, much darker forces were beginning
to brew. By the 1880s one could observe on the continent, in France
and in Southern and Central Europe, a growing reaction against
these very progressive forces. In the middle and upper classes powerful
advocates of dictatorship and violence emerged. In Germany, a
mystical and backward-looking *Volk* ideology fermented (Mosse
1964), spreading even to intellectual classes (Ringer 1969). In France
there was a sickening turn toward nationalist antisemitism. In the
United States, the rigidly segregationist policies of 'Jim Crow' began to
spread through the Southern states, and 'nativism' – cultural prejudice
and social mobilization against foreign-born Americans – became an
imperious collective psychology in the North.

These irrationalist forces fed directly into the First World War,
the cataclysm that separated what afterward looked like an age of
innocence from the wasteland that followed (Fussell 1975).[13] Sometime
between 1919 and 1921, when he was the British Secretary of State,
Winston Churchill jotted down on a piece of War Office stationery
a retrospective whose embittered and apocalyptic tones captured
the profound disturbance this war gave to the vision of progress.

> All the horrors of all the ages were brought together, and not only armies
> but whole populations were thrust in the midst of them. . . . Every outrage
> against humanity or international law was repaid by reprisals. . . . No truce
> or parley mitigated the strife of the armies. The wounded died between the
> lines: the dead mouldered into the soil. Merchant ships and neutral ships
> and hospital ships were sunk on the seas and all on board left to their fate,
> or killed as they swam. Every effort was made to starve whole nations into
> submission without regard to age or sex. Cities and monuments were

smashed by artillery. Bombs from the air were cast down indiscriminately. Poison gas in many forms stifled or seared the soldiers. Liquid fire was projected upon their bodies. . . . When all was over, Torture and Cannibalism were the only two expedients that the civilized, scientific, Christian States had been able to deny themselves: and they were of doubtful utility.

(quoted in Johnson 1983: 14–15)

Seventy years after the war's end, these activities could no longer arouse such astonished indignation. They have become everyday occurrences in the political relations of the twentieth century.

In the chaos and devastation that followed in the wake of the First World War, there emerged at the end of the first third of the century what to earlier progressives would have been a totally unexpected event. This was the outbreak in Europe not of revolutions of the left but of counterrevolutions of the right. In Germany, Austria, Italy, and Spain, radical right-wing movements came to power and began to dismantle what remained of the rational and progressive apparatuses of their respective societies. This reactionary movement reached its zenith in Germany, and the results are well known. Rather than the promotion of civility and inclusion, there was the genocidal murder of large segments of the carriers of progress, not only Jews but also intellectuals, communists, socialists, scientists, free-thinkers, and Christian idealists alike.

Alongside the spread of rational understanding, then, there has emerged in the course of this century brutality and violence on an unprecedented scale. This century invented total war, war to the death, war against not only professional armies but the masses of civilian populations. Americans are usually less sensitive to these developments than others, since none of this century's wars has been fought on its continental soil. It is a critically significant fact, however, that liberal democratic countries have become full participants in the ideology and practice of total war (see Gibson 1986 and Johnson 1983). Faced with Hitler's attack on Britain in the summer of 1940, Churchill wrote that 'when I look around to see how we can win the war I see that there is only one sure path . . . and that is an absolutely devastating, exterminating attack by very heavy bombers from this country upon the Nazi homeland' (quoted in Rhodes 1988: 469). The leader who once had been repelled by total war had now come to embrace it. Even before the dropping of atomic bombs on Japan, allied bombing killed 260,000 Japanese and injured more than 400,000 more (Johnson 1983: 423). In their battle against the ruthless FLN in the first Indo-Chinese war, the French engaged in terror and systematic torture.

In their own Indo-Chinese war, the Americans engaged in blanket bombing, with the intention, in President Johnson's words, of 'bombing Vietnam back to the stone age.' In contemporary America, one of the most democratic nations in the history of the world, the massively funded Central Intelligence Agency organizes secret classes on torture techniques for the military cadres of dictatorial nations; afterward, it gives them the facilities to carry it out.

In part because of the strain of continuous warfare, this century has seen the spread of charismatic executive authority on an unprecedented scale. In Germany, China, and Russia, leaders have become living icons for their sometimes adoring, sometimes terrified, but almost always mesmerized and often surprisingly compliant populations. In democratic countries charismatic executive authority has never disappeared. On the contrary, the cult of the personality seems increasingly essential for national integration and effective government (Harden 1974).

Finally, even when the darkest shadows of antimodernity have been avoided, the twentieth century has been haunted by a sense of disappointment with modern life. In the most successful countries, boredom and ennui often overshadow a sense of individual and collective purpose (see, e.g., Keniston 1964). This has resulted in one of the most revealing phenomena of our time – the continuing attempts by those who have been spared the most awful modern brutality to escape from the very progressive forces, ideas, and institutions that have spared them. People flee from the demands of this-worldly perfection to the romantic alternatives of various addictions – to drugs and alcohol, to escapist religion, to visions of nirvana of a mystical and other-worldly kind.

The Nightmare of Reason

This historical declension of real life in the twentieth century – albeit a 'real world' permeated by ideas – has had a pronounced effect on the world of intellectual thought. Reason has been experienced as a hollow shell, progress as inconceivable, and often actually undesirable. The very possibility that there is a higher point, an 'end' toward which society should strive, has come to be thrown into doubt.

When social theory is caught up in the dream of reason it is postreligious but relies on a metaphysical prop. When it articulates the nightmare of reason, it is postreligious without a metaphysic. Paul Tillich, a great twentieth-century theologian who lived without the dream, described modern individuals as adrift and alone, without the traditional support from God. Yet Tillich maintained that this condition could spur them on to great strength and, indeed, even to greater faith, and he (1952) drew from Sartre the notion that what we need in the present, postmodern situation is 'the courage to be.' Nietzsche drew the opposite conclusion, one more characteristic of the dark line itself. God is dead. Reason is a lie and abstract reasoning is lifeless and corrupt. From this Nietzsche drew a kind of proto-fascist conclusion: we must escape from our present condition by transcending it. One of the ways we can do so is by identifying with an irrational superman.

But let us turn from this prophecy of alternative societies to efforts at creating alternative worlds of thought. Earlier I identified four intellectual currents of embodied reason. Here I will outline the anti-rationalist postures that have developed as alternatives. These alternative orientations crystallize the sharp departures from rationality and progress that have characterized our time.

Twentieth-century philosophy began with logical positivism and the confidence that analytic thought could know the truth. It is ending with hermeneutics, a philosophy which maintains that knowing reality in a manner that separates it from us is epistemologically impossible. Logical positivism was bold, ambitious, predictive. Hermeneutics is modest, exploratory, tentative, regarding the mere description of the object as a herculean task. In the earlier (1922) Wittgensteinean philosophy, words can reflect things; they are based on reality. In the later Wittgensteinean philosophy – *Philosophical Investigations* (1968) being the most representative single work of postpositivist thought – words refer not to reality but to themselves. We do not touch reality; we think within a self-referential cocoon of other thoughts and words. Saussure (1959 [1911]), the founder of structural linguistics and semiotics, made much the same point. There is no way to go from objects, from reality, to the word-thoughts that characterize them. Between words and objects there is only an arbitrary relation. Influenced by logical positivism, earlier philosophy of science was concerned with the conditions for truth, verification, and the evolutionary progress of knowledge. Much of postpositivist philosophy glories in irrationality, asserts incommensurability, and theorizes apocalyptic revolutions.

Earlier I suggested that there does exist in contemporary aesthetics an emphasis on minimalism, realism, directness, and linearity. Much more widely recognized, of course, is the aesthetic movement in the opposite direction, toward surrealism. Particularly in the visual arts and in avant-garde literature there has been the destruction of the notion of a transparent reality. Artists neither refer to nor rely upon the rationality of human beings. Over the *longue durée*, the disconti-nuities are striking: from Ingres to Abstract Impressionism by way of Cubism; from Beethoven to Webern by way of Strindberg; from George Eliot and Tolstoy to Beckett and Pynchon by way of James and Woolf. Interpretation theory reflects a similar trajectory. Earlier critics exam-ined authors' intentions, historical contexts, and thematic development within actual texts. Beginning with New Criticism, these standards and practices became less applicable. The complexity and irrationality of motive, it is now believed, makes authorial intention impossible to discover. Similar difficulties accrue to the study of historical context. With Derrida, our lack of confidence in our own rationality has increased to the point that we are not certain there is a text.

Freud created the psychological alternative to the rationalistic images of developmental and behavioral approaches. Since assump-tions about motives are the bedrock of social theory, this depth psychology has had a particularly powerful impact, whether orthodox, Jungian, or 'humanistic.' Instead of rational motive, psychoanalysis begins with the passionate, moralistic, and irrational actor. In contrast to the self-confident and reactive individual, it suggests that the self is fragmented, contradictory, and difficult to find. Against the notion that reality is either obviously visible or increasingly becoming so, depth psychology emphasizes the difficulty of reality-testing and the omnipresence of distortion. Rather than an innate quality, ration-ality is something that may take years of treatment for an actor to achieve.

The intellectual alternatives to social engineering are at first sight less obvious. Theorists do not argue that society is impossible to change. They do, however, suggest that the standards for promoting and evaluating change are neither rational nor capable of providing accurate evaluations. Oakeshott (1962) has developed this approach in its conservative form, arguing that social change is encrusted by custom and inherently incremental, and that efforts to plan change rationally only blind actors to these facts. Walzer (1983) and other 'internalist' critics of Rawls and Habermas have developed this alter-native more critically. They argue that justice cannot be understood in terms of abstract criteria and transcendental principles. It must be theorized from within the cultural practices of particular spheres of life. Social movements that ignore these structures encourage the domination and violence that has characterized the degenerate line of twentieth-century life.

Social Theory as a Bridge between Two Worlds

Many of the great thinkers who initiated twentieth-century social thought participated in two worlds. They experienced both the dream of reason and the nightmare that followed in its wake. They came to early maturity as believers in science, evolution, and progress. One thinks here of Freud's first career in psychophysiology, Weber's pre-breakdown Darwinian writings in political economy and comparative history, Durkheim's early scientism, and Wittgenstein's logical positivism. At a certain point in their development, however, these thinkers came face to face with the darkness and irrationality of their times. When Weber wrote, just after the turn of the new century, that 'the rosy blush of . . . the Enlightenment [is] irretrievably fading' (1958 [1904–05]: 182), he gave expression to the darker perception that characterized an entire generation.

For many of these thinkers the First World War symbolized their disillusionment. In his lecture to German students immediately in the wake of war, for example, Weber rejected out of hand the evolutionary hope for reason.

> I may leave aside altogether the naive optimism in which science – that is, the technique of mastering life which rests upon science – has been celebrated as the way to happiness. Who believes in this? – aside from a few big children in university chairs or editorial offices.
>
> (1946 [1917]: 143)

Three years before that war began, Durkheim wrote that 'we are going through a stage of transition and moral mediocrity'.

> The great things of the past which filled our father with enthusiasm do not excite the same ardor in us. . . . The old gods are growing old or already dead, and others are not yet born.
>
> (1965 [1911]: 475)

Just after the war began, Freud conceived of it as representing the disillusionment that all thinking people felt with the rationalist promises of the past.

> We are constrained to believe that never has any event been destructive of so much that is valuable in the common wealth of humanity, nor so misleading to many of the clearest intelligences, nor so debasing to the highest that we know. Science herself has lost her passionless impartiality; in their deep embitterment her servants seek for weapons from her. . . .

When I speak of disillusionment, everyone at once knows what I mean. ... We were prepared to find that wars between the primitive and the civilized peoples [and] wars with and among the undeveloped nationalities of Europe or those whose culture has perished – that for a considerable period such wars would occupy mankind. But we permitted ourselves to have other hopes.

We had expected the great ruling powers ... who were known to have cultivated world-wide interests, to whose creative powers were due our technical advances in the direction of dominating nature, as well as the artistic and scientific acquisitions of the mind – peoples such as these we had expected to succeed in discovering another way of settling misunderstandings and conflicts of interests.

(1963 [1915]: 107–8)

Just as Wittgenstein had been 'a happy sunny child' in Vienna, so 'his English acquaintances from before 1914 knew him as capable of great gaiety' (Janik and Toulmin 1973: 177). During the war Wittgenstein fought for Austria on the front lines.

From 1919 on, he became a lonely and introverted figure. He admitted to having been impressed by Oswald Spengler's *Decline of the West*, and he retreated more and more into ethical attitudes of extreme individualism and austerity.

(ibid.)

After the war's end, even as the *Tractatus* made Wittgenstein famous, the author disappeared from the intellectual world. He taught school in a small peasant village and later became a gardener. When he returned to Cambridge and academic life in 1929, he did so with an entirely different outlook on life from that of his early, logical positivist phase. He had given up on progress in the conventional sense. 'When we think of the world's future,' he wrote in 1929 (1980: 3e), 'we always mean the destination it will reach if it keeps going in the direction we can see it going in now; it does not occur to us that its path is not a straight line but a curve, constantly changing direction.' These changes, Wittgenstein was certain, would bring ruin. He had a premonition of disaster: 'The earlier culture will become a heap of rubble and finally a heap of ashes' (ibid.).

Cleansed of their earlier innocence, these thinkers devoted themselves to explaining how this darkness could have come about. Yet if they abandoned the dream of reason, they did not reject rationality as a normative goal. To explain irrationality constituted the principal intellectual challenge of their lives. They would do so in order to preserve the values of modernity in a less naive, more mature form.

Freud spent his later life outlining the pathways of unconscious irrationality. He allowed that the result of psychoanalysis would not be utopia but simply common unhappiness. He insisted, however, that this was far preferable to the fantasies of psychosis. Psychoanalysis could not eliminate the influence of the unconscious, but it could reduce its ability to distort reality. 'Where id was,' Freud suggested hopefully, 'there ego shall be.'

Weber demonstrated how modern rationality had historically arisen from religious commitments, and he believed that 'world flight' would be the most common reaction of modern people once these commitments were withdrawn. He condemned these flights and any attempt to restore the metaphysical world. The secular rationality that was the heir to religious rationalization, he insisted, represented the only possible hope for humankind (Alexander 1989).

In his later work, Durkheim described how the mythical and symbolic underpinnings of modern thought made any conception of narrowly rational behavior obsolete. At the same time, he hoped that his exposure of the social foundation of religion would allow this symbolic dimension of human life to be expressed in a non-deistic form, freeing the cognitive dimension of thought to be disciplined by the scientific method.

The case for a continuing commitment to reason is more complex with Wittgenstein. Alone among this first generation of great theorists, he experienced a second world war. Is it surprising that in 1947, after this second shattering experience, he would ask whether it is so 'absurd . . . to believe that the age of science and technology is the beginning of the end for humanity,' or that he would entertain what he called a 'truly apocalyptic view of the world' in which 'the idea of great progress is a delusion' (1980: 56e)? When he announces his hopes for *Philosophical Investigations*, that great rational reconstruction of ordinary language, he does so in a subdued and pessimistic way:

> I make them public with doubtful feelings. It is not impossible that it should fall to the lot of this work, in its poverty and in the darkness of this time, to bring light into one brain or another – but, of course, it is not likely.
> (1968: vi)

Still, this later theory of the conventionalized nature of ordinary language explained the impossibility of denatured objectivity in an extraordinarily lucid and rational way. Even while he expressed skepticism about 'the idea that truth will ultimately be known' (1980 [1947]: 56e), it is clear that Wittgenstein continued to see 'clarity [and] perspicuity as valuable in themselves' (1980 [1930]: 7e).

The great social theorists of the middle and latter twentieth century matured within the framework created not by progressive rationalism but by Freud, Durkheim, Weber, Wittgenstein, and other thinkers of a similarly postmodern cast. Keynes was weaned on the anti-utilitarian platonism of Moore, and he developed a radically new theory of the irrationality of capitalist investment that could only have been drawn from Freud. Lévi-Strauss grew up on Durkheimian anthropology and structural linguistics. Sartre cut his intellectual eye-teeth on Husserl. Marcuse grew up on Heidegger, Freud, and Lukács. Parsons's intellectual fathers were Weber, Pareto, and Durkheim.

Yet, while these more contemporary thinkers differed from their illustrious predecessors in the fact that they never experienced an epistemological break, their commitment to postmodern thought was nourished by a similar confrontation with the darkness of modern life. Keynes rejected his earlier aestheticism after he was horrified by the barbarism of the Great War and politicized by the stupidity of the peace treaty that followed. In the middle of the 1930s, Lévi-Strauss fled to the Brazilian jungle and immersed himself in savage thought because of the repulsion he felt for the mechanization of modern society and the cold, abstract reasoning it employed.[14] Sartre lived at such a distance from French society that he experienced the Second World War almost as a relief (Hayman 1987: 149–78). He wrote *Being and Nothingness* in a German prisoner-of-war camp, and he took man's confinement in 'non-being' as characterizing modern society as such. The true condition of being, Sartre wrote, is anguish; to talk about ideal values is only bad faith. Parsons conceived of his first great book as a response to the double shadow of fascism and Stalinism – 'various kinds of individualism have been under increasingly heavy fire [and] the role of reason, and the status of scientific knowledge ... have been attacked again and again' (1937: 5). Marcuse regarded even democratic industrial societies as totalitarian. 'The fact that the vast majority of the population accepts, and is made to accept, this society,' he wrote (1964: xiii), 'does not render it less irrational and less reprehensible.'

Neither did these later thinkers accept the nightmare of reason as humankind's necessary fate. Keynes intended to revive the hope for a humane economy in a post-perfectionist form. Lévi-Strauss, despite his fatalistic ruminations, regarded his life's work as a scientific contribution and urged other rational thinkers to resist the temptations of historicist thought. Sartre insisted that human beings do have the capacity for freedom, and he strenuously argued in his literature as well as his philosophy that this responsibility be taken up. Parsons tried to demonstrate through his voluntaristic theory that the internalization of values would provide the basis for a more mediated and secure freedom. Marcuse insisted that transcendence was possible, if only his contemporaries would draw upon their innately human capacity for critical thought.

Conclusion

H. Stuart Hughes (1966) entitled his influential historical study of French social thought in the interwar years *The Obstructed Path*. His thesis was that French society, and French social theory, had strayed off the normal and expected path of rationality and democracy into mysticism, radicalism, alienation, and antimodernity. My argument in this essay has been directed against this kind of 'exceptionalist' view of antimodernity. Rather than as an accurate description of twentieth-century thought, it should actually be viewed as an expression of the dream of reason itself. The line of twentieth-century development has been a tortuous one, and the path of the theory that has reflected on this development has been obstructed. It is not just French theory between the wars that reflected alienation, radicalism, and irrationalism, therefore, but the principal thrusts of twentieth-century theory itself.

Indeed, it is American thought in the twentieth century that has been exceptional, precisely because it has been so untortured and perfectionist, so confident in the unobstructed access to rationality in modern life. In the postwar period, Parsons and Rawls provide perhaps the two best illustrations of this rationalist optimism. Hughes' first important book, *Consciousness and Society* (1958), provides a historical formulation of this American bias in a still influential form. In this classical work, which brought the Whiggish thesis of *The Structure of Social Action* (Parsons 1937) into the domain of intellectual history, Hughes described the growing recognition of the irrational and surrealism in European thought and art merely as a deepening of progressive self-reflection: the bitter often tragic, and enormously destabilizing social and intellectual origins of this turn away from rationality are simply unrecognized.

A taut dialogue between pessimism and optimism, reason and unreason, defines social theory in the twentieth century. Suspended between perfection and apocalypse, what marks off the greatest of this century's theorists is their attempt to mediate these dichotomies. While they have abandoned positivism and no longer see their times as embodying the dream of reason, most have not given up on science as a hope and none has given up on reason as a possibility. They recognize the omnipresence of irrationality with regret. Their theories are devoted to showing how the irrational works, in different spheres, in different modes, with different results. They show this by exercising their reason, and they hope to use their hard-won understandings to find a way to a better life. This life will recognize the ineradicable need for irrational experience and for the concrete, expressive articulation of meaning. By augmenting our rational understanding, however, it may be possible for a form of social life to emerge that meets these needs in a less restrictive way.

This form of life has not yet emerged. As the second millennium of Western history draws to a close, it remains a possibility devoutly to be wished. By reflecting on the unique character of this century, social theory may perhaps contribute to this task.

Notes

1. For the notion of 'transformative capacity' as the rationalizing contribution of the Protestant Reformation, see Eisenstadt (1968). By emphasizing perfectionism and reason, I am adding to this evolutionary approach a more culturally specific element of intellectual history.

2. For the centrality of millennialist ideas in modern revolutions and reform movements, see Walzer (1965) on the English Revolution; Tuveson (1968) and Bloch (1985) on the American Revolution; Miller (1965) on early national reform in America; Yeo (1989) on Chartism and primitive Christianity; and Hyams (1973) on the communist revolutions more generally.

3. At several points in his work, Weber suggested that, via the Enlightenment, the 'charisma of reason' inherited Puritanism's this-worldly asceticism and became the embodiment of the world-mastering heritage of religious rationalization. For the connection of Puritanism to the first great manifestation of 'reason,' the scientific revolution, see Merton (1970 [1939]) and Tenbruk (1974). The connection between religious rationalization and the contemporary ethos of modernity has been almost totally obscured by Weber's instrumental and materialistic theorizing about the industrial society. The Parsonian tradition provides the antidote to this, but its generally optimistic, even pollyanna-ish, thinking about modernity has made its contributions to theoretical reflection much less important.

4. For the religious and eschatological underpinnings of Marx's work, see Lowith (1949); of Hegel's, see Taylor (1975).

5. I doubt, however, that it is possible for Poles to take this progressivist line. For Germans who describe history in this progressive way, see the evolutionary change theories of Habermas and Munch. I will address the extremely interesting issue of national variation in the latter part of this essay.

6. Indeed, participation in these mass socialist parties seemed to have provided tens of thousands of low- and middle-status people not only with a firm conviction of the imminence of the new society but with an experience of actual salvation in this world. See, for example, the autobiography of Julius Braunthal, the Austro-Hungarian socialist leader, which presents Braunthal's participation and expectations in unmistakably millennial terms.

It was a great day in my life when I went . . . to the Working-Class Youth Club to register.
. . . It meant for me the firm resolve to help bring about nothing less than the New Jerusalem
on earth in my own lifetime. . . . For me the fact that the world was constantly changing was
beyond any question. My problem was whether or not the time for the 'final change' in
human society had come. . . . From Marx's *Manifesto* and Friedrich Engels' *Anti-Dühring*,
which were among the first Socialist classics I had read, I believed that humanity had now
entered the final stage of its history.

(Braunthal 1945: 39–40)

7. At first glance, it seems quite extraordinary that, in a century that has been
humbled by the most horrid violence, this turn toward violence in radical philosophy
has been so little remarked upon and so infrequently criticized. Thus, Sartre's *Critique
of Dialectical Reason* (1976 [1968]) has typically been taken by left thinkers (e.g. Poster
1979) as an argument for community – for the movement from serial to fused groups
– rather than as an apologia for violence, which it also is. Aron's *History and the
Dialectic of Violence* (1975) is the only serious critique of this theme in Sartre's work of
which I am aware, and it has been virtually ignored. Aron argues that Sartre's work
became so politicized that theoretical and ideological confusions are fused – 'the taste
for Revolution and a lack of it for reform have become a philosophical truth' (Aron
1975: 185). He attacks the degeneration of reason and the ultimate dehumanization
that this position involves: 'The strange alliance between Reason and violence, whereby
the other – the conservative, the reformist, anyone who says "no" to the revolutionary
apocalypse – takes on the grim traits of the anti-man' (ibid.). 'It is by means of the class
struggle, by the antagonism of groups where everyone wishes the death of the other, that
the dialectical movement, whose completion is marked by the advent of totalizing
Truth, progresses' (ibid.: 187–8).

In regard to the link between Fanon and Sartre, Aron is critical not of anticolonial
violence as a strategic necessity but of its theoretical justification in antirational terms.
'What I hate,' he writes (ibid.: 192), 'is not the choice, *hic et nun*, at a particular
conjunction of circumstances, in favour of violence and against negotiation, but a
philosophy of violence in and for itself, not as means that is sometimes necessary for
a rational politics, but a philosophy that lays claim to an ontological foundation and
psychological function or effectiveness.' The intellectual promotion of violence, of
course, is hardly limited to the left. Highly respected geopolitical thinkers, like
Kissinger, advocate the strategic use of massive deadly force (see Gibson 1986).

That most commentators have been uninterested in the philosophical promotion of
violence may, on further reflection, not be so surprising. It may in fact be the very result
of the omnipresence of violence in this century's life.

8. This is not an anachronistic usage, as Lenin's famous pamphlet *Left-Wing
Communism: An Infantile Disorder* demonstrates.

9. 'The notion that social change can be best achieved through revolutionary
violence is very much an offshoot of the French Revolution and of its socialist heirs.
Sorel's *Reflections sur la violence* took up an uncomfortable and hushed-up subject
and made it the center of a strategy destined to overthrow the bourgeois order. At a time
when the Marxists of the Second International were pussy-footing about the desirability
of a revolution, Sorel took the uncompromising step of affirming its necessity' (Llobera
1988).

10. For a discussion of the historical dialectic between absent and present reason,
see chapter 3, below.

11. Until recently, it was only 'anticommunists' who made such critical claims.
Ironically the most recent documentation of the communist distortion of reason came
from newspapers within Soviet Russia itself. In spring 1988, in the wake of perestroika,
the final history examinations of more than 50 million Soviet schoolchildren were
canceled. In an extraordinary commentary on its front page, laced with expressions of
bitterness, tortured guilt, and hopes for purification, *Izvestia* attacked the entire historiography of Soviet communism as the inversion of the Revolution's rational hopes.

The guilt of those who deluded one generation after another, poisoning their minds and souls with lies, is immeasurable. . . . Today we are reaping the bitter fruits of our own moral laxity. We are paying for succumbing to conformity and thus to giving silent approval of everything that now brings the blush of shame to our faces and about which we do not know how to answer our children honestly. [This process is] a purifying torture of revelation, or, to be precise, a second birth.

(quoted in *Los Angeles Times*, June 11, 1988)

12.

[I]t is now the world of psychologically and morally exhausted societies (largely on a Marxist and post-Marxist pattern) that have lost their energy and appeal. They are seen, along with their philosophy, as antique fortresses jutting out of a wasteland of the past. In fact, their own chances of breaking out of this closure now depend largely on their success in following the new model set by America and its rivals and competitors in the Western imperium. . . . At the time of Nikita Krushchev's reform regime in the early 1960s, and again under Mikhail Gorbachev's drive in the mid-1980s to modernize the Soviet economy and partially open the society, there was discussion of a possible 'convergence' of the two adversary systems. But the pull of convergence was mostly one-sided, not toward the blocked societies of the East but toward the openness of the West.

This polemical statement was remarkable not so much for what it says as for who has said it – not a conservative Cold Warrior but the venerable New Deal liberal, Max Lerner (1987: 11–13), in the left of center American magazine *The New Republic*.

13. 'In the weeks before the Armageddon, Bethmann Hollweg's secretary and confident Kurt Riezler made notes of the gloomy relish with which his master steered Germany and Europe into the abyss. July 7, 1914: "The Chancellor expects that a war, whatever its outcome, will result in the uprooting of everything that exists. The existing world very antiquated, without ideas." July 27: "Doom greater than human power hanging over Europe and our people."' (Johnson 1983: 12).

14. Lévi-Strauss begins *Tristes Tropiques* with an account of his encounter with 'one of those outbreaks of stupidity, hatred, and credulousness which social groups secrete like pus when they begin to be short of space' (1973: 18). He argues that 'experiences such as these [are] starting to ooze out like some insidious leakage from contemporary mankind, which [has] become saturated with its own numbers and with the ever-increasing complexity of its problems' (ibid.). He concludes the book with this melancholic prophecy, not much different from the spirit of Wittgenstein's:

The world began without man and will end without him. The institutions, morals and customs that I shall have spent my life noting down and trying to understand are the transient efflorescence of a creation in relation to which they have no meaning. . . . From the time when he first began to breathe and eat, up to the invention of atomic and thermonuclear devices, by way of the discovery of fire . . . what else has man done except blithely break down billions of structures and reduce them to a state in which they are no longer capable of integration?

(ibid.: 472)

References

Alexander, J.C. (1988) 'Back to Lippman.' *The New Republic* 198 (5), February 1: 15–16.

Alexander, J.C. (1989) 'The Dialectic of Individuation and Domination: Max Weber's Rationalization Theory and Beyond,' pp. 68–100 in Alexander, *Structure and Meaning: Relinking Classical Sociology*. New York: Columbia University Press.

Aron, R. (1957) *The Opium of the Intellectuals*. New York: W. W. Norton & Co.

Aron, R. (1975) *History and the Dialectic of Violence: An Analysis of Sartre's 'Critique de la raison dialectique'*. New York: Harper & Row.

Becker, C. (1932) *The Heavenly City of the Eighteenth-Century Philosophers*. New Haven: Yale University Press.

Bloch, R. (1985) *Visionary Republic: Millennial Themes in American Thought, 1756–1800*. New York: Cambridge University Press.

Braunthal, J. (1945) *In Search of the Millennium*. London: Gollancz.

Durkheim, E. (1965 [1911]) *The Elementary Forms of Religious Life*. New York: Free Press.

Eisenstadt, S.N. (1968) 'Introduction,' pp. 3–45 in Eisenstadt, ed., *The Protestant Ethic and Modernization: A Comparative View*. New York: Basic Books.

Fanon, F. (1965) *The Wretched of the Earth*. London: MacGibbon and Kee.

Freud, S. (1963 [1915]) 'Reflections upon War and Death,' pp. 107–33 in *Freud, Character and Culture*. New York: Collier.

Fussell, P. (1975) *The Great War and Modern Memory*. New York: Oxford University Press.

Gibson, J.W. (1986) *The Perfect War*. New York: Atlantic.

Habermas, J. (1984) *The Theory of Communicative Action, Vol. 1*. Boston: Beacon Press.

Harden, C.M. (1974) *Presidential Power and Accountability*. Chicago: University of Chicago Press.

Hart, N. (1982) 'Is Capitalism Bad for Your Health?' *The British Journal of Sociology*, 33 (3): 435–43.

Hart, N. (1985) *The Sociology of Health and Medicine*. Ormskirk: Causeway Press.

Hayman, R. (1987) *Sartre: A Life*. New York: Simon & Schuster.

Hughes, H.S. (1958) *Consciousness and Society: The Reconstruction of European Social Thought, 1890–1930*. New York: Vintage.

Hughes, H.S. (1966) *The Obstructed Path: French Social Thought in the Years of Desperation, 1930–1960*. New York: Harper & Row.

Hyams, E. (1973) *The Millennium Postponed*. New York: Taplinger.

Janik, A., and S. Toulmin (1973) *Wittgenstein's Vienna*. New York: Simon & Schuster.

Johnson, P. (1983) *Modern Times: The World from the Twenties to the Eighties*. New York: Harper & Row.

Keniston, K. (1964) *The Uncommitted: Alienated Youth in American Society*. New York: Dell.

Koch, S. (1993) *Double Lives*. New York: Free Press.

Lanham, R. (1976) *The Motives of Eloquence: Literary Rhetoric in the Renaissance*. New Haven: Yale University Press.

Lerner, M. (1987) 'Myth America.' *The New Republic* 197 (September 7): 11–13.

Lévi-Strauss, C. (1973) *Tristes Tropiques*. New York: Washington Square Press.

Llobera, J.R. (1988) 'The Dark Side of Modernity.' Paper presented at Madrid conference on the History of Sociology, Madrid, Spain, May.

Lowith, K. (1949) *Meaning in History*. Chicago and London: University of Chicago Press.

Mannheim, K. (1940) *Man and Society in an Age of Reconstruction: Studies in Modern Social Structure*. London: Routledge & Kegan Paul.

Marcuse, H. (1964) *One-Dimensional Man*. Boston: Beacon.

Marshall, T.H. (1964) *Class, Citizenship, and Social Development*. Garden City, New York: Doubleday.

Merton, R.K. (1970 [1939]) *Science, Technology and Society in Seventeenth-Century England*. New York: Harper & Row.

Miller, P. (1965) *The Life of the Mind in America*. New York: Harcourt Brace.

Mosse, G. (1964) *The Crisis of German Ideology*. New York: Grosset & Dunlap.

Oakeshott, M. (1962) *Rationalism in Politics and Other Essays*. New York: Methuen.

Parsons, T. (1937) *The Structure of Social Action*. New York: Free Press.

Pevsner, N. (1977) *Pioneers of Modern Design from William Morris to Walter Gropius*. Harmondsworth: Penguin.

Piaget, J. (1972) *Principles of Genetic Epistemology*. London: Routledge & Kegan Paul.

Poster, M. (1979) *Sartre's Marxism*. London: Pluto.

Rawls, J. (1971) *A Theory of Justice*. Cambridge, Mass.: Harvard University Press.

Rhodes, R. (1988) *The Making of the Atomic Bomb*. New York: Simon & Schuster.

Ringer, F.K. (1969) *The Decline of the German Mandarins: The German Academic Community, 1890–1933*. Cambridge, Mass.: Harvard University Press.

Sartre, J.-P. (1976) *Critique of Dialectical Reason*. London: New Left Books.

Saussure, F. de (1959 [1911]) *Course in General Linguistics*. New York: McGraw-Hill.

Sorel, G. (1950 [1908]) *Reflections on Violence*. New York: Collier.

Taylor, C. (1975) *Hegel*. Cambridge: Cambridge University Press.

Tenbruck, F. (1974) 'Max Weber and the Sociology of Science: A Case Reopened.' *Zeitschrift für Soziologie* 3: 312–20.

Tillich, P. (1952) *The Courage to Be*. New Haven: Yale University Press.

Tuveson, E.L. (1968) *Redeemer Nation*. Chicago: University of Chicago Press.

Walzer, M. (1965) *Revolution of the Saints*. Cambridge, Mass.: Harvard University Press.

Walzer, M. (1983) *Spheres of Justice*. New York: Basic Books.

Weber, M. (1958 [1904–05]) *The Protestant Ethic and the Spirit of Capitalism*. New York: Scribners.

Weber, M. (1946 [1917]) 'Science as a Vocation,' pp. 129–56 in H. Gerth and C.W. Mills, eds, *From Max Weber*. New York: Oxford University Press.

Wittgenstein, L. (1922) *Tractatus Logico-Philosophicus*. New York: Harcourt Brace.

Wittgenstein, L. (1968) *Philosophical Investigations*. New York: Macmillan. Third edition.

Wittgenstein, L. (1980) *Culture and Value*. Chicago: University of Chicago Press.

Yeo, E. (1981) 'Christianity in Chartist Struggle, 1838–1848.' *Past and Present* 91: 109–39.

3

General Theory in the Postpositivist Mode:

The 'Epistemological Dilemma' and the Search for Present Reason

In the postwar period, general sociological theory has been associated with the search for nomothetic knowledge. It has been viewed, by its proponents and critics alike, as the crowning glory of the positive science of society. As the positivist conviction has weakened, the attractiveness of pursuing general theories in social science has waned; indeed, the very viability of the project has come to be seriously questioned. If subjective frameworks inevitably mediate scientific observations, it is reasoned, then efforts at generalization from these observations must themselves have a particularist component. Once the pristine universal status of theory has been undermined in this way, it has seemed only logical to many that social science should not just acknowledge the personal but embrace it. Increasingly, there have been calls for social science to give up its one-dimensional quest for cognitive truth; social science as praxis or moral inquiry (Haan et al. 1983; Wardell and Turner 1986), or as a hermeneutics of the concrete (ibid.; Gibbons 1987; Rabinow and Sullivan 1979) have been offered as alternatives.

On such intellectual grounds, and for historical and political reasons as well, non-empirical discourse in the social sciences has become more relativist than ever before. Some intellectuals have embraced this relativism enthusiastically; others have adopted it in a spirit of resignation, believing that no other alternative to positivism can be defended. My point in this essay is that this *simpliste* choice between scientistic theory and antitheoretical relativism represents not only a false dichotomy but a dangerous one.

I will call the presentation of these alternatives the 'epistemological dilemma,' for it presents the fate of general theory as dependent upon an epistemological choice alone. Either knowledge of the world is un-related to the social position and intellectual interests of the knower, in which case general theory and universal knowledge are viable, or knowledge is affected by its relation to the knower, in which case relativistic and particularistic knowledge can be the only result. This is a true dilemma because it presents a choice between two equally unpalatable alternatives. I argue that neither pole of this dilemma should be accepted. The alternative to positivist theory is not resigned relativism; the alternative to relativism is not positivist theory. Theoretical knowledge can never be anything other than the socially rooted efforts of historical agents. But this social character does not negate the possibility for developing either generalized categories or increasingly disciplined, impersonal, and critical modes of evaluation (cf. Will 1985).

To acknowledge relativism is not necessarily to imply that actors impose on knowledge personal and idiosyncratic imprints. Actors can be bound – by their societies and themselves – to standards that are rooted within, and after a manner are reflections of, broader and more inclusive social institutions and groups. They may also be bound by traditions that have a distinctively rational, impersonal bent. One must differentiate, then, within the category 'relativist.' Evaluative criteria, while contextually relative, can be both more universalistic and less so. The search for truth can be fused with the search for other kinds of knowledge – with the search for beauty and moral purity – or it can be separated from them and controlled in specialized and more impersonal ways. It is possible, in other words, to defend the search for universal truth, and the possibility of gaining valuable approximations to it, in a manner that does not reflect positivist credulity.

In the course of this essay I seek to overcome the epistemological dilemma in a variety of ways. In the section immediately following I present the argument that universalistic standards of evaluation, and impersonal conceptual constructs, are products of millennia-long development in human civilization. Because the effort to gain distance from objects outside of the self – to separate the knower from the known – did not begin with the positivism of the seventeenth-century scientific revolution, the quest for universalism cannot be evaluated on the grounds of a simple objection to philosophical positivism as such. In the course of this discussion I introduce the counterpoint to universalization that, in different guises, is the critical object through-out much of this essay. I suggest that the demand for a turning away from universalism has been intrinsic to cultural history and, in the section following, that this dialectic can be seen throughout the modern history of social thought.

After these general considerations, my focus becomes narrower and more detailed. I show how the epistemological dilemma was reproduced with debilitating consequences in the postwar debate between scientism and theoreticism on the one hand and neo-romantic contextualism on the other. After discussing the deepening skepticism about theory and 'truth' which has marked a range of intellectual movements over the last two decades, I develop a detailed criticism of Richard Rorty's brief for antifoundational relativism. Only after these critical and hermeneutic discussions are completed do I offer, in the concluding section of this essay, a relatively systematic defense of the possibility for general theorizing within a postpositivist frame.

The Dialectic of Universal and Concrete in Cultural History

Social science theory is one important manifestation of the search for universalism, for fair and principled standards of evaluation, that has been one of the principal ambitions of civilizational development. The contemporary debate between general theory and its critics can be seen, therefore, as one version of the conflict between the universal and the concrete that has marked cultural history itself.

To advocate the necessity for general theory is to uphold the possibility of universal thought. Universalism rests upon the capacity for actors to decenter themselves, to understand that the world does not revolve around them, that they are not its creators, that they can study 'it' in a relatively impersonal way. As Nagel writes in his important argument about the paradoxical pursuit of objective knowledge,

> The aim of such understanding is to go beyond the distinction between appearance and reality by including the existence of appearances in an elaborated reality. But this expanded reality, like physical reality, is center-less. Though the subjective features of our own minds are at the center of *our* world, we must try to conceive of them as just one manifestation of the mental in a world that is not given especially to the human point of view.
>
> (1986: 18, original italics)[1]

Yet, paradoxically, this decentered world is at the same time a world view, and the human view of it a human creation. When this agency is forgotten, universalism becomes an objectification that seems not just to decenter human beings but to deny them. Objectivity is viewed not as world mastery but as alienation. The consequence is the return to the concrete.

The process of decentering actors from their world is the process upon which the claims of civilization rest. The earlier the human society, the more its members experience centeredness. The world is whole, it is our world, it is experienced in its subjective immediacy. Actors live in the dreaming, in circular narrative time, in myth, conventions, parables, stories.[2] As Weber first demonstrated, and as many others have substantiated since, as societies become larger and more complex, experience becomes more fragmented. Reality is posited more as something that exists outside the actor, that is removed from immediate experience and the concrete. As it becomes more universal, time flattens out; reflection and self-consciously constructed recipes, maps, and hypotheses take their place alongside myths as organized orientations for social action.[3]

With the great monotheistic religions – particularly with Judaism and Christianity – but also with Buddhism, Hinduism, and Confucianism, this reality is expressed as a higher truth that not only stands completely outside of subjectively experienced time and place but that actually creates them. This reality, expressed as God, is so universal that in Judaism it could not even be personalized through a name, so abstract it could not be worshiped through any concrete form.[4] The same kind of decentering and objectifying process occurred in ancient Greece (Jaeger 1965; Voegelin 1957), where nature assumed the status of an impersonal force, challenging the pantheon of personal divinities. For both secular and religious society, the universal forces that decenter men and women are at the same time sources for the exercise of their reason. If it is men and women who have created the universal, then they must, after all, have the capacity to understand it.

For the Greeks, the connection between impersonal nature and the exercise of reason is easy to see. It is perhaps more difficult in the case of religion. It is easier when we understand that the will and motives of the impersonal religious force are also conceived by believers as forms of reason. God's reasons are presented to believers not only through the deep order of the natural and social worlds but through divine laws. As radically decentered beings, men and women strive to emulate the abstract model of divinity in order to understand its order and submit to its laws. For the ancient Jews, to submit to this universal personalization was to gain salvation. Salvation can be called religious 'truth,' for it is based on understanding rather than on immediate experience. For the Greeks, effacing oneself before impersonal nature gained access to truth in a more secular and obviously rational way.

This interplay between expanding religious abstraction and secular universalism continued to develop in the modern world. Depersonalization brings individuation, not simply domination.[5] It was the great world religions that gave birth to the very conception of autobiography.[6] Cosmic abstraction brings metaphysical dualism; such dualism is the key to the experience of the separated 'self.' Thus, even while the world is increasingly experienced as objective and impersonal – as rational and rationalized – actors can experience an intimate connection to the objective forces from which they have become estranged. Insofar as this experience can be sustained, there exists what I will call present reason.

The experience of present reason is difficult to maintain. In the course of its progress, impersonal reason is continually negated by the demand for the concrete. As soon as the existence of the universal is posited, it is denied. This negation is generated because depersonalization is experienced as having caused reason to be absent. Actors experience the fear of obliteration from the forces that they have themselves created, from the isolated and demanding self, from the impersonally organized society, from an omnipotent God, from the rationally reorganized forces of nature.

This is not a deception, but rather another form of truth. The dialectic of present and absent reason forms the main topic of Hegel's *Phenomenology*. Insofar as human beings posit reason as outside of themselves, they create the conditions for the alienation of reason from its human origins. Religion becomes an orthodoxy in which the faithful lose touch with their own spiritual life. Philosophy becomes a dogma that is casuistic, obfuscatory, elitist, and merely abstract. When decentered reason becomes objectified in colossal weapons of death that obliterate human beings, the alienation of reason assumes more than a metaphysical form (see chapter 2, above). Because reason appears to be absent from the objects created by rational human beings, people deny its very existence. In response to this alienation of reason, truth is sought within, not without, in the concrete rather than the abstract. Reason is abandoned for experience, rationality for the irrational. This countermovement is expressed by cabbalistic movements in Judaism, by Gnosticism in Christianity, by antinomianism in Puritanism, and by sophistry, skepticism, and idealism in philosophy.

Universal and Concrete in Social Thought

In the realm of thought this dialectic has been conceptualized as
the relation of the knower to the known. The scientific revolution
of the early modern period decentered the human being, the knower,
in a particularly dramatic way. Social thought followed in its wake,
as thinkers from Hobbes to the French philosophers strove to find
the social physics corresponding to Newton's heavenly ones. These
decentering movements of thought were experienced as liberating but
also as forms of alienation. Romanticism created a countermovement
that continues to inform reactions against universalism today. Fichte,
Hegel, and the early Marx were not the only thinkers who believed
that self and world division were only necessary steps on the way to
a higher experience of unity.[7] Romantic literary and theoretical
protests against objectification were also firmly rooted in English
thought, as M.H. Abrams (1971) has shown in his discussions of
Wordsworth, Coleridge, and Blake.

Still, it was British thinkers who produced political economy and
utilitarian social science and Germans who created hermeneutics,
the great intellectual countermovement whose call for the recentering
of the knower within the known has become increasingly influential
in recent times. While I will suggest later that Dilthey, at least, did
not intend to give up on scientific generalization, his program for
Geisteswissenschaft clearly emphasizes intuition and experience over
reason and abstraction. It places activities governed by impersonal
laws – including much of political, economic, and geopolitical life
– outside the bounds of interpretive social thought.

When Nietzsche condemned abstract reason as the invention of
monotheism and the Greeks, he was not wrong; however, in his
feverish effort to get behind (and beyond) reason to the sensate and
concrete, to embrace particularism at any cost, he pushed Romanticism
into a radically destructive form. When it takes less nihilistic forms,
its anti-epistemological message is much the same. When he rejected
Husserl's transcendental phenomenology for existentialism, Heidegger
was insisting on the disaster of depersonalization. Following Husserl
led only to understanding how impersonality is rationally constructed,
not to the demand for its abolition. Heidegger wanted philosophy to
be more personal and direct, an ontology of 'being there' (*Dasein*).

Following Heidegger and Hegel, Sartre called for a radical recentering of existence and questioned the very reality of the depersonalized
world. In his early work he described what was outside the individual
as nothingness; in his later work he called it the concrete inert. Both

are conceptions of the world in which abstractions have no meaning, in which it is impossible to experience the world outside of the self in a real and satisfying way. In this critical respect, the later Wittgenstein is no different. Words do not refer to things outside of consciousness but to other words. When we speak of the world as red we speak not of redness as such, of the world out there, but rather we refer to a linguistic concept whose referent we accept because convention relates the word to other concepts with similar objects. Chained within the subjective though not private world of our language games, we do not have any access to the impersonal world itself.

It is not my intention in this essay to deny the intellectual significance, much less the moral importance, of this Romantic and idealistic movement in modern thought and culture. There is a pathology inherent in the universalism that civilization upholds, and it is precisely that reason itself is often experienced as absent. To 'treat' this pathology, rational actors must be reminded that they are the creators of the world view that allows them to comprehend nature, self, and society in a universalistic and impersonal way. Romanticism in its various forms has been the teacher of this lesson, for every generation fortunate enough to experience its tutelage.

I do wish to maintain, however, that in important respects the world outside of the self can, in fact, be comprehended. Human beings create the world view that allows them to conceive of this world, but they do not create this world as such. Nor do they invent the society whose regularities this decentering allows them to see, regularities which, if not lawful in the same sense as physical laws, exhibit powerful and consistent patterning. The countermovement against impersonal rationality allows us not to forget that it is we who are seeing this society and world; it is not seeing itself through us. This is the achievement of Romantic social thought in its modern guise. Yet, we can decenter ourselves from this personal process of objective knowing in turn. Insofar as we do so, we can understand and explain what this process of constructing rational perception involves. This understanding, however, does not threaten the universality of perception. To the contrary, it can become another, equally universalistic theory – a theory of knowledge and perception – in its own right.

Scientism and Theoreticism in the Postwar Period

These broad considerations are central to the problem of general theory and its critics. One can argue about what exactly 'theory' is, whether it is a model, a set of interlinked propositions that produces testable hypotheses, a frame of reference, a set of classifications, a conceptual scheme. One cannot argue, however, with the notion that, no matter how defined, theory implies an abstraction from the concrete. The more general the theory – the greater its interpretive and explanatory reach – the more general the abstraction. Theory is the quintessence of the decentering process that distinguishes the modern world.

The universalism of general theory cannot be justified if this universalism is understood, and experienced, as a decentering that demands the alienation of reason. General theory is not something that simply reflects the objective out there. Positivism and empiricism reduce theory in just this way, viewing it merely as the studied reflection of the natural world. For this reason, their justifications for theory have been particularly vulnerable in the contemporary period, for in this recent period the agentic contribution to our perception of the objective world has become increasingly well understood. In the present context, general theory can be justified only in a postpositivist way, as the case for present reason.

Positivism and empiricism take their warrant for universal theorizing from the role it seems to play in the sciences of nature. I say 'seems to play,' for in the practice of natural science the exercise of reason is camouflaged in a particularly effective way. In its natural science form, the practice of general theory has become, at least in its normal science mode, a process of absent reason. Scientists experience themselves as mirroring nature.[8] Their own exercise in rationality – the manner in which it is this rationality itself which has allowed perceptual access to a world which mathematics and scientific method can model – is forgotten. For many decades absent reason also characterized the philosophy of natural science. Effacement, abnegation, objectivity, transparency – when these terms describe the relation of scientists to nature their agentic construction of the natural world is ignored. Theories are held to be proven or falsified by exposing their human-made tenets to the force of non-human empirical facts.

This perspective on natural science practice, articulated philosophically by logical positivism, carried forcefully into the heyday of positive social science in the decades that followed the Second World War. The unified science movement, a position articulated by Neurath but shared by virtually the entire social scientific community, suggested no significant difference between natural and social science. The increasing technical efficiency of statistical methods made it appear that access to the social equivalent of unadorned nature would soon be approximated. With these methods, social scientists would not have to construct generalizations on the basis of their interpretive insights, intellectual power, and wit; on the basis simply of their commitment to the ironclad experimental codes of science, generalizations would emerge out of the data themselves.

This vision of absent reason can be found even in the work of sophisticated theorists like Talcott Parsons. While Parsons appreciated Weber's search for a universalistic version of the *Geisteswissenschaften*, presenting a subtle and powerful interpretation of it in his first major work (Parsons 1937: 579–639), he conceived his own theorizing on the model of Newtonian mechanics. He was not troubled by the possibility, which he himself recognized, that general theory placed the constructions of the knower onto the very perception of the known. To the contrary, Parsons confidently presented his action theory as a powerful reflection of 'the real,' even if a reflection that had been mediated in an analytic, a priori way.[9] This utopian rationalism was not the product of Parsons's functionalism. Writing at the high point of French communist ascendancy in the early 1960s, Louis Althusser (1969) confidently separated his own version of Marxist social science theory from mere bourgeois ideology. Postwar semiotics agreed to the idea that truth was accessible without the intervention of subjective frames. In 'Myth Today,' Roland Barthes (1959) illustrated how social structural pressures distorted merely denotative analogies into redolent myths, without giving any thought to the question of how his own thought could have escaped the same mythic fate.[10]

Contextualism as the Neo-romantic Alternative

It is not surprising that in the course of the 1960s there emerged in reaction against such absent reason an extraordinary neo-romantic critique. Optimism about the objectively progressive course of the postwar world had begun to fade; renewed racial, ethnic, and class conflicts, and the emergence of newly strengthened pimordial attachments, made the unthinking commitment to universal and social and intellectual structures more difficult. When they protested against 'meaningless abstraction' in their newly expanded universities, college students were experiencing the absence of reason in the very heart of intellectual life; they viewed the university not as the expression of human creativity and imagination but as an objectified machine. They indicted science for its reification in weapons of war.

The classical embodiments of rational social theory also were challenged in an antinomian way. Against the reconstruction of Weber by Parsons and Bendix as the embodiment of rational sobriety, Mitzman (1970) claimed that charisma, pathos, and eros formed the revealing underside to Weber's rationalizing theme. Against Rieff's (1961) moralist Freud and Jones's (1963) scientific one, Norman O. Brown (1966) created a Freud of play and joy, while Russel Jacoby (1975) indicted American revisionists for ignoring the critical and erotic Freud that Marcuse (1954) had earlier unearthed. Garfinkel (1967) became dissatisfied with Husserl's epistemological stance, fearing that it too easily endorsed the existence of impersonal forms; inspired by Heidegger and Wittgenstein, he pushed ethnomethodology into a more radically antinormative mode, away from the belief in, and the hope for, consensual normative constraints as they were embodied in theorizing of a Parsonian form (see Alexander 1987: 257–80).

By the end of the 1960s, an antitheoretical orientation had begun to emerge throughout Western intellectual life.[11] I will call this broad movement contextualism. Thus, in what became an extraordinarily influential quarrel with functionalist theory, Clifford Geertz (1973a [1964]) attacked the notion that cognitive truth was relevant to the study of ideology, arguing against Parsons for an interpretive and relativist approach that emphasized the close link between political action and the rhetorical creation of meaning. Thomas Kuhn (1970 [1962]) rebelled against absent reason in natural science in an equally constructivist and contextualist way. While not denying the possibility of doing natural science, he identified the decentered scientist as a kind of 'normal science' idiot while describing creative and revolutionary science in a subjective and recentered way. Also beginning to get serious attention was the work of Peter Winch (1958), which in questioning the very possibility of a social science went further than either Geertz or Kuhn. Following Wittgenstein, Winch argued that social scientists were imprisoned by linguistic-conceptual worlds that made it impossible to create even relatively independent knowledge about the actions and intentions of those outside one's cultural group.

The Deepening Skepticism about Theory and 'Truth'

With the exception of Winch, these early contextualist reactions did not reject the possibility of universalism or the value of general theory. They had not, in other words, become fully confined by the epistemological dilemma. Those who followed them did, and were.

In the 1970s and 1980s the neo-romantic reaction deepened. What are taken to be the epistemological implications of contextualism – conventionalism and skepticism – have been explicitly formulated; in many quarters, theory has given way to the investigation of the concrete. Arguing from the mere existence of context, social scientists and philosophers have concluded that universalistic modes of argument are impossible. The facile and ultimately false dichotomy between positivism and relativism has thus inserted itself as a principal rubric in contemporary debate. The possibility that the context within which we operate is itself the very tradition of objective reason has been ignored.

This movement from the acknowledgment of context to the embrace of relativism and the abandonment of theory is nowhere more clear than in the intellectual odyssey of Clifford Geertz. In his 1960s essays on ideology and religion, Geertz had emphasized interpretive over scientific reason in order to avoid the sociological reductionism so prevalent in the social sciences of that day. Ideology and religion could be viewed as cultural systems only if their relation to social actors was evaluated by some criterion other than scientific truth. Ideological and religious actors, in other words, should not be mistaken for scientific ones. By the time he collected these earlier essays in his enormously influential *Interpretation of Cultures*, however, Geertz was arguing that scientific theorizing should not be the goal of analysts themselves. Not universalistic theory but 'thick description' of concrete behavior should be the goal of the human studies (Geertz 1973b).

The essays that appeared subsequent to this publication contain intriguing interpretations of cultural life, but they manifest virtually none of the theoretical ambitions, or the conceptual precision, of Geertz's earlier work. When he introduced his second collection of essays, *Local Knowledge*, published one decade after the first, Geertz (1983: 3–6) averred that in this latter set of essays he had, indeed, simply taken to their logical conclusion the implications of the first: 'In anthropology, too, it so turns out, he who says A must say B, and I have spent much of my time since [that first collection] trying to say it.' Employing the logic of the epistemological dilemma, Geertz identifies the social scientific search for theoretical generalization with the pretensions of the natural sciences. Citing the 'growing recognition that [this] established approach . . . was not producing the triumphs of prediction, control, and testability that had for so long been promised,' he condemns such efforts at 'laws-and-causes social physics' as reflecting 'a technological conception of those [human] sciences.' One must choose either positivism or particularistic relativism: Geertz is condemning not simply empiricist social science but any attempt to theorize about society as such. 'Calls for "a general theory" of just about anything social,' he asserts, 'sound increasingly hollow.' General theory 'has never seemed further away, harder to imagine, or less certainly desirable than it does right now.'

Once positivist and theoretical social science have been rejected, the only alternative Geertz can foresee is a return to the concrete. Social analysis must 'turn from trying to explain social phenomena by weaving them into grand textures of cause and effect to trying to explain them by placing them in local frames of awareness.' Ethnography, not generalizing social science, is the discipline best suited to this particularist task. 'To an ethnographer, sorting through the machinery of distant ideas, the shapes of knowledge are always ineluctably local, indivisible from their instruments and their encasements. One may veil this fact with ecumenical rhetoric or blur it with strenuous theory, but one cannot really make it go away.' Geertz concludes by warning his readers that, while his approach is a hermeneutic one, 'one will not find very much in the way of "the theory and methodology of interpretation" . . . in what follows.' Nor surprisingly, Geertz believes that 'there are enough general principles in the world already.' He does not wish to see hermeneutics 'reified into a parascience.' What the essays in *Local Knowledge* offer instead of theorizing are 'actual inter-pretations of something.' In this relativizing task, Geertz aligns himself with 'the views of such philosophers as Heidegger, Wittgenstein, Gadamer, or Ricoeur, such critics as Burke, Frye, Jameson, or Fish, and such all-purpose subversives as Foucault, Habermas, Barthes, or Kuhn.' These are, of course, precisely the figures – Habermas excepted – I have earlier identified as central to the contextual reaction against universalist thought (cf. Friedman 1987).

It is revealing, in this regard, that later developments in Thomas Kuhn's intellectual career manifest the epistemological dilemma in strikingly similar ways as those in Geertz's. Despite his quite legitimate protests that he had not intended to produce an irrationalist theory, Kuhn's revision of his paradigm concept (1970) made it impossible to identify it with theoretical presuppositions of a universal bent (see Alexander 1982b). Neophytes learn to exercise their scientific skills not by understanding intellectual frameworks but by mimicking the plots of specific problem solutions, which Kuhn calls 'exemplars.' Scientific results are controlled not, in the first instance, by universal-istic theories or impersonal methods but by a 'disciplinary matrix,' which Kuhn is careful to define not as a set of ideas but as a social network of situated human relations. In his subsequent monographic work Kuhn (1978) seemed to have given up on efforts at theoretical clarification altogether. Eschewing even the claim to exemplify his theory of scientific revolution, he returned to detailed historical description of a specific scientific case.

Equally revealing of the increasingly radical implications of contextualism is the poststructural movement beyond semiotics and structuralism. Since Saussure set forth semiotic philosophy in his general theory of linguistics, its key stipulation has been the arbitrary relation of sign and referent: there can be found no 'rational reason,' no force or correspondence in the outside world, for the particular signs that actors have chosen to represent their world. As I briefly indicated in my discussion of Barthes, early elaborations of the semiotic position exempted from this critique of objective reference semioticians themselves. It should not be surprising, perhaps, that the founder of the American pragmatic tradition of semiotics, Charles Peirce, was confident that practical experience eventually aligned scientific symbols with objective truth. What is striking, however, is that the same assurance of universalism marked the French semiotic school. Saussure showed no anxiety about his ability to perceive linguistic systems in a realistic way. Lévi-Strauss triumphantly described his structuralist interpretations as exemplifying the science of myth.

Contemporary inheritors of this semiotic and structuralist tradition were disappointed with the fate of what they conceived to be truth and reason in the 1960s. In addition to their experience of absent reason, they had well-justified concerns with the epistemological naivety of their theoretical predecessors. In accord with the logic of the epistemological dilemma, poststructuralists moved to extend the arbitrary relativism of the semiotic field to the semioticians themselves. Acknowledging the arbitrary reference of 'reality,' they felt compelled to reject out of hand the very concept of an objectively differentiated world exercising an independent influence on the knower. Experience replaces reason, relativism and the embrace of hypercontextualism displace the search for universalistic truth. Emancipation is a logical impossibility, domination a condition that cannot logically be overcome.

Baudrillard's (1983) concept of the simulacrum represents the *reductio ad absurdum* of the poststructuralist position, the inevitable conclusion of an insistence not only on the referential arbitrariness but also on the particularism of symbolic codes. Where the early Barthes saw myth as the corruption of realistic reference at the hands of objective social power, Baudrillard sees the play of signifier and signified as a closed circuit into which the reality of social needs can never intrude. The contrast between Lévi-Strauss and Bourdieu can be seen in much the same way. Lévi-Strauss's overweening rationalism led him to cut symbolic thought short before the entry of the modern world. The *bricoleur* was replaced by the scientist. With Bourdieu, we can see, once again, how a latter-day follower of structuralism responds to the earlier faith in objectivity with cynical disappointment. Denying the very possibility of reference to critical universalism, the perceptual structures of bourgeois and proletarian actors alike are for Bourdieu (1984) mere particularistic reflections, primitive codes from which there is no escape.

Derrida and Foucault supply the deep justification for such poststructural argument. Whereas Bourdieu seems blithely to exempt himself from his own relativizing strictures, Derrida (1981) has insisted that the knower is simply a literate *bricoleur*. Reality, in turn, can be nothing other than a text, a symbolic construction that is itself related to other texts – not to history or social structure – in arbitrary ways. Indeed, texts cannot themselves be accepted as representations, even of arbitrarily signified referents. Composed not just of presences but of absences, texts do not exist as complete wholes.

To this reconstruction of the epistemological dilemma in its most nihilistic form, Foucault adds a history and sociology. Against the possibility of contemporary universalism, he makes a double critique. First, there is his substantive historical demonstration of absent reason. The rationalization of modern society, as manifest particularly in the thought and activity of the scientifically trained professions, is a fraud (e.g. Foucault 1977, 1978). Professionals actually engage in the manipulation of reason; their ministrations are forms of surveillance, their goal technical control. Enlightenment universalism amounts to the particularism of power; it results in the suppression of subjectivity, not in the exercise of present reason.

Foucault's second critique is an analytical one. In his later work he insists on the virtually complete identity of knowledge, or discourse, with power. In doing so, the very possibility of decentered experience is denied. The subject, Foucault is fond of repeating, is completely constituted by discourse. In this way, discourse becomes both the basis for power and merely its manifestation in another form. Because truth is relative to discourse, it is impossible to appeal to universalizing standards against worldly power: 'Truth isn't outside power, or lacking in power. . . . Each society has its regime of truth, its "general politics" of truth: that is, the types of discourse which it accepts and makes function as true' (Foucault 1980: 131). To set about rationally to evaluate the logical consistency, theoretical implications, or explanatory value of a given discourse is obviously a waste of time.

The simple and dangerous dichotomy is firmly set. The only alternative to the fallacy of absent reason, to positivism, is a thoroughly relativist sociology of knowledge, an archeology of the historical conditions of discourse.[12]

The Apotheosis of Antitheoretical Relativism: The Philosophy of Richard Rorty and Its Postmodern Reprise

Nietzsche based his own genealogy of morals on his contempt for advocates of a belief in truth and the ascetic ideal. In their place, he 'enthrones taste . . . as the sole organ of knowledge beyond Truth and Falsity, beyond Good and Evil,' as Habermas puts it in his brilliant exploration of the disturbing underside of critical theory. Richard Rorty, while on his own account a good 'postmodern bourgeois liberal' (1985a), reluctantly embraces this Nietzschean frame. He does so because, like Nietzsche, he experiences the history of Western ratiocination not as the radically imperfect expression of present reason but as the alienation of subjectivity from itself. When Rorty describes the scientific revolution, it is the pathology of absent reason of which he writes.

> This is reality conceived as somehow represented by representations which are not merely ours but its own, as it looks to itself, as it would describe itself if it could. . . . This fantasy of discovering, and somehow knowing that one has discovered, Nature's Own Vocabulary *seemed* to become more concrete when Galileo and Newton formulated a comprehensive set of predictively useful universal generalizations, written in suitably 'cold,' 'inhuman,' mathematical terms.
>
> (1982a: 194, italics added)

This perception of absent reason leads Rorty to embrace the dichotomy between scientism and relativism. 'The urge to tell stories of progress, maturation and synthesis might be overcome,' he writes (1986: 48, italics added), 'if we once took seriously the notion that we only know the world and ourselves *under a description*.' Rorty is caught on the horns of the epistemological dilemma. If we acknowledge context, he believes, there 'is no possibility of evaluating the worth of various perspectives in a universalistic way.

> If we once could feel the full force of the claim that our present discursive practices were given neither by God, nor by intuition of essence nor by the cunning of reason, but *only* by chance, then we would have a culture

which lacked not only a theory of knowledge, not only a sense of progress, but *any* source of what Nietzsche called 'metaphysical comfort.'

(ibid.: italics added)

To embrace fully such relativism, indeed, one must avoid not only progressive theories but theorizing as such. 'A Nietzschean must not want any substitute for theories,' Rorty explains (ibid.). To theorize is to imply the possibility of at least partly circumventing the particularism of context. This is impossible, for a Nietzschean 'views the very idea of "theory" as tainted with the notion that there is something there to be contemplated, to be accurately represented in thought.' The possibility of accurate representation is what Rorty wants to avoid. He succeeds remarkably well.

Rorty sees the history of philosophy as directed to 'the relation between universals and particulars' (1979: 149).[13] Because *Philosophy and the Mirror of Nature* is an argument against the possible existence of the concrete, it is necessarily an argument against the history of philosophy as well. The problem began long ago, with the Greeks. Plato's and Aristotle's search for universal categories and impersonal knowledge did not mark the beginning of human emancipation from an anthropomorphically distorted world; this search, rather, simply produced another kind of equally magical and distorted myth. 'The metaphor of knowing general truths by internalizing universals,' Rorty suggests (p. 42), became 'the intellectual's substitute for the peasant's belief in life among the shades.'

One of the peculiarities of Rorty's book is that this key proposition – that universal properties do not exist – is taken more as the basis upon which to draw other conclusions than as a point that needs to be demonstrated in and of itself. Rorty demonstrates that, after 2,500 years, philosophers still have not agreed about what such universals are, or about how they can be proved. He also discusses recent discoveries in the postpositivist philosophy and history of science and points to the skeptical conclusions of such contextualist philosophers as Wittgenstein, Heidegger, and, more questionably, Dewey. Finally, Rorty argues that the split between mind and body cannot exist. He introduces a long parable about the visit to earth of Antipodeans, a mythical people from the other side of the galaxy whose vast knowledge of micro-neurology has demonstrated exactly how thoughts are produced by electrical impulse and physical laws. 'Now that they have taught us micro-neurology,' Rorty (p. 81) has his backward friends on earth suggest, 'cannot we see that talk of mental states was merely a place-holder for talk of neurons?' Because we have bodies, in other

words, there is no need for the concept of mind or for the theories
they produce. 'To suggest that the mind is the brain,' Rorty insists,
'is to suggest that we secrete theorems and symphonies as our spleen
secretes dark humors' (pp. 43–4). Rorty's parable is amusing but
ultimately terrifying in its antirationalist implications.

It might be argued that Rorty's failure to justify his assumption that
universals do not exist places the intellectual edifice he is constructing
on rather flimsy foundations. We will see that Rorty himself would
offer to this fundamental objection the most skeptical of replies.
Because universals do not exist, an effort to construct intellectual
foundations is a hopeless enterprise from the start. At any rate, it is the
implication that Rorty draws from this assumption against universals
that makes his work interesting.

Because there are no universals, we can talk in good faith only about
experience, not abstract norms; we can refer only 'to common sense
and common practice for details about what counts as justification'
(p. 151). The real problem, as Rorty sees it, is 'not to abjure such
hypostatized universals but to explain why anyone had taken them
seriously' (pp. 68–9). He laments (p. 38) the passing of the traditional
world – 'there would not have been thought to be a problem about
the nature of reason had our race confined itself to pointing out
particular states of affairs – warning of cliffs and rain, celebrating
individual births and deaths.' Unfortunately, for 'no particular reason,'
some philosophers – but not many normal human beings – got it
into their heads that 'knowledge of universals' held the key to personhood and freedom. With the entrance of the Greeks, the slide down the
slippery slope began. Among philosophers at least, it has come to the
point that 'to suggest that there are no universals . . . is to endanger
our uniqueness' (p. 43).

The conclusion Rorty draws from the nonexistence of universals is
that foundational arguments – general theoretical ones, in the language
of social science – are impossible to make. It is revealing that, despite
his explicit condemnation of epistemology as such, this antifoundational
argument is made precisely in epistemological terms. Philosophers
who espouse universals have justified their importance by describing
them as objective entities. Against this, Rorty insists over and over
again that it is impossible to have 'pre-linguistic awareness' (p. 181).
His (epistemological) point is that there is 'no transcendental standpoint of our present set of representations from which we can inspect
the relation between these representations and their object' (p. 293).
He concludes that the '"epistemological" quest for a way of refuting
the skeptic and underwriting our claim to be talking about nonfictions

[is] hopeless.' The epistemological claim is hopeless because it is empiricist. It reflects the absence of reason. Rorty points to the coercive implications that flow from this loss. Such philosophers, he writes, believe that 'knowing a proposition to be true is to be identified with being caused to do something by an object' (p. 157). According to this view 'the object which the proposition is about *imposes* the proposition's truth' (original italics).

Rorty's claim is that philosophers seeking objectivity see themselves as reflectors, or mirrors, of reality; hence, they set out to establish the 'foundations of knowledge.' Foundational arguments are universals that establish the grounds for truth in what are conceived of as objectively rational ways, 'truths which are certain because of their causes rather than because of the arguments given for them' (p. 159). Because they move 'beyond argument to compulsion from the object known,' foundational arguments are inhuman; they claim that 'anyone gripped by the object in the required way will be *unable* to doubt or to see an alternative' (italics added). Foundationalism, Rorty insists, is 'the end-product of an original wish to substitute *confrontation for conversation* as the determinant of our belief' (p. 163).

Rorty is right to demand that reason be present, and he is also right that this can be achieved only if a hermeneutic rather than mechanistic stance is achieved.

> If the study of science's search for truth about the physical universe is viewed hermeneutically it will be viewed as the activity of spirit – the faculty which *makes* – rather than as the application of the mirroring faculties, those which *find* what nature has already made.
>
> (p. 344, original italics)

Rorty is wrong, however, to think that this can be accomplished only by abandoning the search for universals as such. The problem lies with his conviction that every argument against skepticism and for universalism is an 'epistemological quest,' that it is based upon reflection theory and the absence of reason. Philosophers who seek truthful foundations may perceive themselves as mirroring reality, but the interest and power of their arguments do not stand or fall on whether this claim can itself be true. These philosophers can be seen, rather, as rational agents who create frameworks within which to interpret a world whose objectivity and impersonality they take on faith. To the degree that they succeed, they falsify Rorty's epistemological syllogism, his claim that the proposition 'there is no neutral ground on which to stand' follows logically from the notion 'there is no such thing as pre-linguistic awareness' (p. 181).

Rorty says that when foundationalists make their arguments they are playing the language game of 'philosophy-as-epistemology.' But surely he is himself playing the same game from the other side of the net. Rorty characterizes foundationalism as the demand for 'some transcendental standpoint outside our present set of representations from which we can inspect the relations between those representations and their objects' (p. 293). He believes that to deny the transparency of reality is to deny the interest and importance of universalistic ambition. Because he is caught within the epistemological dilemma, he cannot differentiate the levels and complexity of present reason in an appropriate way. Acknowledging representational subjectivity does not mean abandoning the possibility of differentiating our representations from objects in the outside world. The possibility for so comparing 'objective' and 'subjective' is produced by the development of human culture itself, which can be seen as progress because it has allowed an increasingly decentered construction of nature and social life. Reason can be exercised in a present way.

Because Rorty cannot conceptualize this fine-grained alternative to positivist credulity, he can only recommend that we return to the concrete. Rather than evaluating knowledge, he recommends, we should explore its social origins. Rather than criticizing society in light of universalist norms, we should criticize universalist norms in light of their social base. Because 'justification is a matter of social practice' (p. 186), we must explain 'rationality and epistemic authority by reference to what society lets us say, rather than the latter by the former' (p. 147). Rorty's recommendation that philosophy be abandoned for intellectual and cultural history – 'the division of labor between the historian and philosopher no longer made sense' (p. 272) – is only the logical, Wittgensteinian conclusion. Because 'the way people talk can "create objects,"' it follows that 'when we want to know how we know about such objects as these, we do and should turn not to the epistemologist but to the intellectual historian' (1986: 42).

> The historian can make the shift from the old scheme to the new intelligible, and make one see why one would have been led from the one to the other if one had been an intellectual of that day. There is nothing the philosopher can add to what the historian has already done to show that this intelligible and plausible course is a 'rational' one.
>
> (1979: 272)

It is an either/or choice, ironically dictated by Rorty's location within the epistemological straitjacket from which he is trying to escape. This logic is particularly clear in his attack on anything other than a historical approach to science. If a nonhistorical, objectivistic reference for scientific concepts is impossible, then the effort to evaluate the truth of this concept must be abandoned. 'We have the following dilemma: either the theory of reference is called upon to underwrite the success of contemporary science, or else it is simply a decision about how to write the history of science (rather than the provision of a "philosophical foundation" for such historiography)' (pp. 287–8). 'Once we understand (as historians of knowledge do) when and why various beliefs have been adopted or discarded,' Rorty (p. 178) insists, there is simply nothing 'called "the relation of knowledge to reality" left over to be understood.'

Once the problem of the relation of thought to reality is abandoned (cf. Rorty 1982b: 15), there is nothing much left for philosophers in the traditional sense, or for theorists in general, to do. Having given up on the traditional conception of truth-telling, Rorty suggests, the philosopher should become an 'informed dilettante,' the 'polypragmatic' who can spread a little understanding by providing what are destined to be personal translations between discourses whose relative truth can never be compared (p. 317). In this way, philosophy can become an 'edifying' profession, even a 'poetic' one (p. 360), which follows from the belief that 'our culture should become one in which the demand for constraint and confrontation is no longer felt' (p. 315). Compromise is possible because no principled positions are at stake – 'edifying philosophers have to decry the very notion of having a view, while avoiding having a view about having views' (p. 371). Once the trappings of rationality are avoided – things like 'inquiry' and notions like an 'exchange of views' – a return to intimacy, love, and real community will result. 'One way to see edifying philosophy as the love of wisdom is to see it as the attempt to prevent conversation from degenerating into inquiry, into an exchange of views. Edifying philosophers can never end philosophy, but they help prevent it from attaining the secure path of a science.'[14]

This aestheticized and antitheoretical vision, which believes itself incapable of distinguishing between telling stories and telling the truth, provides an analytic-philosophical rationale for the poststructuralist theory I described above (see Rorty 1985b). This connection surfaces most clearly in the postmodernism of Jean-François Lyotard. Lyotard contends that the age of the great 'metanarratives' is past; the beliefs that such abstractions as science, education, democracy, and revolution would provide emancipation are myths that are no longer believed. Whereas modernism is defined as the search after such abstract will-o'-the-wisps, postmodernism marks a return to the concrete. In place of abstracting and transcendence, there is 'heterogeneity' and 'local determinism' (Lyotard 1984: xxiv). Rather than metanarratives, which through abstraction promote the mythical ideal of rational self-reflection, there remain only local narratives, from within which recourse to an extra-discursive principle is impossible.

Lyotard, too, is caught by the epistemological dilemma. Arguing from Hegel's relativizing of rational scientific thought in the *Phenomenology*, he moves from the simple existence of context to the impossibility of knowing as such.

> The speculative apparatus maintains an ambiguous relation to knowledge. It shows that knowledge is only worthy of that name up to the extent that it reduplicates itself ('lifts itself up,' *hebt sich auf*; is sublated) by citing its own statements in a second-level discourse . . . that functions to legitimate them. This is as much as to say that . . . denotative discourse bearing on a certain referent (a living organism, a chemical property, a physical phenomenon, etc.) does not really know what it thinks it knows. Positive science is not a form of knowledge.
>
> (ibid.: 38)

Lyotard draws a sharp distinction between science – defined in its positivist mode as the knowledge that 'does not really know what it thinks it knows' – and narrative, or centered knowledge. The positivist scientist dismisses narratives because, confidently assessing validity, he 'concludes that they are never subject to argumentation or proof' (ibid.: 27). With the end of metanarratives, this demand for abstract legitimation has ceased. 'Because narrative knowledge does not give priority to the question of its own legitimation, [it] certifies itself in the pragmatics of its own transmission without having recourse to argumentation and proof.' What is left for the postmodern theorist to do? 'All we can do,' Lyotard concludes, 'is gaze in wonderment at the diversity of discursive species' (ibid.: 26). At this juncture, Huyssen's lament about 'the list of "no longer possibles"' (1986: 288) seems very much to the point.

The Postpositivist Case for Theory

When Rorty puts hermeneutics forward as the alternative to theory and foundationalism, he emphasizes that he is not suggesting it as a 'successor subject' to fill the vacancy left by foundationalist philosophy. Indeed, 'hermeneutics is an expression of hope that the cultural space left by the demise of epistemology [e.g. foundationalism] will not be filled' (1979: 315). According to Rorty, in other words, hermeneutics is not a more sensitive or interpretive approach to universalism or rational understanding; it is the very opposite, the type case of an immersion in the sensuous concrete. With hermeneutics, Rorty believes, 'the demand for constraint and confrontation is no longer felt.' This understanding of hermeneutics, however, like Rorty's understanding of science, is distorted by the epistemological dilemma that confines his thought. We have seen how this condition makes it impossible to defend objectivity in even a conditional way, to defend the search for universal grounds and the possibility that some approximation of them can be achieved. It is the ambition of this final section to suggest, this time in a positive rather than in a critical form, how such a search can proceed and how this possibility of proximate universality can be understood.

I will introduce this discussion by examining a recent development within hermeneutical social theory itself (cf. Ingram 1985). The possibility that hermeneutical understanding may not, after all, be the antithesis of reason has recently been recognized by even some of the most severe critics of 'mainstream' social science. Shifts can be traced, for example, in the critical and hermeneutic philosophy of Richard Bernstein, which exemplify this recognition in the most vivid way. The central ambition of Bernstein's earlier work, which culminated in *The Restructuring of Social and Political Theory*, published in 1978, was to question the very possibility of a social science (see Alexander 1981). Attacking confidence in explanatory theorizing as profoundly misplaced, Bernstein issued a call for practical theory and contextual interpretation. In *Beyond Objectivism and Relativism* (1983), however, Bernstein's ambition is now very different. He wants to demonstrate that hermeneutics is antithetical neither to social science nor to the search for universals.

In his earlier work, Bernstein presents Kuhn's incommensurability thesis in a sympathetic way, urging his readers to agree that 'the differences among competing paradigms are as radical as Kuhn suggests' and that 'there is no set of standards for proving the superiority of one paradigm over another' (1978: 87). He goes on to praise the novelty of Kuhn's description of paradigm change as a conversion experience depending upon techniques of persuasion, an antirationalist position that surely confused the psychology of science with the normative structure within which scientific interaction proceeds. In his later work, however, Bernstein treats Kuhn's notion of incommensurability in a dramatically different way. He insists not only that the concept must be carefully distinguished from 'incompatibility' and 'incomparability,' but that the claim that Kuhn himself conflates these terms 'is not only mistaken but perverse' (1983: 82). Not only does Kuhn make these distinctions, but he does so, Bernstein would now have us believe, in order to demonstrate the manner in which 'rational debate and argumentation between proponents of rival paradigms' is possible (ibid.: 85).

Whatever its merits as interpretation, these revisions demonstrate the new movement to defend rationality that characterizes Bernstein's recent work.[15] His intention is to escape the epistemological dilemma. Thus, whenever he contrasts rationality and contextualism, he qualifies his characterization of the former in a manner that points to a new, third term. While apparently paraphrasing Kuhn and Feyerabend on the decision-making process by which one scientific statement is judged to be more 'logical and rational' than another, Bernstein writes that it is not 'free-floating standards of rationality detached from actual historical practices to which we can appeal' (ibid.: 67, italics added). In such judgments, he continues, 'we are not appealing to permanent, atemporal standards of rationality,' to 'a permanent set of ahistorical standards of rationality' (ibid., italics added). After making these careful qualifications, Bernstein impatiently rejects what he calls a 'false dichotomy' – 'either permanent standards of rationality (objectivism) or arbitrary acceptance of one set of standards or practices over against its rival (relativism)' (ibid.: 68).

Bernstein now introduces the missing third term – 'reasons embedded in . . . social practices.' Rather than free-floating, reason is a practice imbedded in science; when scientists argue about truth, they refer not to some supra-social reality but to this imbedded reason – to 'the best possible scientific reasons that can be given.' To suggest that it is institutionalized, however, does not suggest that science is irrational. To the contrary, 'a scientist is always under the obligation to give a rational account of what is right and wrong in the theory that is being displaced and to explain how his or her theory can account for what is "true" in the preceding theory.' By this point, it is clear that Bernstein's target is not positivism but skepticism. Indeed, he ends up by defending the possibility of social science theory against hermeneutics itself. 'However much one recognizes the importance of the hermeneutical dimension of the social sciences,' he warns, 'one must also forthrightly confront those aspects of these disciplines that seek to develop theoretical and causal explanations of social phenomena' (ibid.: 160). Bernstein even chides Gadamer, the heroic figure of his book, for what he takes to be the latter's hermeneutic rejection of scientific method, insisting that 'method is more like hermeneutic understanding than Gadamer frequently acknowledges' (ibid.: 169).

The third term that Bernstein inserts into the debate over science is the notion of present reason, the alternative to the epistemological dilemma which I have explored in a variety of ways above. My argument has been that, even while rationality is acknowledged to be an agentic accomplishment, objectivity can also be seen as an eminently worthy goal. To achieve grounded rationality, social actors promote a decentered understanding of the social and natural world, establish norms and frameworks that sanction personalization and that reward not only the ability to see the world as 'out there' but the willingness to 'subordinate' one's personal desires to that world's exploration.

It is time now to establish some general criteria for just how such a hermeneutically rooted version of universality can be established.

While present reason establishes the framework for understanding this world, it does not create this world itself. As Frederick Will (1985: 131) puts it in his modified brief for realism, action is 'affected by, controlled by, or more exactly, constituted in part by determinants external to, independent of, the individuals engaged in them.' For this reason, correspondence between framework and reality must ultimately be conceived of as the criterion governing every validity claim. Obviously, I am not myself proposing here a realist program. Since the world, in the brute pre-Kantian sense, cannot be seen as such, correspondence can be nothing other than the relationship between 'reason-created' conceptual structures and reasonable 'observational statements' about the world. Whether this differentiation can be confidently made is, then, the first criterion of whether universality, and some conditional conception of objectivity, can be achieved.

Has this criterion been met in contemporary natural and social science? The answer must certainly be yes. It has been one of the clearest achievements of Western and more recently modern intellectual life to create a world of observational statements which most practitioners at any given point in the development of their disciplines recognize as having an impersonal status. Scheffler (1976: 39) expresses this perspective in the following: 'We simply have a false dichotomy in the notion that observation must be either a pure confrontation with an undifferentiated given, or else so conceptually contaminated that it must render circular any observational test of a hypothesis.' The fact that Rorty (1979: 276n.) himself approvingly quotes this very passage to declare his own departure from idealism indicates the extent of consensus on this criterion. In social science, of course, there is a smaller body of agreed-upon observational statements than in natural science. Agreement about observations, however, is different from acknowledging that they exist in an impersonal realm which is conceived as separate from theoretical claims. This latter conception, even in social science, commands near unanimous consent. It is inscribed in, and sustained by, practical prohibitions against contaminating empirical data and by support for the experimental method broadly understood, whereby it is agreed that empirical variations can be compared with an experimenter's personal expectations. Observational tests of preconceptions – whether explicitly or implicitly 'experimentally controlled' – are omnipresent in the practice of virtually every social scientist.

Whether impersonal worlds are acknowledged to exist is the first criterion for universality. Whether practitioners feel themselves bound to these frameworks points to the second. Insofar as scientists do not agree about the nature of their worlds – either about observations or about the differentiated rules that interpret, document, model, and explain them – they will be unable to consider one another's claims as reasonable. Not only will they appear, instead, as particularistic and personal arguments, but they will in part be so. The more individuals share conceptions of their impersonal worlds, by contrast, the more individual practice can be subject to extra-personal control, the more it submits itself to universal criteria of evaluation. The more shared ground, the more neutral this ground not only seems but is in fact. The ground is not neutral in the sense of absent reason, but in the sense of a historical practice that neither party feels it can either own or control.[16]

The possibility of reaching consensus, then, is the second criterion of scientific objectivity. It was Merton's insight into the intrinsic connection between impersonality and consensus (1973 [1942]) that led him to identify universalism, communism, disinterestedness, and organized skepticism in his classic definition of the scientific ethos half a century ago. If Merton ignored the process by which interpretation allows the construction of reality, he clearly understood that the socially generated framework for this construction has to assume an impersonal form if the consensus and objectivity that are such distinctive characteristics of modern science are to be achieved.[17] In *Theoretical Logic in Sociology* I paid much more careful attention than Merton had to the interpretive process of reality construction. The criteria for evaluating these constructions, however, remained for me a central concern. With the notions of consensus and universality, I am telescoping the criteria for 'postpositivist objectivity' I offered in that earlier work (Alexander 1982a: 113–26).

In what remains of this discussion, I want to suggest that social science succeeds in developing the conditions for consensus, and therefore meets this second criterion of objectivity, more often than its relativist critics realize. Ultimately, I will argue that it does so because of the existence of 'theories,' multilayered impersonal worlds that create the conditions of agreement. Within theories, social scientists share broad traditions and research programs; moreover, in the context of contemporary social science, even competing theories crosscut one another in important ways. I will begin, however, by pursuing the notion that these impersonal worlds are not theories but lifeworlds. I will show that, contrary to the radical relativism implied by the epistemological dilemma, hermeneutical philosophy is premised on the notion that these lifeworlds are not only impersonal but that they typically assume a universal and consensual form.

Since Dilthey defined the *Geisteswissenschaften*, hermeneutics has taken as given the existence of an impersonal natural world. For Dilthey natural science did not seem to involve the exercise of reason. By contrast, he was extremely sensitive to the subjectivity of the social world and to the impact of this subjectivity on the methods of the human studies. 'Though experience presents us with the reality of life in its many ramifications,' he writes (1976 [1910]: 186), 'we only seem to know one particular thing, namely our own life.' Since Dilthey posits a 'direct relationship between life and the human studies,' the subjective personalism he places at the center of life makes relativism a critical issue for the human sciences. As he puts it, there is 'a conflict between the tendencies of life and the goal of science' (ibid.: 183).

> Because historians, economists, teachers of law and students of religion are involved in life they want to influence it. They subject historical personages, mass movements and trends to their judgment, which is conditioned by their individuality, the nation to which they belong and the age in which they live. Even when they think they are being objective they are determined by their horizon, for every analysis of the concepts of a former generation reveals constituents in them which derive from the presuppositions of that generation.
>
> (ibid.)

It is not well understood that, while Dilthey begins with a powerful insight into the inevitable personalization of data and methods in the human studies, he does not think that methodological depersonalization or shared and binding universal understandings are impossible. He immediately follows the statement quoted above, for example, by insisting: 'Yet every science implies a claim to validity,' and he wishes to apply these goals to the relativistic human sciences themselves: 'If there are to be strictly scientific human studies they must aim more consciously and critically at validity' (ibid.). At least in the latter part of his career, Dilthey took as his task to demonstrate how the very personalization of human life made depersonalization and binding norms one of its central features.

Dilthey believed that it was precisely the ineluctable centrality of experience that made the supersession of particularism a continuous human project. Because experience is personal, mutual understanding becomes problematic and hence of ultimate importance. Precisely because we are primarily experiencing the world, we are always trying to understand others and not only ourselves. This leads us to strive for common knowledge and to construct categories. Thus, Dilthey can insist, in what would otherwise seem an enigmatic passage, that 'understanding alone surmounts the limitation of the individual experience.' It does so because 'extending over several people, mental creations, and communities, it widens the horizon of the individual life and, in the human studies, opens up the path which leads from the common to the general' (ibid.). Because human understandings 'possess an independent existence and development of their own,' individual actors are bound by universals, by generalized 'judgments of value, rules of conduct, definitions of goals and of what is good' (ibid.: 179). Not only does the universal 'objective mind' exist, but, Dilthey insists, it is accessible to hermeneutic understanding. In their role of social and cultural analysts, individuals exercise the same sure sense of understanding as when they are lay participants. 'Because we are at home everywhere in this historical and understood world,' Dilthey writes, 'we understand the sense and meaning of it all' (ibid.: 191). It is the existence of generals – contextually universalistic understandings – that allows Dilthey to argue for the possibility that, even within hermeneutics, validity claims can have an objective reference.

> What persons have in common is the starting-point for all the relations between the particular and the general in the human studies. A basic experience of what men have in common permeates the whole conception of the mind-constructed world. . . . This is the presupposition for understanding. . . . The degree of methodological uncertainty achieved by understanding depends on the development of the general truths on which the understanding of this relationship is based.
>
> (ibid.: 187)

This same confidence that subjectivity and contextuality actually create shared and binding norms – commensurability in the science studies phrase – rather than detract from them is at the heart of Gadamer's existential hermeneutics, which owes much more to Dilthey than Gadamer seems inclined to admit. Universal, depersonalized norms

are possible – in life as well as in method – because on the level of social
life there is openness and community between individuals, who relate
to one another more in the mode of 'I and thou' than 'I and it.'

> In human relations the important thing is, as we have seen, to experience
> the 'Thou' truly as a 'Thou,' i.e., not to overlook his claim and to listen to
> what he has to say to us. To this end, openness is necessary. . . . Anyone
> who listens is fundamentally open. Without this kind of openness to one
> another there is no genuine human relationship. Belonging together always
> also means being able to listen to one another.
>
> (Gadamer 1975: 325)

Because individuals are open to each other, they have a chance of
mutual understanding. This act of understanding means acknowledging the decenteredness of human reality and accepting some at least of
its impersonal claims: 'Openness to the other, then, includes the
acknowledgement that I must accept some things that are against
myself, even though there is no one else who asks this of me.' (ibid.)

This is where tradition enters in, but for Gadamer it is not the source
of the unexamined, hence arbitrary, reference that the contextual
reaction to positivism suggests. Where these recent contextualists seem
almost eager to embrace skeptical implications – with the implication,
for example, that the project of justifying democracy is impossible
– for Gadamer this was hardly the case. Half a century after Dilthey
and one German Reich later, Gadamer is far more sensitive than
the founder of hermeneutic philosophy to the possible arbitrariness
of binding norms. Dilthey demonstrates that there is commensurability and assumes that this provides the context for sustaining critical
evaluation. Gadamer demonstrates in detail how it is that shared bonds
become standards for the exercise of critical reason. He argues that
common norms are accepted as binding – hence become 'traditional'
– not simply because actors wish to be understood but because they
recognize their validity claims. Actors are open to tradition in the
same way that they are open to other persons, and with often the same
results: 'I must allow the validity of the claim made by tradition,
not in the sense of simply acknowledging the past in its otherness, but
in such a way that it has something to say to me' (Gadamer 1975:
324). If I decide it has something to say, it is because I recognize that
traditions can 'be a source of truth,' that there are 'justified prejudices
productive of knowledge' (ibid.: 247).

> The authority of persons is based ultimately, not on the subjection and
> abdication of reason, but on recognition and knowledge – knowledge,

> namely, that the other is superior to oneself in judgment and insight and
> that for this reason his judgment takes precedence. . . . Authority cannot
> actually be bestowed, but . . . must be acquired, if someone is to lay claim
> to it. It rests on recognition and hence on an act of reason itself.
>
> (ibid.: 248)

In these passages, the language of hermeneutics echoes with the
sounds of the Enlightenment. Authority is a 'claim' that makes implicit
'validity demands.' Authority is recognized if these claims – in 'an act
of freedom and reason' – can 'be seen, in principle, to be true' (ibid.:
248–9). Even the preservation of tradition is 'act of reason, though an
inconspicuous one'. Indeed, 'preservation is as much a freely-chosen
action as revolution and renewal' (ibid.: 250).

There could be no more relevant argument against the epistemological dilemma than this. Gadamer's hermeneutics has been taken – not
just by Rorty but by most of the contextualists I have discussed
– as the quintessence of the concrete and personal against the abstract
and universal. Yet Gadamer himself argues that this cannot be the
case. 'It seems to me,' he writes, 'that there is no such unconditional
antithesis between tradition and reason' (ibid.). The reason that is
exercised vis-à-vis tradition in everyday life is exercised by the interpreter of society as well. Universalism and objectivity are intrinsic to
the exercise of the modern human sciences; they mark its coming of
age. 'At the beginning of all historical hermeneutics,' Gadamer insists,
'the abstract antithesis between tradition and historical research,
between history and knowledge, must be discarded' (ibid.: 251).
Interpretive understanding is not simply personal and empathic; it
necessarily involves an impersonal reference that allows a critical and
universalistic response.

> This placing of ourselves is not the empathy of one individual for another,
> nor is it the application to another person of our own criteria, but it always
> involves the attainment of a higher universality that overcomes, not only
> our own particularity, but also that of the other . . . We have continually to
> test all our prejudices.
>
> (ibid.: 272–3)

In light of this forcefully expressed self-understanding of hermeneutics, it seems clear that the distance Habermas has traveled with his
theory of communicative action is not quite so great as he (1977) and
others have represented. The notion of immanent validity claims is already
there in Dilthey; it became explicit in the notion of understanding and
interpretive method developed by Gadamer.

What Habermas has done to hermeneutic philosophy is important nonetheless. He suggests that it has overemphasized the likelihood of fully mutual and consensual understanding of the spontaneous exercise of rational control. Actors are imbedded in social arrangements that systematically distort communication in ways of which they cannot be fully aware. On these grounds, Habermas argues that rational understanding must also be exercised, and often is, in a more self-conscious and less spontaneous way than through the exercise of understanding alone. This leads Habermas from hermeneutics as such – even when it is rightly understood – to a historically grounded advocacy of social science theory. In pursuit of theory, Habermas rephrases Gadamer's approach to traditional rationality in a manner that emphasizes its impersonality. Because 'reflexivity and objectivity are fundamental traits of language,' he writes, hermeneutics is actually suggesting that 'pre-understanding can be thematized.' Through self-reflection, 'interpretive schemes . . . are formulated in everyday language . . . which both enable and pre-judge the making of experiences.' Self-reflection, thematization, and interpretive schematization are interpretive practices that will at some point be applied to themselves: 'The rational reconstruction of a system of linguistic rules . . . is undertaken with the aim of explaining linguistic competence' (1987: 177–9).

Rationally reconstructed linguistic rules are one form of general knowledge – they are theories of language. In making this transition from the objectivity of commonsense communication to thematization of the rules for communicative understanding, we have moved from hermeneutics to social science. We can see that this has not been a leap but a logical step. The movement toward universalism is inherent in contextual interpretation itself, for actors make efforts to understand their own understanding in increasingly general ways. The universalistic result of each interpretive effort might be conceived of as a deposit of rationality. If these deposits are taken up by future efforts, they may become rational traditions; eventually, upon further reconstruction, they may become abstract theories.

Theories are couched at various levels of generality. For this reason, 'theories' present themselves in a variety of forms (Alexander 1982a), as arguments about presuppositional logic, as schematic interactive models, ideological prescriptions, methodological predictions, causal hypotheses. These theories do not reflect absent reason; they do not exist 'out there' and impose themselves on credulous human beings. They do reflect thoughtful efforts, sometimes generations and centuries long, to understand and develop approximations of the society that surrounds human life. It is not only moral or aesthetic edification that prompts this effort but the desire for objective understanding itself.

Indeed, it is a simple thing to demonstrate that moral and aesthetic arguments – so often taken by contextualists as the very paradigms of anti-universalist, grounded discourse – have themselves aimed at developing general theories and have been guided by earlier theorizing in turn. One could illustrate this with even the most vulgar and popular of the arts. When French New Wave film critics developed their director-centered evaluative standards in the postwar era, they advanced what they called the 'auteur theory' and relied on André Bazin's (1967) ontological theories about cinema in turn. In the film criticism that followed, auteur theory was treated as a generalization and guided the practice and interpretation of film-making for decades (see, e.g., Sarris 1968), despite the efforts of critics like Pauline Kael to refute it by offering falsifying data. In more sophisticated aesthetic domains, the generalizing references and the objective force of what is taken to be 'true argument' are much more explicit. When William Empson (1935) helped to launch 'New Criticism' in *Seven Types of Ambiguity*, he did not rely simply on textual intuition but on Freud's theories about ambivalence, and the claims he made for the universal validity of his new theory appeared to be sustained for several decades thereafter. When Harold Bloom (1973) made his influential riposte in *The Anxiety of Influence*, he rested his case upon other Freudian tenets and a more historical theory of knowledge production, but he aimed at producing a conceptual scheme that was just as generalizing and ambitious.

For moral argument, of course, it is that much easier to demonstrate the significance of general theory. Does John Rawls (1971) forsake propositions, models, and abstract conceptions simply because his concern in *A Theory of Justice* is practical and prescriptive? It could be argued, of course, that the theoretical abstraction of Rawls's argument is produced by his mistaken sense of the transcendental – in current moral philosophical language, 'externalist' – nature of his project. Yet while he has subsequently acknowledged (McMurrin 1987) the historically specific moral underpinnings of his project, his central propositions look much the same. Michael Walzer (1983) has offered the most forceful hermeneutical alternative to Rawls. Despite the groundedness of Walzer's moral reasoning, however, *Spheres of Justice* presents an attempt to build a systematic, empirically documented, and highly general moral theory (cf. Warnke).

Neither aesthetic nor 'practical' theory can or actually wishes to avoid strenuous references to validity claims; nor can they or wish they to avoid the effort to substantiate these claims by building arguments of the most generalized sort. In giving such reasons and making such arguments, they reflect their deep entrenchment within a depersonalized and decentered world. This universalistic mode is abandoned, indeed, only when there is a change in genre. Here we have the famous 'imitative fallacy,' that form should resemble substance. When the analysis of morality becomes an exercise in moral jeremiad, or when the argument for erotic and aesthetic freedom becomes an exemplification of poetic playfulness, moral or aesthetic argument may be edifying or satisfying but it certainly will not have the same claim to be true.[18]

While the centrality of general theorizing can be demonstrated even in such paradigmatically interpretive works, such theoretical reference does not create a comforting sense of objectivity. 'Theories' may create, or crystallize, the impersonal worlds that are the necessary conditions for agreement, but within the social and humanistic sciences, at least, fully satisfying agreement rarely occurs. The disciplines of the human sciences are organized theoretically around broad and competing traditions and empirically around competing research programs (Alexander and Colomy 1995b). These traditions and programs originate in the charismatic reason of figures who at some later point have been accorded classical status (Alexander 1989b). In periods of fission, the existence of such cleavages often leads to skepticism and discouragement. This, indeed, has been one of the principal reasons for the deepening movement toward contextualism of the present day.

Two responses can be made. The first follows directly from the argument thus far. These traditions and programs are not just sources of disagreement but powerful means of intertwining impersonal theoretical controls with disciplinary practice. While there is dissensus between programs and traditions, there is relative agreement within them. It is for this reason that, within the parameters of a school, practitioners can sometimes reach remarkable levels of mutual theoretical understanding and conceptual, even empirical, precision. The objectivity of such practices is conditional but not ephemeral. Dominant and mature research programs often create entirely new realms of observational statements; they also set standards of explanatory scope and internal coherence that competing programs must meet. In the competition between such programs and traditions is found whatever progress the human sciences can provide (cf. Alexander and Colomy 1995a).

The second response to the prospect of continual disagreement is to suggest that these groups are neither as internally coherent nor as externally hermetic as the model of theoretical cleavage suggests.

Kuhn exaggerated the incommensurability of paradigms because he viewed scientific orientations as expressive totalities, emphasizing the consistency between the different components of science. Yet the components of science – the different kinds and levels of theory – are relatively autonomous (Alexander 1982a); even within a single theorist's own work, let alone a particular school, commitments at different levels of the scientific continuum do not tightly cohere. While this variability reduces the possibility of objective controls over practices within a school, it increases the likelihood that there will be universal and shared references between schools.

In the history of natural scientific thought (Alexander 1982a: 25ff), scientists of similar metaphysical orientations have often diverged radically over issues on the more empirically oriented side of the scientific continuum, such as proper models or correct propositions. On the other hand, scientists have agreed about empirical observations while disagreeing fundamentally about general presuppositional issues. If such crosscutting commitments, or 'weak ties,' occur even within the relatively controlled settings of the physical sciences, they are that much more frequent in the social. In both the natural and social sciences, moreover, powerful cross-cleavage agreements emanate from the methodological level, where common commitments to rationalist notions of evidence and logic can usually be found. These and other historically grounded yet deeply institutionalized agreements – which range from intellectual ambitions to topic selection procedures – form the shared disciplinary matrices (Toulmin 1972) within which theoretical traditions and research programs must find their place. In his slashing attack on Louis Althusser's contention that empirical historical research can be reduced to mere ideological particularities, E.P. Thompson demonstrates the controlling power of these broader disciplinary universals. 'His comments,' Thompson writes about Althusser, 'display throughout no acquaintance with, nor understanding of, historical procedures; that is, procedures which make a "history" a *discipline* and not a babble of alternating ideological assertions: procedures which provide for their own relevant discourse [about] proof' (1978: 205–6, original italics).[19]

These final considerations bring us back, fittingly, to the question of 'foundations.' To engage in foundationalism is to put forward general theoretical arguments, to create criteria for truthfulness that are so universally compelling that they produce agreement about validity claims between practitioners in a field. Rorty, we have seen, rejects foundational argument on the grounds that, because theory cannot mirror reality in an epistemological sense, there is no possibility of permanently uncontested truth. But surely this misses the point. It is precisely the perspectival quality of social science that makes its own version of foundationalism, its more or less continuous strain of general theorizing, so necessary and often so compelling. It is natural science that does not exhibit foundationalism, for the very reason that its access to external truth has become increasingly secure. Commensurability and realism delegitimate foundationalism, not increase its plausibility. In natural science, attention can plausibly be focused on the empirical side of the continuum. In social science, by contrast, practitioners cannot so easily accept 'the evidence of their senses.'

Discourse becomes as important a disciplinary activity as explanation. Discourse is general and foundational. It aims at thematizing the standards of validity that are immanent in the very practice of social science. Responding to the lack of disciplinary confidence in empirical mirroring, theoretical discourse aims to gain provisional acceptance on the basis of universal argument. It is, therefore, the very impossibility of establishing permanent foundations that makes foundationalism in the social sciences so critical. This is the postpositivist case for general theory. It is also the case for present reason.

Notes

1. For a developmental perspective on the concept of decentering, see Piaget (1972). For the historical framing of societal generalization and depersonalization and their relation to human freedom, see the evolutionary theory of Parsons (1966, 1973) and Bellah (1970), which carries through on certain key themes in Weber and Durkheim and is pushed further and formalized by Habermas (e.g. 1984).

2. For Weber's understanding of civilization and dualism, see particularly Parsons's (1963) classic Introduction to Weber's *Sociology of Religion*. For civilization as an evolving, increasingly abstract and ascetic construct, see Elias (1975 [1939]). For Aboriginal consciousness as a fused and interpenetrated 'dreaming,' see Bellah (1970). For the interpenetration of levels in primitive thought, see Lévi-Strauss (1967).

3. I stress 'organized social action' because the subjective, phenomenological dimension remains central to the construction of action and order in modern societies, just as, in earlier and more simple societies, actors had to sustain a strong sense of the objectivity of the world outside them. Indeed, to demonstrate this necessary interrelation of objectivity and subjectivity is the very point of phenomenological theory. Such a demonstration is also one of the main ambitions of Wittgenstein, at once the most influential relativist in modern thought and one of the most forceful critics of the notion of private language (e.g. Wittgenstein 1968: para. 272). Neither for Husserl nor for Wittgenstein is there the philosophical possibility of seeing the world out there as it really is. To recognize this possibility social theory and philosophy must develop a historical conception of the human capacity for perception, one which emphasizes its cultural and social organization.

4. This is one of the principal themes of Weber's comparative religion.

5. This theme is developed in Alexander (1989a).

6. For this hypothesis and some fascinating historical documentation, see Georg Misch (1973 [1907]).

7. For this argument, see Hegel's *Phenomenology of Mind* and Marx's *Early Philosophical Manuscripts*. For a broad and important discussion of Romantic idealism as a countermovement, see Charles Taylor (1975).

8. I use Rorty's (1979) phrase ironically, to emphasize that it is the practitioners, not the philosophers of science, who are compelled to understand objectivity in a mirroring, subject-less stance.

9. For this position, see particularly Parsons (1954) and Parsons and Shils (1951). In his earlier work, Parsons (1937) developed the concept of analytic realism, which recognized the agentic contribution of the scientist but insisted (in a Kantian fashion) that the world could be mirrored nonetheless. Rather then transcending the dichotomy, however, this concept finesses it. A more Hegelian, less Kantian conception is needed.

10. After all, if the pressure of a particular historical conjuncture leads a popular audience to attach a new connotatively social 'signified' to what had initially been merely a denotated referent, why should Barthes's environment not affect him in the same way? Can he really distance himself from the history that mythologizes other semiotic patterns in an objective way? Is he not merely reading in his own antibourgeois sentiment? Barthes's implicit response (1959: 156–9) is that he is the 'scientific' student of myth. It is this unthought-out, implicit scientism of early semiotics that detonated later poststructural considerations.

11. It was not visible at that time, however, because of the continuing influence of critical theory, which insisted on the reality, if not the desirability, of the external world.

12. For a powerful critique of the political and epistemological implications of Foucault's work, which takes it as the archetype of an antihumanism, see Taylor (1986).

13. Unless otherwise indicated, all following page references are to Rorty (1979).

14. It is probably not fair, then, for Cornell West (1985: 267) to call Rorty's philosophy 'a form of ethnocentric posthumanism.' Not fair, at least, in the sense that Rorty's aim is to create the basis for universal community and love. However, Rorty's rejection of universalism and embrace of the concrete make it impossible for him to respond in principle to West's charge that 'for Rorty . . . we are North Atlantic ethnocentrists in solidarity with a civilization (or set of contemporary tribal practices) – and possibly a decaying and declining one – which has no philosophical defense' (ibid.).

15. Nor is Bernstein alone in this shifting emphasis. As the contextualist movement has gained acceptance, the full ramifications of its relativism are beginning to lead to reconsiderations in different quarters of the social sciences. Cf. the important critique of deconstructive history in Gossman (1989).

16. This connection between the possibility for conditional objectivity and the ability for those engaged in a knowledge practice to sustain agreement about the frameworks for knowing is emphasized by Goldstein (1976), in a work on historiography that is highly pertinent to the present argument.

17. In the drive to personalize and relativize science, this dimension of Merton's contribution has been almost completely neglected, as, of course, has virtually the entire issue of scientific universalism as such. It is an incredible paradox that in an age when scientific technology has put the entire human world at fatal risk the philosophy, history, and sociology of science have focused increasingly on relativistic idiography. Surely some attention must be paid to the opposite question: How has impersonal knowledge succeeded in so successfully exploring the objective world that it has learned to mimic it through humanly constructed machines? Cf. Boudon (forthcoming: 11): 'In spite of the "post-modernist" reflection on science, science appears as ever growing, and its quick progress is evidence. So the dominant style of the reflection on science seems to have nothing to do with science.' Also relevant is Boudon's observation (ibid., italics added) that the 'ultra-empiricism' of contemporary science studies – which are almost exclusively ethnographic – make the objective dimension of natural scientific practice difficult to understand: 'Is real what can be observed *hic et nunc*? . . . The fact that most scientists believe (and are entitled to believe) that discussions can in principle be concluded on an objective basis cannot so easily be *observed*.'

18. Compare, in this latter regard, Marcuse's *Eros and Civilization* (1954) with Brown's *Love's Body* (1966).

19. In his essay on historiography, Gossman (1989: 49–50, 57) similarly emphasizes the critical role of the emergence of the disciplinary, professional organization in promoting the rational dimension of historical debate.

References

Abrams, M.H. (1971) *Natural Supernaturalism*. New York: Norton.

Alexander, J.C. (1981) 'Looking for Theory: "Facts" and "Values" as the Intellectual Legacy of the 1970s.' *Theory and Society*, 10: 279–92.

Alexander, J.C. (1982a) *Theoretical Logic in Sociology, Vol. I: Positivism, Presuppositions, and Current Controversies*. Berkeley and Los Angeles: University of California Press.

Alexander, J.C. (1982b) 'Kuhn's Unsuccessful Revisionism: A Rejoinder to Selby.' *Canadian Journal of Sociology* 7 (2): 66–71.

Alexander, J.C. (1987) *Twenty Lectures: Sociological Theory since World War II*. New York: Columbia University Press.

Alexander, J.C. (1989a) 'The Dialectic of Individuation and Domination: Max Weber's Rationalization Theory and Beyond,' pp. 68–100 in Alexander, *Structure and Meaning: Relinking Classical Sociology*. New York: Columbia University Press.

Alexander, J.C. (1989b) 'On the Centrality of the Classics,' pp. 8–67 in Alexander, *Structure and Meaning: Relinking Classical Sociology*. New York: Columbia University Press.

Alexander, J.C., and P. Colomy (1995a) 'Neofunctionalism Today: Reconstructing a Theoretical Tradition,' in Alexander, *Neofunctionalism and Beyond*. New York and Oxford: Blackwell.

Alexander, J.C., and P. Colomy (1995b) 'Traditions and Competition: Preface to a Postpositivist Approach to Knowledge Accumulation,' in Alexander, *Neofunctionalism and Beyond*. New York and Oxford: Blackwell.

Althusser, L. (1969) *For Marx*. Harmondsworth: Penguin; New York: Vintage.

Barthes, R. (1959) 'Myth Today,' pp. 109–59 in Barthes, *Mythologies*. New York: Hill & Wang.

Baudrillard, J. (1983) *Simulations*. New York: Semiotext(e).

Bazin, A. (1967) *What is Cinema?* Berkeley: University of California Press.

Bellah, R.N. (1970) 'Religious Evolution,' pp. 20–50 in Bellah, *Beyond Belief*. New York: Harper & Row.

Bernstein, R.J. (1978) *The Restructuring of Social and Political Theory*. Philadelphia: University of Pennsylvania Press.

Bernstein, R.J. (1983) *Beyond Objectivism and Relativism*. Philadelphia: University of Pennsylvania Press.

Bloom, H. (1973) *The Anxiety of Influence*. London: Oxford University Press.

Boudon, R. (forthcoming) 'On "Postmodern" Skepticism,' in C. Cansino and E. Gellner, eds, *Democracy and Modernity: Essays in Honor of J.-G. Merquior*.

Bourdieu, P. (1984) *Distinction: A Social Critique of the Judgement of Taste*. Cambridge, Mass.: Harvard University Press.

Brown, N.O. (1966) *Love's Body*. New York: Vintage.

Derrida, J. (1981) *Positions*. Chicago: University of Chicago Press.

Dilthey, W. (1976 [1910]) 'The Construction of the Historical World in the Human Studies,' pp. 168–245 in Dilthey, *Selected Writings*. New York and Cambridge: Cambridge University Press.

Elias, N. (1975 [1939]) *The Civilizing Process*. New York: Urizen Books.

Empson, W. (1935) *Seven Types of Ambiguity*. London: Chatto & Windus.

Foucault, M. (1977) *Discipline and Punish: The Birth of the Prison*. New York: Pantheon.

Foucault, M. (1978) *The History of Sexuality, Vol. I: An Introduction*. New York: Pantheon.
Foucault, M. (1980) *Power/Knowledge: Selected Interviews and Other Writings, 1972–1977*. New York: Pantheon.
Friedman, J. (1987) 'Beyond Otherness or: The Spectacularization of Anthropology.' *Telos*, 20 (1): 161–70.
Gadamer, H.-G. (1975) *Truth and Method*. New York: Seabury.
Garfinkel, H. (1967) *Studies in Ethnomethodology*. Englewood Cliffs, New Jersey: Prentice Hall.
Geertz, C. (1973a) 'Ideology as a Cultural System,' pp. 193–223 in Geertz, *The Interpretation of Cultures*. New York: Basic Books.
Geertz, C. (1973b) 'Thick Description: Toward an Interpretive Theory of Culture,' pp. 3–32 in Geertz, *The Interpretation of Cultures*. New York: Basic Books.
Geertz, C. (1983) 'Introduction,' pp. 3–16 in Geertz, *Local Knowledge*. New York: Basic Books.
Gibbons, M.T., ed. (1987) *Interpreting Politics*. Oxford and New York: Blackwell.
Goldstein, L.J. (1976) *Historical Knowing*. Austin: University of Texas Press.
Gossman, L. (1989) 'Toward a Rational Historiography.' *Transactions of the American Philosophical Society* 79 (3): 1–68.
Haan, N., R.N. Bellah, P. Rabinow, and W.N. Sullivan, eds (1983) *Social Science as Moral Inquiry*. New York: Columbia University Press.
Habermas, J. (1977) 'A Review of Gadamer's *Truth and Method*,' pp. 335–63 in F.R. Dallmayr and T.A. McCarthy, eds, *Understanding and Social Inquiry*. Notre Dame, Ind.: University of Notre Dame Press.
Habermas, J. (1984) *The Theory of Communicative Action, Vol. I: Reason and the Rationalization of Society*. Boston: Beacon.
Habermas, J. (1987) 'The Hermeneutic Claim to Universality,' pp. 175–202 in M.T. Gibbons, ed., *Interpreting Politics*. Oxford and New York: Blackwell.
Huyssen, A. (1986) 'Mapping the Postmodern,' pp. 178–240 in Huyssen, *After the Great Divide*. Bloomington: Indiana University Press.
Ingram, D. (1985) 'Hermeneutics and Truth,' pp. 32–53 in R. Hollinger, ed., *Hermeneutics and Praxis*. Notre Dame, Ind.: Notre Dame University Press.
Jacoby, R. (1975) *Social Amnesia*. Boston: Beacon.
Jaeger, W. (1965) *Paideia: The Ideals of Greek Culture*. New York: Oxford University Press.
Jones, E. (1963) *The Life and Work of Sigmund Freud*. New York: Doubleday.
Kuhn, T. (1970) *The Structure of Scientific Revolutions*. Chicago: University of Chicago Press.
Kuhn, T. (1978) *Black-Body Theory and the Quantum Discontinuity, 1894–1912*. New York: Oxford University Press.
Lévi-Strauss, C. (1967) *The Savage Mind*. Chicago: University of Chicago Press.
Lyotard, J.-F. (1984) *The Postmodern Condition: A Report on Knowledge*. Minneapolis: University of Minnesota Press.
Marcuse, H. (1954) *Eros and Civilization*. Boston: Beacon.
McMurrin, S.M., ed. (1987) *Liberty, Equality, and Law: Selected Tanner Lectures on Moral Philosophy John Rawls et al*. Salt Lake City, Utah: University of Utah Press.
Merton, R.K. (1973 [1942]) 'The Normative Structure of Science,' pp. 267–78 in Merton, *The Sociology of Science*. Chicago: University of Chicago Press.
Misch, G. (1973 [1907]) *The History of Autobiography in Antiquity*. London: Routledge & Kegan Paul.
Mitzman, A. (1970) *The Iron Cage*. New York: Knopf.
Nagel, T. (1986) *The View from Nowhere*. New York: Oxford University Press.
Parsons, T. (1937) *The Structure of Social Action*. New York: Free Press.
Parsons, T. (1954) 'The Present Position and Prospects of Systematic Theory in Sociology,' pp. 212–37 in Parsons, *Essays in Sociological Theory*. New York: Free Press.
Parsons, T. (1963) Introduction to Max Weber, *Sociology of Religion*. Boston: Beacon.

Parsons, T. (1966) *Societies: Evolutionary and Comparative Perspectives.* Englewood Cliffs, New Jersey: Prentice Hall.

Parsons, T. (1973) *The System of Modern Societies.* Englewood Cliffs, New Jersey: Prentice Hall.

Parsons, T. and E. Shils, eds (1951) *Toward a General Theory of Action.* Cambridge, Mass.: Harvard University Press.

Piaget, J. (1972) *The Principles of Genetic Epistemology.* London: Routledge & Kegan Paul.

Rabinow, P. and W. Sullivan, eds (1979) *Interpretive Social Science: A Reader.* Berkeley and Los Angeles: University of California Press.

Rawls, J. (1971) *A Theory of Justice.* Cambridge, Mass.: Harvard University Press.

Rieff, P. (1961) *Freud: The Mind of the Moralist.* New York: Doubleday.

Rorty, R. (1979) *Philosophy and the Mirror of Nature.* Princeton, New Jersey: Princeton University Press.

Rorty, R. (1982a) 'Method, Social Science, Social Hope,' pp. 191-210 in Rorty, *Consequences of Pragmatism.* Minneapolis: University of Minneapolis Press.

Rorty, R. (1982b) 'The World Well Lost,' pp. 3-18 in Rorty, *Consequences of Pragmatism.* Minneapolis: University of Minneapolis Press.

Rorty, R. (1985a) 'Postmodernist Bourgeois Liberalism,' pp. 214-21 in R. Hollinger, ed., *Hermeneutics and Praxis.* Notre Dame, Ind.: Notre Dame University Press.

Rorty, R. (1985b) 'Habermas and Lyotard on Postmodernity,' pp. 161-75 in R.J. Bernstein, ed., *Habermas and Modernity.* Cambridge, Mass.: MIT Press.

Rorty, R. (1986) 'Foucault and Epistemology,' pp. 41-50 in D.C. Hoy, ed., *Foucault: A Critical Reader.* Oxford and New York: Basil Blackwell.

Sarris, A. (1968) 'Toward a Theory of Film History,' pp. 19-37 in Sarris, *The American Cinema: Directors and Directions 1929-1968.* New York: Dutton.

Scheffler, I. (1976) *Science and Subjectivity.* Indianapolis: Bobbs-Merril.

Taylor, C. (1975) *Hegel.* Cambridge: Cambridge University Press.

Taylor, C. (1986) 'Foucault on Freedom and Truth,' pp. 69-102 in D.C. Hoy, ed., *Foucault: A Critical Reader.* Oxford and New York: Blackwell.

Thompson, E.P. (1978) *The Poverty of Theory and Other Essays.* London: Merlin.

Toulmin, S. (1972) *Human Understanding, Vol. I.* Princeton, New Jersey: Princeton University Press.

Voegelin, E. (1957) *The World of the Polis.* New Orleans: Louisiana State University Press.

Walzer, M. (1983) *Spheres of Justice.* New York: Basic Books.

Wardell, M.L., and S.P. Turner, eds, (1986) *Sociological Theory in Transition.* Boston: Allen & Unwin.

Warnke, G. (1993) *Justice and Interpretation.* Cambridge, Mass.: The MIT Press.

West, C. (1985) 'The Politics of American Neo-pragmatism,' pp. 259-72 in J. Rajchman and C. West, eds, *Post-Analytic Philosophy.* New York: Columbia University Press.

Will, F.L. (1985) 'Reason, Social Practice, and Scientific Realism,' pp. 122-42 in R. Hollinger, ed., *Hermeneutics and Praxis.* Notre Dame, Ind.: Notre Dame University Press.

Winch, P. (1958) *The Idea of a Social Science and Its Relation to Philosophy.* London: Routledge & Kegan Paul.

Wittgenstein, L. (1968) *Philosophical Investigations.* New York: Macmillan. Third Edition.

4

The Reality of Reduction:
The Failed Synthesis of
Pierre Bourdieu

Pierre Bourdieu has become the most influential 'critical theorist' in the world of social science.[1] In an age marked by the death of communism his oeuvre may be viewed as the most impressive living embodiment of a neo-Marxist tradition that, triumphant only a decade ago, currently is struggling to survive. Indeed, despite the author's own claims to the contrary (e.g. Bourdieu 1990b: 22 and 123–39), and his impressively omnivorous ingestion of vast portions of theoretically antagonistic ideas, Bourdieu's work cannot be understood unless it is seen as the latest in the long line of brilliant reconstructors of a system of thought he himself has rarely defended but which, nonetheless, penetrates to the very marrow of his social science.[2]

Perhaps it is the failure to recognize the cultural thrust of every important form of twentieth-century Marxism that has made Bourdieu's own Marxist lineaments so invisible to so many. His American interpreters (e.g. Brubaker 1985; DiMaggio 1979: 1469; Ringer 1992), for example, tend to deny or overlook this fundamental theoretical link. Cultural Marxists themselves have had no such trouble, recognizing and sometimes criticizing Bourdieu's work as part of the century long effort – extending from Lukács and Gramsci to the later Sartre and Habermas – to create a neo-Marxist theory of superstructural forms.[3] Stuart Hall (1978: 29), a key figure in the British cultural studies school that originated in Birmingham, has hailed Bourdieu for promising to develop 'an adequate Marxist theory of ideology.' Nicholas Garnham and Raymond Williams (1980: 211) also have recognized that, 'while Bourdieu has concentrated his attention upon the mode of domination, upon what he calls the exercise of Symbolic Power, his theory is cast in resolutely materialist terms.'

Yet there is a paradox here. For, perhaps more than any other social scientist in the critical tradition, Bourdieu has moved well beyond the merely revisionist effort to tinker with one part or another of Marx's original thought. Rather, like Habermas, he has sought heroically to reconstruct historical materialism and even to create a new theory that, while resembling original Marxism in critical respects, simultaneously seeks to displace it in significant ways.[4] Indeed, if we were to employ the kind of metasociology of knowledge to which Bourdieu himself often so recklessly resorts, we might say that being a Bourdieuian has become a mark of distinction precisely because of the crisis engulfing the neo-Marxist tradition. In a period that has subjected materialist social theory to relentless epistemological critique, it is vital to recognize that his own critical approach accepts the importance, if not the authenticity, of symbolic action and cultural systems. At the same time, however, Bourdieu's work gives full play to the materialism and corrosive cynicism of our time. In an age when utopian hopes have become routinized, when liberation movements have given way to fundamentalist revivals and socialist regimes to market economics, Bourdieu's understanding of action and order implies that this must be so. No matter what the ideals of an actor, a group, or an age, Bourdieu's theory of practice suggests, they are bound to be degraded by the strategic will to power that underlies, and undermines, every dimension of social life.

Still, the sociology of knowledge can never substitute for the analysis of knowledge. Bourdieu, it must be said, not only reflects the contradictions of our time but tries to resolve them. He recently described his theory (Bourdieu 1994: 10) as 'a philosophy of action' that has broken decisively with 'a series of very socially powerful oppositions, individuality/society, individual/collective, conscious/ unconscious, interested/disinterested, objective/subjective.' From the beginning, indeed, it has been the self-conscious ambition to resolve and even dissolve a series of classical theoretical antinomies that has established the originality and importance of Bourdieu's work and, for his devoted followers at least, has marked its brilliant success.

> Bourdieu's near-encyclopedic oeuvre throws a manifold challenge at the current divisions and accepted modes of thinking of social science [because of] its persistent attempt to straddle some of the deep-seated antinomies that rend social science asunder ... by honing a set of conceptual and methodological devices capable of dissolving these very distinctions.
> (Wacquant in Bourdieu and Wacquant 1992: 3 and passim).[5]

Long before the micro–macro link (Alexander et al. 1987) became a faddish phrase, and a decade before the 'new theoretical movement' (Alexander 1988a) emerged from the second phase of postwar social theory, Bourdieu already had begun a remarkably ambitious project to sublate three of the most obdurate dichotomies of the theoretical world: structure/agency, symbolic/material, and interpretive/strategic. In his style of work as well as its content, moreover, Bourdieu seeks to bridge long-standing epistemological disputes as well. He brings together, more effectively perhaps than any other living writer, abstract general theory and middle-range empirical studies. He also has something important to say about the conflict between critical and positive theory. As one dense empirical study after another has issued from his pen, it has become increasingly clear that Bourdieu's understanding of critical theory, like Habermas's, shares a welcome characteristic with Marx's own: he seeks not to displace positive social science but to incorporate and recreate it.

Despite the fundamentally critical nature of the discussion that follows – indeed, precisely because of it – one must begin, therefore, by recognizing the exhilarating and exemplary ambition of Pierre Bourdieu, and by expressing admiration for the austere yet still febrile sensibility of this French master who has produced studies that are not only enlightening but *très amusant*.

Nonetheless, I will argue in the essay that Bourdieu's sociology is irredeemably flawed, in theoretical as well as in empirical terms, and ultimately in ideological and moral terms as well. It distorts the nature of action and order and misunderstands the basic institutional and cultural structures, let alone the moral and human possibilities, of contemporary life.

Since the early 1960s, Bourdieu has taken aim at two intellectual opponents: structuralist semiotics and rationalistic behaviorism.[6] Against these perspectives, he has reached out to pragmatism and phenomenology and announced his intention to recover the actor and the meaningfulness of her world. That he can do neither, I will suggest, is the result of his continuing commitment not only to a cultural form of Marxist thought but to significant strains in the very traditions he is fighting against. The result is that Bourdieu strategizes action (re-incorporating behaviorism), subjects it to overarching symbolic codes (reincorporating structuralism), and subjugates both code and action to an underlying material base (reincorporating orthodox Marxism).

In the reflections that follow, I begin by considering Bourdieu's polemic against structuralist cultural theory and how this false critique lays the basis for Bourdieu's conception of 'habitus,' which while apparently embracing phenomenology actually casts subjectivity in a determinate, antivoluntaristic form. It is in silent recognition of this reduction, I will suggest, that Bourdieu emphasizes the strategic, economizing dimension of action in turn. Only after these considerations on Bourdieu's general theoretical model of action and order do I take up the framework that Bourdieu develops for his more empirical research. Examining a broad although by no means complete sample of his instutional studies, I argue that Bourdieu's 'social fields' are far less autonomous from economic structures than has commonly been assumed, and conclude that his portrait of modern society can provide neither the theoretical nor the empirical resources for understanding, much less appreciating, the pluralist and democratic dimensions of contemporary societies.

The Misleading Critique of Cultural Theory

In a refrain that constitutes the primary polemical theme of his work, Bourdieu accuses symbolic structuralism of being a form of 'objectivism' (OTP: 1)[7] that eliminates agency because its 'mechanical interlocking of pre-set actions' (LOP: 107) conflates 'the model [for action] and its execution' (ibid.: 33). At the same time, however, Bourdieu makes a directly contrary criticism. He attacks structuralism, not because it is objectivist, but because it is idealist: it is a 'hagiographic hermeneutics' that 'reduc[es] all social relations to communicative relations' (OTP: 1).[8]

This paradoxical criticism – which equates mechanism with communication – is intellectually problematic, although we will soon see that it plays a pivotal logical role in Bourdieu's theorizing. Yet in social terms the association of objectivism and idealism is hardly anomalous. From the mid-1960s, the period during which Bourdieu's own project emerged, precisely the same charges were raised against a perspective that was becoming equally discredited in political-cum-theoretical ways, namely structural-functionalism. Bourdieu's early attack on role theory (OTP: 2), which relates its failures to the objectivism of symbolic structuralism, shows the close connection between these historically contemporaneous critiques. Like Dahrendorf (1968), Garfinkel (1967), and Turner (1962) before him, Bourdieu claims that structuralism portrays action as dogmatically following formal and explicit rules.

> To slip from *regularity*, i.e., from what recurs with a certain statistically measurable frequency and from the formula which describes it, to a

consciously laid down and consciously respected *ruling*, or to unconscious regulating by a mysterious cerebral or social mechanism, are the two commonest ways of sliding from the model of reality to the reality of the model.

(LOP: 39, original italics)

The result, he asserts, is that actions are described by structuralists as if they 'had as their principle conscious obedience to consciously devised and sanctioned rules' (ibid.).

If this antistructuralist criticism is taken in a weak form, there is no denying it a certain merit. It is true that pristine culturalism says little about action, even if it does not necessarily dismiss it in the principled manner Bourdieu suggests. In this sense, Bourdieu's insistence on the role of time, place, strategy, and improvisation (OTP: 8–10) is a useful, if not particularly original, restatement of the phenomenological and ethnomethodological arguments that concrete action must have its place. But Bourdieu's attack on structuralism goes well beyond the simple effort to restore to the concrete and temporally rooted elements a distinctive and acknowledged place. He means not only to modify theories that employ symbolic codes as explanation but to dismiss the usefulness of symbolic theory as such. He is making a strong claim, not a weak one. This claim rests on the assertion that cultural theory assumes 'consciousness' and 'obedience,' leaving the actor neither intuitive nor autonomous.

This is the same distorted understanding of structuralism in which Garfinkel (1967) had earlier engaged when he accused the structural-functionalist actor of being a 'cultural dope,'[9] and it allows Bourdieu, as it allowed Garfinkel, to equate his alternative to structuralism with the riposte against logical formalism that Wittgenstein made in his famous discussion of what it means to follow a rule. Wittgenstein (1968 paras 206–38) argued for the centrality of tacit knowledge, which he equated with knowledge gained 'practically,' via action, in contrast with knowledge gained through formal or conscious attempts to follow explicit rules.

Even if we forget for the moment that formal logic and conscious rule-following have little to do with cultural theory, it still seems fair to ask: what's new? Notions about the 'practicality' of action originated neither with Bourdieu nor with Garfinkel; they express, rather, the broad commitments of a particular theoretical tradition. In European philosophy, the fundamental early critique of 'structuralist' and 'abstract' theorizing about action and order was Husserl's phenomenological demonstration of the nature and function of intentionality. Husserl and Heidegger were critical, formative influences on the phenomenologies of Schutz and the early Garfinkel, and on such thinkers as Sartre and Merleau-Ponty. Wittgenstein's work, while differing in specifics, parallels these developments, influenced perhaps by the early phenomenologists and certainly influencing the later ones in turn. In American philosophy, of course, parallel remonstrations for the practicality of action were made by the Pragmatists.

While our interest here is in the systematics of social theory, not in its historiographics or intellectual history, Bourdieu's place in this broad tradition is important to note precisely because it exposes the weakness of some of his central claims. For there is a persistent thread in Bourdieu's theorizing in which his argument against structuralism amounts to little more than the 'weak' suggestion I have noted above, namely that rules must be distinguished from the acts which are informed by them, a notion that leads to the perfectly reasonable insistence that action *qua* action – action in its contingency – has an independent theoretical significance that cannot be ignored. Once we are aware of the tradition of practical action theory within which Bourdieu works, however, we can see not only that the articulation of alternative understandings of action preceded him but that these criticisms of structuralism that he has produced had already been lodged, and in a fundamental manner, in the early, now classical works of Peircean pragmatism (e.g. Peirce 1985 [1931]; Morris 1946). Indeed, at about the same time that Bourdieu began to formulate his theory these already well-known Pragmatist criticisms had begun to generate a series of important responses. On the one hand, neo-structuralists like Eco (1985), Benveniste (1985), and Sahlins (1976, 1981) argued that such criticisms of Saussurian semiotics are mistaken because they take the structuralist emphasis on symbolic code for an ignorance of acts. On the other hand, these neo-structuralists developed more pragmatically sensitive versions of structuralist theory.

It is fair to say, I think, that neither structuralism nor functionalism implies formal, rule-governed action or excludes the independent consideration of action as such. Insofar as structuralism ignores *parole*, it does so only in order to assert the greater priority, not the exclusivity, of *langue*.[10] How else, after all, can we explain Lévi-Strauss's (1969) famous *bricoleur*, that messy spinner of tales who sits comfortably within everyday life and grabs from myth what he needs to construct the narratives of his local world? Indeed, there are illuminating passages in Bourdieu's own writing (e.g. OTP: 110–12; LOP: 85–8) that demonstrate how symbolic codes provide elasticity even while their structure is maintained. They are able to do so, Bourdieu suggests, precisely because the abstraction of their categories allows a wide range of concretely differentiated actions to be signified by the same signifier. Similar points have been made by contemporary neo-structuralists. Theorists like Ecco, Benveniste, and Sahlins – and other more social scientific thinkers who have used semiotics to explore the changing contours of historical and contemporary life (e.g. Hunt 1984; Jameson 1980; Sewell 1980) have developed detailed accounts of how sign structures become involved in action sequences, in practical processes that mediate cultural determinacy and contingent event. Eco's well-known term for this mediation – semiosis – has become emblematic for such an understanding of action that blends pragmatic considerations with a sense of structured cultural constraint.

Moreover, while linguistic structuralism is certainly the most significant element in Bourdieu's anticultural polemic, his attack on kinship structuralism suffers from a similar refusal either to understand or to recognize the theory's breadth and complexity, and it undermines his theoretical alternative in just as fundamental a way. In various biographical accounts (e.g. IOW: 20; LOP: 15–17), for example, Bourdieu claims to have become disillusioned with structuralism primarily because it could not account for the failure of observed marriage patterns to conform closely to legitimate rules and norms. He concludes that cultural codes do not have broad effects on actual behavior, which must be seen, instead, as practical in force and intent. In fact, however, structural anthropologists have long been aware of the problems that Bourdieu points out, making concerted efforts to demonstrate that such empirical variations in no way vitiate the influence of broader cultural codes. They have done so (see, e.g., the influential discussions by Needham 1972 and Goode 1981) by clarifying the relationship between the relatively autonomous levels of kin classification ('prescription'), jural rules ('preference'), and statistical patterns ('practice'). Once again, Lévi-Strauss himself acknowledged, at a very early point in the development of his structural theory (1969: xxiii–xxiv, xxx–xxxiii), that the existence of prior and more general kinship 'systems' does not preclude choice and agency from entering into the actual patterning of marriage transactions themselves.

That Bourdieu has distorted culturalism and ignored important developments in contemporary neo-structuralist thinking is not important in itself. These mistakes are important, rather, for what they reveal about Bourdieu's more general theoretical intent. If we may speak, contra Bourdieu, of theoretical dispositions that exist on the level of ideas alone, we wish to ask: what is Bourdieu's theoretical interest in portraying structuralism as ideal and determinate, and as a theory that implies formal and conscious obedience to rules?

Bourdieu constructs this vulgarized enemy-tradition, it would seem, 'so that' he can present his own version of *practical* action as the only viable alternative for theories that wish to maintain some reference to supra-individual, collectivist forms. By portraying cultural theory as objectivist and determinist, by attacking symbolic structuralism as the principal source of antivoluntaristic theory, Bourdieu means to suggest that collective theory is coercive only in its culturalist form. In so doing, he is preparing his reader for an alternative version of collectivist theory that can maintain the voluntarism of action without giving culture pride of place.

Misinterpreting one's theoretical opponents in a manner that opens up a protected space for a reductionist alternative is common practice in the history of social thought (Alexander 1995a). Rational choice theorists, for example, have consistently distorted cultural theory in the same way as Bourdieu. By representing it as a form of objectivist determinism, they can argue that only an anticultural understanding of action can allow voluntarism to be maintained. Marx also distorted the cultural tradition to make way for his reductionist alternative, but he did so in an entirely different way. Portraying cultural theory as thoroughly voluntarist and individualist – as 'idealist' – he could introduce collectivist materialism as the only viable theoretical alternative. It is clear, in fact, that Bourdieu's interpretive 'deception' brings together both the behaviorist and the Marxist distortions of the common enemy, 'cultural idealism.' It does so, we will see, so that a theory that is collective but ultimately instrumental can be justified in its place.

Bourdieu's energetic critique of cultural theory as deterministic is deceptive in this sense: when the outer layer of his theorizing is peeled away, one finds that a renewed interest in the creativity or voluntariness of action is not at all what he actually has in mind. When he calls his own approach a theory of 'practice' or 'practical action,' we have every right to expect, in light of his critique of structuralism, that this approach will have both an anticultural *and* an anticollective cast. But this is not the case. Bourdieu's intention, it turns out, is not to qualify the autonomy of cultural norms vis-à-vis action and its other, non-cultural environments, thereby giving to culture a less determinate cast. His intention, rather, is to submerge cultural norms, to demonstrate that they are determined by forces of an entirely different, decidedly material kind. Bourdieu wishes not to free up creative and interpretive action but to attach it to structures in a noninterpretive way.

Bourdieu's theory of practice, then, is too practical by half. Overwhelmed by demands for practicality, his actors are in a state of continuous adaptation to – not communication with – their external environments. We will see, in fact, that Bourdieu actually conceives of actors as motivated by a structure of dispositions which merely translates material structures into the subjective domain.

The Subjectification of Objective Force: Habitus

The self-neutralizing character of Bourdieu's agency is displayed in the way that he develops his pivotal concept of habitus. A 'system of structured, structuring dispositions' (LOP: 52), habitus identifies the internal and motivated character of action, which is said to carry the imprint of social structure but to be actively creative at the same time. As a 'generative principle of regulated improvisations,' habitus 'reactivates the sense objectified in institutions' by 'continuously pulling them from the state of dead letters' and by 'imposing the revisions and transformations that reactivation entails' (ibid.: 57). Again, Bourdieu seems to be suggesting that human effort, in the form of affectively and cognitively structured motivation, must be given a new and more powerful theoretical role.

> The notion of habitus allowed me to break away from the structuralist paradigm without falling back into the old philosophy of the subject or of consciousness. ... I wished to put forward the 'creative', active, and inventive capacities of habitus and of agent (which the word usually does not convey) but to do so by recalling that this generative power is not one of universal mind ... but that of an acting agent.
>
> (Bourdieu 1985: 13)

This, however, is not really the case. Like Bourdieu's other key concepts, habitus turns out not merely to be loosely defined – the criticism so beloved by scientism – but to be ambiguous in what can only be called a systematic way. Despite Bourdieu's repeated claim that habitus is akin to Chomsky's generative grammar, it turns out to be more like a Trojan horse for determinism. Time and time again it is explained not as a site for voluntarism – for improvising within certain limits – but as the reflection and replication of exterior structures. Bourdieu allows that persons act from within the habitus, but habitu-ated action, he insists, actually prefigures structure. Habitus allows structure to pass from the visible and (theoretically and ideologically) vulnerable position of a phenomenon that possesses external form into the invisible and protected physiognomy of subjective, noumenal space. Far from an alternative to social structural explanation, habitus merely operationalizes it.[11]

The problem with the concept of habitus lies, indeed, in Bourdieu's insistence that 'dispositions . . . are the product of economic and social processes that are more or less completely reducible to these constraints' (LOP: 50). True, Bourdieu employs this concept to insist that socialization intervenes between economic environment and social action. Habitus is presented as an unconscious motivational structure that is formed in earlier, family life. It is not formed, however, around 'relatively autonomous' values or ideals. This standard of the relative autonomy of culture (Alexander 1990) is fundamental for understanding the weaknesses in Bourdieu's theory. Values possess relative independence vis-à-vis social structures because ideals are immanently universalistic. This is so, in the first place, because they have an inherent tendency to become matters of principle that demand to be generalized in 'unpractical' ways. It is also so in a more historical sense, for social differentiation itself involves the growing organizational independence of religious and secular values, and of their intellectual carrier groups, vis-à-vis the more particularistic centers of economic and political life (Eisenstadt 1981; Walzer 1983). For Bourdieu, however, socialization does not transmit values that are in tension with life-as-it-is-found-to-be-lived; rather, it produces values that are immediate reflections of the hierarchical structures of material life.

> Through the economic and social necessity that they bring to bear on the relatively autonomous world of the domestic economy and family relations, or more precisely, through the specifically *familial manifestations of this external necessity* . . . the structures characterizing a determinate class of conditions of existence produce the structures of the *habitus*, which in their turn are the basis of the perception and appreciation of all subsequent experiences.
>
> (LOP: 54, italics added)

What we have here is a materially reflective rather than culturally mediated conception of socialization and family life. What results, not surprisingly, is an account of the actor's habituation to external material conditions and the hegemonic ideals of the dominant economic class. When Bourdieu speaks of 'the internalization of externality' as enabling 'the external forces to exert themselves, but in accordance with the specific logic of the organisms in which they are incorporated, i.e. in a durable, systematic and non-mechanical way' (LOP: 55), he is speaking frankly about his theory. Habitus has no independent power to direct action, in the way that 'self' has for Mead or 'personality' for Parsons. Habitus does not lead us to a social psychology or to the issues of identity, character, conformity, and independence. What it initiates, instead, is an endless and circular account of objective structures structuring subjective structures that structure objective structures in turn.

> The 'subject' born of the world of objects does not arise as a subjectivity facing an objectivity: the objective universe is made up of objects which are the product of objectifying operations structured according to the same structures that the *habitus* applies to them. The *habitus* is a metaphor of the world of objects.
>
> (LOP: 76–7)

Bourdieu is not merely asserting, then, that 'agents are possessed by their habitus more than they possess it' (OTP: 18), a 'weak' position taken by any theory that posits the social construction of agency. His point is that the social internalized are not rules but the political-economic structures and powers that rules merely obfuscate.

The reductionism of habitus dovetails neatly with Bourdieu's reductionist attack on the symbolic autonomy of language, which is yet another version of his broad attack on structuralist theory. 'The constitutive power which is granted to ordinary language,' Bourdieu insists, 'lies not in the language itself but in the group which authorizes it and invests it with authority' (ibid.). While paying formal obeisance to language theorists like Saussure and Chomsky, Bourdieu's own approach fails to recognize that the meaning of words is derived from relations of difference inside each linguistic set. Because he fails to acknowledge the meaningful specificity of language *qua* language, he is unable to recognize the possibility that symbolic systems modeled on language can exert an independent force against, rather than in support of, institutional and economic life. As the symbolic code which structures the self, 'habitus' must be treated in exactly the same way.

What follows from this assertion of the dependence of habitus is that the analyst must focus on real political-economic causes rather than on their 'ephemeral,' merely 'subjective' representations. In the following passage Bourdieu disputes ethnomethodology's focus on the interpersonal negotiation of legitimacy, but his criticism has more general implications.

> One is entitled to undertake to give an 'account of accounts,' so long as one does not put forward one's contribution to the science of pre-scientific representation of the social world as if it were a science of the social world. But this is still too generous, because the prerequisite for a science of

commonsense representations which seeks to be more than a complicitous description is a science of the structures which govern both practices and the concomitant representations, the latter being the principal obstacle to the construction of such a science.

(ibid.: 21)

Bourdieu insists, once again, that the structures behind accounts can only be of a material kind. In doing so, he makes it clear that his theoretical objective is to eliminate the significance of motive and subjectivity, not to underline their importance.

Only by constructing the objective structures (price curves, chances of access to higher education, laws of the matrimonial market, etc.) is one able to pose the question of the mechanisms through which the relationship is established between the structures and the practices or the representations which accompany them, instead of treating these 'thought objects' as 'reasons' or 'motives' and making them the determining cause of the practices.

(ibid.)

That Bourdieu himself never offers 'an account of accounts' underscores the manner in which his interest in an alternative to anthropological structuralism is primarily an interest not in the nature of contingent action but in structuralism of a more materialist kind. His frequent references to the creativity of the agent are summarily abstract, highly generalized statements which amount to no more than a gloss when compared to the detailed and systematic theorizing developed by ethmnomethodology and its more positivist variant, conversation analysis. To acknowledge and attempt to theoretically incorporate the ad hocing procedures first identified by Garfinkel (1967) and the turn-taking procedures detailed by Schegloff (1992) and others would demonstrate that there is, indeed, a space of indeterminacy – a space for practice or use in Wittgenstein's sense – between institutionalized expectations of any kind and any particular individual act. That Bourdieu is correct in criticizing these microtheorists for ignoring the more structured environment of action does not negate the specific significance of their contribution. Whereas Garfinkel began with a phenomenological critique of the objectivity of structural-functionalism and an encounter with Wittgenstein to develop an (overly) voluntaristic theory of action, Bourdieu transformed similar criticisms and sympathies into a theory that merely redeployed objective order and eliminated the attention to interaction as an order *sui generis*.

The habitus does not have its own emergent properties, its own logic, its own internal complexity. Because it does not possess any real independence, it cannot provide a vehicle for establishing a true micro–macro link (Alexander et al. 1987: 257–98). The theory of practice, then, is nothing other than a theory of the determination of practice, and it is precisely the theoretical function of habitus to show how and why this must be so: 'Practical taxonomies . . . are a transformed, misrecognizable form of the real divisions of the social order' (OTP: 163).

Because this sense of ineluctable determinism contradicts Bourdieu's declared aim of bringing the actor back into social theory, it is not surprising that he continually complains (IOW: 113) that 'the charge of reductionism thrown at me' is unfair. He protests, 'I am taken to task for overlooking the specific logic and autonomy of the symbolic order, thereby reduced to a mere reflection of the social order.' In fact, he insists, he has written that 'the space of symbolic stances [i.e. the habitus] and the space of social positions are two independent, but homologous, spaces.'[12] Even in such efforts at self-defense, however, we are only reminded of how Bourdieu's habitus theory simply misses the relevant theoretical point. True, he is careful to specify that subjective dispositions are not simply direct reflections of exterior life: they are mediated in the sense that they are transformed, via early family experience, into a socialized habitus. Yet, as the unrelenting necessitarian tone of the above quoted passages demonstrates, it is the very 'homologous' character of habitus that guarantees its subordination, that is, the determination in both a causal/empirical and analytical/theoretical sense of the symbolized interior order to external structural force.

While public lectures and expository interviews provide theorists with opportunities for clarification and illustration, they also allow retrospective reconstructions of one's intellectual life and work in order to re-represent one's theory vis-à-vis critical attack. For Bourdieu, such self-defense often involves precisely the mea culpa I have just described: assertions that his frequent reference to the 'homologous' nature of symbolic orders gives the lie to charges of determinism. Even in such tightly controlled and self-conscious intellectual exercises, however, Bourdieu seems unable to keep himself from affirming determinism 'in the last instance.' He begins one public lecture, for example, by asserting his claim for voluntarism: 'These symbolic struggles, both the individual struggles of daily life and the collective, organized struggles of political life, have a specific logic, which grants them a real autonomy from the structures in which they are rooted' (IOW: 135). This assertion is then immediately undercut by an argument that draws upon habitus in a thoroughly reductionist way.[13]

> Symbolic power relations tend to reproduce and to reinforce the power relations which constitute the structure of the social space. More concretely, the legitimatization of the social order . . . results from the fact that agents apply to the objective structures of the social world structures of perception and appreciation that have emerged from these objective structures and tend therefore to see the world as self-evident.
>
> (ibid.)

In the late 1960s and early 1970s, when Bourdieu retheorized the ethnographic observations of Kabyle peasants he had conducted in the late 1950s, he spoke of them as 'agents endowed with schemes of perception of a determinate sort, which are themselves determined, negatively at least, by the material conditions of existence' (OTP: 116). For the Kabyle there is an intrinsic 'relationship between a mode of production and a mode of perception' (ibid.). On the one hand, this means that the 'Kabyle peasant does not react to "objective conditions" but to the practical interpretation which he produces of these conditions, and the principle of which is the socially constituted schemes of his habitus' (ibid.). On the other hand, Bourdieu wishes to focus attention on 'the economic and social conditions of the production of the dispositions [that are] generating both these practices and also the collective definition of the practical functions in whose service they function' (OTP: 115). The mundanity of peasant life, in other words, is a perfect setting to demonstrate how the ideality of the habitus and the practicality of everyday necessity neatly coincide.

> The Kabyle woman setting up her loom is not performing an act of cosmogony; she is simply setting up her loom to weave cloth intended to serve a technical function. It so happens that, given the symbolic equipment available to her for thinking her own activity – and in particular her language, which constantly refers her back to the logic of ploughing – she can only think what she is doing in the enchanted, this is to say, mystified, form which spiritualism, thirsty for eternal mysteries, finds so enchanting.
>
> (ibid.)

In the later ethnographic studies of art, popular culture, intellectual life, and status conflict in modern societies – which we will examine in some detail below – Bourdieu displays the same inability to conceptualize a distance, or critical space, between mental structures and the social conditions from which they emerge. 'Different conditions of existence,' he asserts (D: 170), 'produce different habitus.' Thought is no more than an inverted reflection of life.

> The habitus is not only a structuring structure, which organizes practices and the perception of practices, but also a structured structure: the principle of division into logical classes which organizes the perception of the social world is itself the product of internalization of the division into social classes.
>
> (ibid.)

Acts of solidarity, sympathy, and even love are analyzed not as motivated or volitional but as predetermined results of outside pressures.

> The concordance between a socially classified person and the socially classified things or persons which 'suit' him is represented by all acts of co-option in fellow-feeling, friendship or love which lead to lasting relations.
>
> (ibid.: 241)

These most human of humanity's traits turn out not to be edifying expressions of the independent self, but strategies by which the habitus creates links with an other, who turns out merely to represent himself.[14]

The difficulties Bourdieu encounters here are familiar ones. In its effort to explain the supposed stability of capitalist societies, cultural Marxism from Lukács to Marcuse and Althusser always has had difficulty in conceptualizing cultural countermovements, for it has been unable to theorize a cultural world that truly has relative autonomy from the base.[15] Bourdieu's habitus concept merely restates this difficulty in a more precise, microsociological way. In habitus theory, domination is not an 'empirical' fact: it results from systematic theoretical inattention to the conditions of autonomy. Actors are 'dominated agents' (ibid.: 471) *in principle*, that is, on good theoretical grounds.

> Dominated agents, who assess the value of their position and their characteristics by applying a system of schemes of perception and appreciation which is the embodiment of the objective laws whereby their value is objectively constituted, tend to attribute to themselves what the distribution attributes to them, refusing what they are refused ('That's not for the likes of us'), adjusting their expectations to their chances, defining themselves as the established order defines them, reproducing in their verdict on themselves the verdict the economy pronounces on them, in a word, condemning themselves to what is in any case their lot.
>
> (ibid.)

Or, as Bourdieu puts the matter more simply in a more recent publication:

> If it is fitting to recall that the dominated always contribute to their own domination, it is necessary at once to be reminded that the dispositions which incline them to this complicity are also the effect, embodied, of domination.
>
> (Bourdieu 1989: 12)

With the signal and revealing exception of behaviorism, the thrust of virtually every school of modern developmental psychology has demonstrated that personality growth involves the 'generalization' of motivational structures, that is, their movement away from any precise correlation with external conditions. Individual development depends upon a shift within the actor's cognitive and moral frameworks – in the actor's capacities to think, to feel, and to evaluate – from concreteness to increasing abstraction. This movement involves changing the cognitive and moral reference from things and persons to rules, to rules about rules, and finally to the possibility of some form of real individuality and independence that involves the actor's ability to rethink the very rules that, according to tradition and group constraint, must be applied to the social situation at hand.

How this internal universalization of internal cognitive and moral development relates to the unevenness and specificity of particular social and cultural formations has, of course, proved to be an enormously difficult problem, which Piaget did not address and neither Parsons nor Habermas effectively resolved. Because of the manner in which Bourdieu has formulated habitus, however, the problem as such does not even exist. Habitus binds actors tightly to the social world; it does not allow them to generalize vis-à-vis it. Bourdieu glories in the concreteness of habitus, which is said to motivate the actor to reproduce what she inherits and which utterly neglects the kind of critical thinking that the idea of cognitive and moral generalization implies. In any real sense there is no 'self' in Bourdieu's theory at all. There is merely the intersection of time and space, a site for social implantation in its most primitive form.

It is at this point in Bourdieu's conceptual architecture that the body comes in. Reading these discussions in a merely empirical way, one can praise Bourdieu for taking Merleau-Ponty's suggestion and focusing attention on this understudied domain of social life. At the same time, however, Bourdieu's focus on the body must also be understood in a more specifically theoretical way. Insofar as he reduces the habitus to the socialized body, Bourdieu finds a material location for internalized dispositions that allows him to ignore the complexities and subjectivities that the category of 'self' implies. With the body, in other words, Bourdieu can be even more practical than before.[16] Rather than speaking of the symbolic and psychological processes involved in such self-forming processes as identity, fantasy, projection, or role-playing, Bourdieu can argue that 'all that is involved [in socialization] is the practical transference of incorporated, quasi-postural schemes' (OTP: 116).

Asserting that 'practical belief is not a "state of mind" ... but rather a state of the body,' Bourdieu (LOP: 68) employs his special kind of sociologized biologism – much as he employs habitus more generally – to enforce determination rather than reduce it: 'The body [is] an automaton that "leads the mind unconsciously along with it"' (ibid.). Socialization does not depend on symbolic interaction and a learned ability to interpret another's sensibility and intention; it involves, rather, simply the child's contact with 'the paternal body and the maternal body' (ibid.: 78). The result, habituated 'practical sense,' is 'social necessity turned into nature [and] converted into motor schemes and body automaticisms' (ibid.: 69).

Is it any wonder, then, that Bourdieu attacks Piaget for not realizing that the ability to generalize from one situation to another is produced simply by 'bodily gymnastics' rather than by 'explicit comprehension' (ibid.: 89)? The physicality of the habitus, Bourdieu insists, can produce 'the equivalent of an act of generalization' through the notion of the socialized body – 'without recourse to concepts' (ibid.). Bourdieu considers it a theoretical triumph to have shown that the actor's generality is 'unrepresented,' that is, a physical disposition rather than a cognitive and moral capacity for re-presenting the discrete experiences of everyday life. As compared with Piaget, Bourdieu proclaims that his explanation of generality 'dispenses with all the operations required by [notions about the actor's] construction of a concept.' Without concepts, of course, there can be no critical thought. But this does not bother Bourdieu. It has been the theoretical function of habitus to explain why a critical distance from social structure is impossible to attain.[17]

Because Bourdieu purports to incorporate the psychodynamic, self-referential element so forcefully into his social theory, it is important to emphasize how sharply his approach to habitus and embodiment differs from psychoanalytic thinking about the self, even of the most sociological kind. While psychoanalytic object relations theory sees the self, or ego, as created from internalized and socially situated others, it understands this social self as increasingly differentiated from these residues, indeed, as forming a distinctive 'identity' by struggling against these earlier object internalizations. Ego psychology documents a similar struggle for differentiated autonomy. Thus, while Erik Erikson (1950) emphasized trust and connection, he introduced the notion of 'identity crisis' and, with it, a social understanding of the individual specificity of contemporary social strains. Erikson's position was elaborated by even more explicitly sociological psychologists, for example in Keniston's investigations of uncommitted youth (1965) and political radicals (1968; cf. Weinstein and Platt 1969).[18] In more recent psychoanalytic theory, theorists like Kohut (1978) have increasingly emphasized the self as a distinctive identity that has analytic independence from its internalized objects, even while stressing the importance of the interrelatedness of self and environment. Even in the thinking of Melanie Klein (1965), who initiated a psychoanalytic tradition that emphasized the body, the breast and the body ego have been regarded as reference points from which the self must differentiate, not as mirror-images with which the self is identified, as in Bourdieu's notion of being 'embodied in.'

I have compared Bourdieu's habitus theory with psychoanalytic and developmental theories of self to illustrate the different kind of emphasis that a real interest in the empirical autonomy of self would involve. In this regard, one must also refer to two other traditions in which self autonomy is conceptualized, one more philosophical, the other more empirical and socio-cultural.

In *Search for a Method* (1963) – his separately published introduction to *Critique of Dialectical Reason* – Sartre demonstrated how nondeterministic the phenomenological insistence on reflexivity can be, even within a quasi-Marxist frame. Rather than automatically reproducing domination, Sartre's conception of the actor insists on role distance, self-consciousness, and a projective orientation to the future (cf. Terrail 1992), concepts which can acknowledge subordination but also open up the possibilities of resistance. Sartre could partially achieve the restoration of intentionality to Marxism because his later thought remained rooted in existential phenomenology. Moreover, while his effort to incorporate Marxism significantly reduced the independence of the actor, it did so via a philosophical-anthropological reference to the limitations imposed by 'scarcity' rather than by pointing to the effects of an external agent or institution. In this way, Sartre's theory was saved from the kind of totalizing objectification that permeates even culturally Marxist work. When Bourdieu theorizes the habitus, by contrast, he conceives of the economic 'moment' in a much more conventional form of economic force and material force. For both these reasons, Bourdieu is unable to maintain reflexivity or intentionality in anything like the manner that Sartre achieved.[19]

The second way to conceptualize self autonomy in a more satisfactory way is to acknowledge the role of cultural internalization while understanding that it allows the self access to collective representations that can be resources for its independence from socially dominant values and institutions. Moscovici has created a contemporary school of social psychology around precisely this insight. In his research on 'social representations' (Farr and Moscovici 1984), for example, he has investigated what might be called the social psychology of the relative autonomy of culture. These studies demonstrate how the internalization, externalization, and creation of social stereotypes may not merely reinforce crowd psychology (Moscovici 1985) but may also allow for the nonconformist and principled influence of minority sentiments (Moscovici et al. 1985) in contemporary societies. In a more philosophical vein, similar arguments have been developed by Charles Taylor (1989).

The case I have made in this section – that habitus represents a mimetic and reflective position vis-à-vis social structure rather than an agonistic and independent one – does not rest on an argument that Bourdieu has adopted an 'equilibrium theory' of self as compared to an approach that emphasizes conflict or allows for social change. The latter considerations refer to more empirical levels of explanation than do arguments about Bourdieu's presuppositions and his general models of self, society, and culture. In fact, the conflation of these two levels has sometimes undercut criticisms of habitus by confusing them with charges that the 'reproductive' implications of the concept force Bourdieu to adopt a static, equilibrium view of society (Frow 1987; Jenkins 1986). This confusion has, in turn, prompted the defense of habitus (most forcefully by Brubaker 1985: 759–60) via the demonstration that Bourdieu has, in fact, employed habitus to explain empirical conflict and social change. The fact that he has done so, however, does not indicate that habitus allows voluntarism, identity, or contingency to open up the deterministic cast of his theory.

Bourdieu has, indeed, succeeded in 'explaining' critical movements of social change, and he has employed the habitus concept to do so. What he has done is to describe change as resulting from the conflict between a generation's or cohort's habitus – formed in childhood – and the socio-economic environment it faces at the time of adulthood. This conflict is not portrayed, however, as resulting from an autonomization of self, which would be connected to the relative independence of culture or to cognitive generalization and a differentiating rather than fusing understanding of internalization. The dislocated or separated habitus is described, rather, as emerging from systemic, objectively generated discontinuities that have developed in the social structures of particular societies over extended periods of time.[20]

This notion of temporally generated structural discontinuities allows Bourdieu to explain rebellion against a particular kind of social structure at a particular time and to identify particular groups of actors as the apparent agents involved – without giving up for a moment the objectivist and determinist slant of his habitus theory. Responding to what he characterizes as criticisms of 'the "durability" of habitus and the charge of "determinism" which goes with it' (1988b: 8), Bourdieu counters by noting that he recognizes that habitus 'becomes active only in the relation to a field.' He means here to suggest that a separation between habitus and its immediate environment is possible, that 'the same habitus can lead to very different practices and position-takings depending on the state of the field (ibid.).'[21] Because he continues to insist on the objectivity of the field, however, Bourdieu can argue that this independence of habitus and field does not imply any new subjectivity. When an actor or group whose habitus was formed at point A changes its behavior at point B, this has nothing whatever to do with a shift in subjective identity: 'One should be careful not to describe as an effect of the conversion of habitus what is nothing more than the effect of a change in the relation between habitus and field' (ibid.). In other words, changed behavior of a once formed character depends on shifts in the actor's external environment.

While several different empirical applications of this reductionistic and deterministic account of rupture can be found (e.g. Bourdieu et al. 1979: 4–5), the case to which Bourdieu returns time and time again is the student and faculty rebellion of 'May '68.' He explains this monumental upheaval in French society as a crisis of succession between academic generations stimulated by broader demographic shifts. Insisting on the structural rather than the subjective, he writes that 'crises (notably that of May 1968) divide the field along pre-existing lines of fracture' (HA: 128). It was long-term shifts in the market for educated labor that created the underlying strain: 'The specific contradiction in the mode of reproduction in its educational aspects [took] on an increasingly critical form with the growing number of those who [saw] their chances of reproduction threatened' (ibid.: 163). The student habitus formed according to one set of expectations – high-status intellectual employment – but at a later point in the life of that generation faced an economic-cum-educational organization which made reality very different. This clash made equilibrium impossible: 'The automatic harmony between expectations and probable trajectories, which led people to see as self-evident the order of succession, was broken, and the university order founded on the concordance between internalized temporal structures and objective structures was ... challenged' (ibid.: 156). The massive protests which resulted had little to do with psychological identity or socialized independence, and everything to do with interest and a sense of objective deprivation. 'Refusing to accept their exclusion,' Bourdieu writes, the students of May '68 found 'themselves falling back on a protest against the legitimacy of the instrument of their exclusion, which threaten[ed] the whole of their class' (ibid.: 163; cf. ibid.: 128–93, passim).

In other publications Bourdieu returns to the same analysis and reaches the same conclusions. His theoretical interest is in denying the voluntaristic, self- or value-generated dimension of critical change.

> This is what is shown by my analysis of the May '68 movement. . . . It's no coincidence if a number of the May '68 leaders were great innovators in intellectual life and elsewhere. Social structures don't run like clockwork. For example, the people who don't get the job that was so to speak statutorily assigned to them . . . will work at changing the job so that the difference between the job they had expected to get and the job they actually get disappears. All the phenomena associated with the 'overproduction of graduates' and 'devaluation of degrees' . . . are major factors of renewal because the contradictions which stem from them lead to change.
>
> (IOW: 45)

Even in Bourdieu's efforts to make this crisis model more complex, the subjective element falls away. While he carefully argues for the temporal and empirical independence of these 'habitus crises' in different social domains, he insists that for a general, societal crisis to emerge there needs to be an overlapping of discontinuities, a situation that is possible only because each refers, ultimately, to the same underlying economic contradiction.

> Without ever being totally coordinated, since they are the product of 'causal series' characterized by different structural durations, the dispositions and the situations which combine synchronically to constitute a determined

conjuncture are never wholly independent, since they are engendered by the objective structures, that is, *in the last analysis*, by the economic bases of the social formation in question.

(OTP: 83, italics added).[22]

The students and assistant lecturers in sociology thus represent one of the cases of the coincidence between the dispositions and the interests of agents occupying homologous positions in different fields which, through the synchronization of crises latent in different fields, has made the generalization of the crisis possible. . . . The crisis as conjuncture, that is to say as conjunction of independent causal series, supposes the existence of worlds which are separate but which participate in the same universe. . . .The meeting of these series supposes their relative dependence as regards the fundamental structures – especially the economic ones – which determine the logics of the different fields.

(HA: 173–4)

It is revealing that Bourdieu's effort to explain individual psychological crises fails in the same way. Because personal crises involve psychological anxiety, they present a potential challenge to Bourdieu's resolutely collectivist reduction of the self. Bourdieu interprets such crises, however, in precisely the opposite way. He suggests (1988b: 8) that because habitus is conceived as the product of 'social conditionings' rather than 'character,' it can be understood as encountering 'structures of objective chances' that both reinforce and challenge it. It is, then, simply a deficit of objective reinforcement that explains why the self-as-habitus is subject to continuous anxiety and change. Acknowledging that habitus can 'be built . . . upon contradiction, upon tension, even upon instability,' Bourdieu can insist, nonetheless, that the source of such tension can be nothing other than the objective economic situation. For example, if the children of the 'subproletariat' are psychologically 'unstable,' it is because they 'bear inscribed in their habitus the instability of the living conditions of [a] family doomed to insecurity in their conditions of employment, housing, and thereby of existence' (ibid.).

From Habit to Strategy

This deterministic retelling of structure as practice is camouflaged and transmuted by yet another theoretical move pretending to resuscitate action by fighting the good fight against 'objectivist idealism.' In his habitus theory, Bourdieu was able to regain *terra objectiva* despite acknowledging the real constraining influence of internalized norms by making them superstructures homologous with the external base. In the theoretical move we will consider here, he achieves a similar aim but in a simpler way: he discards the very notion of internalized normative control itself. In thinking about action Bourdieu now argues that what we must do is 'to substitute strategy for rule' (OTP: 9).

With this second approach to practice Bourdieu transforms Wittgenstein into Bentham and embarks upon an enterprise that is more ingenuous, and more revealing of what I have claimed to be his originating theoretical intent. For in this part of Bourdieu's work, the alternative to rule is neither improvisation nor habitus but rational calculation – strategization – exercised on an extraordinarily wide plane.[23]

Even when Bourdieu insisted on the practicality of action-as-habitus, he described it as symbolic in motivation and intent. When he focuses on the practicality of action-as-strategy, however, action slides from communication to exchange. What we have is the behaviorist interpolation of pleasure and pain decked out as the struggle for social existence: 'Every exchange contains a more or less dissimulated challenge, and the logic of challenge and riposte is but the limit toward which every act of communication tends' (OTP: 14). Voluntarism – the relative autonomy of the actor from collective constraint – emerges not, as in the habitus theory, from subjectivity and lived experience but from the realistic impossibility of knowing with certainty what the response will be to a thoroughly strategic act. 'In the relative predictability and unpredictability of the possible ripostes,' Bourdieu suggests, agents find 'the opportunity to put their strategies to work' (ibid.: 15). Effective action, like successful war, must contain the element of surprise. Voluntarism is reduced here to unpredictability, recalling Keynes's similar insistence that every calculation about the future involves information not available to an actor in present time. Yet, whereas Bourdieu concludes that the actor's response to this knowledge deficit will be to engage in frantic calculation and deceit, Keynes (1965 [1936]: 135–64, 194–209) suggests that the objective inability to know the future in anything more than a probabilistic way opens the theoretical door to irrational motivation ('animal passions') and to the concept of trust. For Bourdieu, even the most traditional peasant plays the game of life like the stock market. For Keynes, even the most hardened capitalist plays the stock market like the game of life.

Altruistic behavior – the reproduction in action of common moral norms – thus becomes impossible in any substantive sense of the word. Since for Bourdieu exchange is no more than a dissimulated challenge, it comes as no surprise when he defines altruism as merely the most clever of the disguises that calculating egoism can take. Indeed, he claims that altruism itself is one of those 'second-order strategies' whose function is to transform 'the primary profit of practice' into action 'whose purpose is to give apparent satisfaction to the demands of the official rule' (OTP: 22). In this way, he explains, it is possible 'to compound the satisfactions of enlightened self-interest with the advantage of ethical impeccability' (ibid.). Exhibitions of altruism, then, are nothing other than 'officializing strategies,' calculations which have the purely ideological function 'to transmute "egoistic," private, particular interests . . . into disinterested, collective, publicly avowable, legitimate interests' (ibid.: 40). We are in Alice's Wonderland, a topsy-turvy world where altruism is egoism and egoism must give the appearance of altruism in turn. In this world, action is instrumental by definition.

> Practice never ceases to conform to economic calculation even when it gives every appearance of disinterestedness by departing from the logic of interested calculation (in the narrow sense) and playing for stakes that are non-material and not easily quantified.
>
> (ibid.: 177)

In Mauss's (1954 [1923–4]) famous essay on the gift, he had argued in precisely the opposite way, demonstrating that every exchange was regulated by cultural forms and real commitments to mutual obligation. Bourdieu is haunted by Mauss's ghost. His work (e.g. LOP: 98–111) is marked by repeated attacks on the very conception of collective obligation, and by continuous efforts to demonstrate that gift-giving must be viewed, instead, as the highest, most wily stage of selfish efforts at domination.[24] Surely, the *reductio ad absurdum* of this argument is Bourdieu's conception of symbolic violence. It is only when 'the direct application of overt physical or economic violence is negatively sanctioned,' he writes, that gifts and generosity come into their own. They replace 'overt (physical or economic) violence' with 'symbolic violence' (OTP: 191–2). According to this logic, gift-giving is merely a thinly veiled sublimation for violent physical attack.

With this theoretical indifference to the ethical possibilities of a historical movement away from physical domination, Bourdieu denies the implications of the civilizing process that thinkers like Freud and Elias so well understood: it is precisely the *failure* to sublimate violence into more symbolic kinds of aggression that creates the psychological conditions for the most drastic upheavals in contemporary life. I will suggest below, indeed, that Bourdieu's failure to appreciate the positive elements of abstract obligation – which sublimates force via law and allows competitive conflicts within civil society rather than violent conflicts outside of it – makes it impossible for Bourdieu to understand democracy itself.

The Oxymoron of 'Unconscious Strategy'

Bourdieu's relentless drive for the hard edge, the strained, Veblenesque effort to avoid sentimentality at all costs, eventually leads his conception of practical action into a real theoretical bind. In the work on habitus, he displaces the 'objective idealism' of symbolic structuralism with an emphasis on structured affect, which even if a Trojan horse for materialism at least has the virtue of recognizing the real existence of motivation of a nonrational and emotional kind. In his strategization theory, however, Bourdieu seems to displace habitualized emotion, replacing it with crass calculation that gives to the external conditions of action much more explicit pride of place. If order is described in a collective yet external way, it seems, action must be rationalized after all.

For what Bourdieu makes perfectly clear by his emphasis on strategy is that neither affective disposition nor symbolic schema is, in fact, the real motivational source for action. Into this strain of his theorizing the conception of action-as-typification – the phenomenological notion which describes unconscious intention weaving affect and schema into the orderly continuity of contingent interaction – is never allowed to intrude. After all, one can acknowledge the typifying dimension of action as equal to the strategic only if one conceptualizes action's internal environments (the psychological and cultural ones) as affecting action independently of its external environment (the social system). Once Bourdieu's theory is strategized, this becomes impossible. Affect and schema, glutinized into habitus, are treated, in effect, as objective environments in relation to which actors' calculations are exercised mechanistically. Despite their internal ontological location, they are external in an epistemological sense, for they do not mitigate, qualify, or condition the nature of calculation itself. As a result, motivation is conceptualized as rational in a merely strategic way.

Bourdieu's point is that action must be practical. We must look, he insists, to its functions in the real world, not to the internal structures of the ideal world to which it pays merely formal obeisance. 'As soon as one moves from the structure of language to the functions it fulfills, that is, to the uses agents actually make of it,' Bourdieu warns, 'one sees that mere knowledge of the code gives only very imperfect mastery of the linguistic interactions really taking place' (OTP: 25; cf. Bourdieu 1991a). Yet, surely, codes may be less than omnipresent and omniscient without giving up a degree of symbolic control. The power Bourdieu wants to give to objective considerations, in other words, goes well beyond acknowledging that they have a role. He insists that 'everything takes place as if, from among the class of "signifieds" abstractly corresponding to a speech sound, the receiver "selected" the one which seems to him to be compatible with the *circumstances* as he perceives them' (OTP: 25, italics added). Bourdieu understands perception objectively rather than subjectively. Segueing his way from perception to objective structures, he leaves structures in the subjective, semiotic sense entirely behind:

> Reception depends to a large degree on the objective structure of the relations between the interacting agents' objective positions in the social structure (e.g. relations of competition or objective antagonism, or relations of power and authority, etc.).
>
> (OTP: 25)

There is a theoretical contradiction, then, between two different versions of Bourdieu's practical action theory. One stresses the role of nonrational action and objectively constructed habitus, the other the role of rational motivation having an objective result. Bourdieu cannot resolve this contradiction truly; to do so, he would have to cut through the mystifying camouflage that gives his theory its apparently synthetic form. What he does, instead, is conceptualize a form of action that is theoretically oxymoronic. We might call this the notion of action as 'unconscious strategy,' a compound whose theoretical function is to make more palatable the vulgar reduction of action to strategization. Whereas rational choice theory typically stipulates only one environment for its actor, that of material conditions, Bourdieu's recognition of the affective-symbolic habitus requires that the environment for his strategic action be more complex. The actor calculates in relation to both material and symbolic conditions, and the latter are situated within, not outside, his self. If an object of action is considered to be unconscious and nonmaterial, however, that action cannot also be said to be 'rational' according to the conventional criteria of social theory. Bourdieu's trouble stems from the fact that, despite this prohibition, he will not allow such action to be called nonrational either.

Bourdieu is caught in a dilemma that he does not face and cannot resolve. Because of this he is forced to make the incongruous suggestion that strategization, which is omnipresent, proceeds largely in an unconscious way (e.g. OTP: 36; HA: 94). What he is objecting to about rational actor theory is not its insistence on rationality but its association of rationality with an '"intention" of "consciousness"' (LOP: 50), an association that in his view makes it not only naive but restrictively economic.[25] Economistic rational choice theory suggests either that ends are 'consciously posited' (ibid.) or that economic reasoning is conscious and prior to the act. The result is that economics is 'unaware that practices can have other principles than mechanical causes or conscious ends.' The alternative, according to Bourdieu, is to recognize that practices 'can obey an economic logic without obeying narrowly economic interests.' Reason can, indeed, be seen as 'immanent in practices,' but it is not located in 'decisions,' that is, in the claim that choices are made in a manner that is consciously calculated. Yet neither does the rationality of action emerge from the 'determinations of mechanisms external to and superior to the agents.' Action is reasonable and rational because, without conscious calculation, it remains structured by the need to 'achieve the objectives inscribed in the logic of particular field at the lowest cost' (ibid.). It can be described as consistent with 'genuinely intentional strategies' even 'when it is in no way inspired by [any] conscious concern' (D: 246). Action, then, is 'reasonable without being the product of a reasoned design,' informed by an 'objective finality' without being actually determined mechanistically, 'intelligible and coherent' without involving intelligent, coherent, and deliberate decisions, and 'adjusted to the future' without being oriented toward a projection or plan (LOP: 50–51).

What an extraordinarily supple concept Bourdieu's conception of practical action is! Once it has postulated calculation as unconscious, it can achieve all the advantages of rational actor theories without taking account of the criticisms that have been lodged so persistently against it for hundreds of years.

'Unconscious strategy' is oxymoronic because the same action cannot be completely rational and nonrational at the same time. In presuppositional terms, habitus refers to normative standards of evaluation, or at least to standards of evaluation that can and must be normativized. Norms, if they are indeed norms, can bind action only on nonrational, subjective, and nonindividual grounds. They cannot do so – the habitus cannot work – if actors have the ability to weigh the adherence to norms solely according to the external and objective consequences of their acts. To presuppose this possibility would be to combine a conception of collective and internal order with a rational conception of action.

To suggest such a combination violates not only theoretical logic but simple common sense. For conceptions of order and action must be complementary. Internalized, normative order and rational action are like oil and water; they can be placed beside one another but they cannot mix. If actors are simply calculating creatures, the objects of their calculation may certainly be norms; if so, then these same norms cannot form the character (habitus) of the calculating agents as well. Norms which are merely objects of calculation can only be the norms of others, not of the actor herself. Norms which are entirely objects of calculation can no longer be understood as having a subjective role; rather, they play the same theoretical role as other kinds of external, objective things. One might put the matter this way. While the empirical referent of the concept 'norm' retains the ontological status of norm, that is, an antimaterial, subjective, mentalistic identity, it does not retain the epistemological status of norm: it no longer refers to a mode of orientation but to an object of orientation. As the whole tradition from Kant to Habermas suggests, norms create order only when they bind action via internal commitments, in relation to which an exclusively rational calculation is impossible.[26]

For the sake of argument, we might allow that what Bourdieu means by calling even unconsciously motivated actions rational is simply that all actions have a rational effect, not that they are rationally caused. We might unpack Bourdieu's oxymoron, in other words, by recalling his earlier discussion of the necessity to move from structures to functions and to the uses that actors make of the elements that move them. But surely this is the worst kind of functionalist reasoning, arguing from effect to cause without demonstrating feedback loops in-between. It was to avoid just such teleology that Bourdieu first introduced the notion of habitus as an alternative to utilitarian thinking. Yet habitus now is employed in such a way as to demonstrate utilitarianism's omnipresence.[27] On the one hand, it continues to mark the presence of emotional and cultural referents inside the actor; on the other, these referents now function merely to allow a pervasively calculating view of action to take an unconscious, and uncriticized, theoretical role.

The unconscious location of the utility-maximizing impetus in Bourdieu's work has been remarked upon by other critics. Honneth (1986: 57) comments, for example, that 'to avoid . . . having to assume that acting subjects possess the actual intention of utility maximization, Bourdieu proceeds from the idea that the positionally based utility calculus of social groups is manifest in their collective perceptual and evaluative schemata on an unconscious level.' The result, he suggests, is that Bourdieu can now claim 'that even if they subjectively orient their actions in other ways, social subjects act from the economic viewpoint of utility.' These and other similarly pointed criticisms (cf. Ferry and Renaut 1990: 78; Jenkins 1982: 275) err, however, when they identify habitus as itself the carrier of unconscious utility rather than discussing the latter as an emphasis that parallels and seriously undercuts the former. Habitus cannot be equated with the utility maximization of ongoing action; it is the emotional reflection of the actor's objective position at a much earlier point in time. The habitus is defined as being oriented not in any direct sense to objects in the actor's contemporary world but, rather, to internalized expectations that have derived from an earlier world. Only by assuming the dominance of strategic calculation can action be portrayed as oriented to contemporary external objects at the same time.

To criticize unconscious strategization in this way, in other words, glosses what is most troubling about the very concept of 'practice.' We have seen that, while it was presented initially as a conceptual alternative to 'objective idealism,' practice actually carries three fundamentally different meanings in Bourdieu's theory. As an expression of the lifeworldly, particularizing focus of action, practice allows Bourdieu to challenge any conception of typifying action as abstract rule-following. His reductionist portrayal of the formation of habitus, on the other hand, allows him to portray practice not only as down-to-earth but as oriented primarily to economic and stratificational issues. Finally, when Bourdieu turns 'from rule to strategy,' action becomes practical because it is neither emotional nor moral but cognitive, calculated, and strategic in the short-range sense. The latter conception assumes an unconscious position not because Bourdieu conflates it with the nonrational habitus but because he wishes to avoid the narrow economism and self-evident superficiality of exchange theory.

Theoretical logic exerts an ineluctable force, but this force is typically misunderstood by the theorists upon whom it acts. Bourdieu certainly is not himself aware that, by virtue of his reductionistic theoretical logic, he has been led to adopt the oxymoronic position

I have called unconscious strategization. Because he does not know this, he can hardly search for a better way to formulate the synthesis he wishes to achieve, which eludes him as a result. In fact, Bourdieu views this notion of unconscious strategization not as a theoretical failure but as a crowning theoretical triumph. He proclaims that, instead of a naive exchange theory – 'the ethnocentric naiveties of economics' (OTP: 177) – he has succeeded in proposing a sophisticated, post-Freudian one. Instead of seeing unconscious strategization as a residual category of last resort that allows him to make the best of a bad theoretical situation, Bourdieu hails it as a conceptual heuristic of enormous importance.

For it is this theoretical oxymoron that provides the invisible theoretical fulcrum of Bourdieu's macrosociology. From this ingenious but impoverished version of the micro–macro link Bourdieu drives the instrumental reduction of action – practice as profit-seeking – into every realm of social life. He contends that every society is defined by an overarching 'economy of practices,' that is, an economy of 'rational practice[s]' that 'can be defined in relation to all kinds of functions' (LOP: 50). The problem with economic theory is not, finally, that it is conceptually imperialistic but, in a strange way, that it is not ambitious enough. 'The theory of strictly economic practice is simply a particular case of a general theory of the economics of practice,' Bourdieu writes in his first major theoretical treatise (OTP: 177), and he has reiterated this central point ever since.

Via the concept of the economy of practices we are led to the heart of Bourdieu's research program. He intends 'to carry out in full what economics does only partially, and to extend economic calculation to all the goods, material and symbolic, without distinction, that present themselves as rare and worthy of being sought' (LOP: 51). Bourdieu promises, in short, to do no less than to ferret out the economy of practices in every arena of social life. There are, he writes confidently, a 'whole universe of economies, that is, of fields of struggle' (ibid.).[28] These fields of struggle are, in fact, the primary objects that his research program takes up. We turn now to Bourdieu's empirical sociology of the field, and to the struggles he describes.

'Field Theory' and Homology: The Reduction of Institutional Autonomy

It has been argued by some commentators (e.g. Brubaker 1985), as well as by Bourdieu (e.g. 1985: 17–19) himself, that by introducing the 'theory of the field' Bourdieu has complexified his model of contemporary society, in a sense de-Marxifying it. With this theory, the argument goes, Bourdieu intends to emphasize the independent, non-economic character of differentiated social spheres and the necessity for a more pluralistic, nonsynchronous, and antireductionistic theory to understand them. In a 1985 interview with German theorists, for example, Bourdieu pointed to the influence on his thinking of Weber's notion of *Vielseitigkeit*, which he translated as 'the many-sidedness of social reality.' This conception of social fragmentation, Bourdieu writes,

> was doubtless the basis of . . . the work that I am preparing on the theory of fields – and which could be called 'the plurality of worlds' [which] will end with a consideration of the plurality of logics corresponding to different worlds, that is, to different fields as places in which different kinds of common sense, different commonplace ideas and different systems of topics, all irreducible to each other, are constructed.
>
> (IOW: 21)

In order to interpret this assertion, we must shift our level of generality. Up until this point, we have examined presuppositional questions of action and order and their effect on the most general models of social life. We must move now to more specific, empirical questions about how these general commitments become translated into propositions about the structure of contemporary society. When this shift in reference is undertaken, it becomes clear that the field concept is not a departure but a specification and elaboration of Bourdieu's more general commitments, which have not been altered in any way. As the field theory becomes a more important focus in Bourdieu's sociology, we observe not a new theoretical development but the unacknowledged process of self-revision that so often marks the work of important thinkers, and important traditions, as they achieve sufficient influence to merit critical scrutiny.

Bourdieu fails to introduce into his field theory notions of action and order that are less reductionistic and more multidimensional than the parts of his work we have examined thus far. Interests are still the name of Bourdieu's game, not culturally habituated motives which exhibit a critical capacity because they are produced by socialization within a relatively autonomous culture. This point is hammered home again and again. 'Interest is . . . a condition of the functioning of a field,' Bourdieu suggests, 'insofar as it is what "gets people moving," what makes them get together, compete and struggle with each other' (IOW: 88). Even 'when one breaks away from economism in order to describe the universe of possible economies,' he assures us, 'one is able to satisfy the principle of sufficient reason according to which there is no action without a *raison d'être*, i.e., without interest, or, to put it another way, without investment in a game' (LOP: 290). Or, finally and most bluntly:

> The notion of interest . . . was conceived as a instrument of rupture intended to bring the materialist mode of questioning to bear on realms from which it was absent and on the sphere of cultural production in particular. It is the means of a deliberate (and provisional) reductionism.
>
> (Bourdieu 1988b: 1)

When Bourdieu speaks about the autonomy and plurality of fields, he does not mean to make his model of society pluralistic, in either the sociologically liberal sense of Parsons (cf. Alexander and Colomy 1990) or, more recently, Boltanski and Thevenot (1991), or the philosophically liberal sense of Walzer (1983). What he means, instead, is to open up the possibility that institutional domains can be studied as arenas of struggle without immediately treating them as simple epiphenomena of production and consumption relations of capitalist economies, a status that would leave them without empirical interest and without independent social effect.

There is, to be sure, a line of reasoning in Bourdieu's work that describes fields as 'products of a long, slow process of autonomization' (LOP: 67). One even can see a tendency – increasing as the *Marxisant* period of the 1960s and 1970s drew to a close – to conceptualize fields as independent institutional spheres dominated by elites whose power is based on their autonomy as such. When Bourdieu writes about scientists in 1985, for example, he describes their 'stake [in] the existence of a science of the social capable of affirming its autonomy against all forms of power' (IOW: 169; cf. also on science, Bourdieu 1991c: 6). This marks a significant departure from Marxist propositions about the concrete organization of empirical social life. If this line of reasoning were carried through consistently, it would push Bourdieu toward that instrumentalizing strain of Weberian work in which the concept of 'closure' plays such a central role. Neo-Weberian sociologists like Parkin, Collins, Rex, and Dahrendorf have written extensively about the struggles for institutional control and resource monopoly that the search for social closure entails.[29] While this strand of the Weberian tradition manifests an instrumentalizing and reductionist understanding of action and order whose zeal nearly matches Bourdieu's own, at least it has the virtue of recognizing the empirical reality of social differentiation and the boundaries it places upon economic power.

There are occasions, indeed, when one of Bourdieu's (e.g. 1991c) discussions of field actually takes on just such a decracinated Weberian form. Generally, however, the argument that Bourdieu's work should be seen as Weberian in either scope or intent – arguments made by Bourdieu himself or his interpreters (e.g. Brubaker 1985; Ringer 1992; van den Berg 1991) – is flawed in fundamental ways. In the first place, it fails to distinguish between the different and often incompatible strands of Weber's own work, one more materialist, the other more multidimensional. For example, in the key article where Bourdieu (1985) asserts the Weberian origins of field theory, he cites as the crucial instigating event his reading of Weber's sociology of religion. The image of the latter that Bourdieu identifies as having stimulated him, however, is sharply reductionist and materialist. It is a reading that recalls other 'sympathetic' Marxist interpretations, which are less efforts at the interpretation of Weber than polemical appropriations of his ideas by thinkers who remain neo-Marxists. Bourdieu himself seems to recognize the politics of his interpretation, acknowledging that he has made a '"structuralist" reinterpretation' (1985: 18), which 'attributes routinely to Weber himself . . . concepts such as those of religious field or of symbolic capital and a mode of thinking all of which are clearly alien to the logic of his thought' (ibid.). When Brubaker (1985: 748) praises Bourdieu for following 'the "generalized" or "radical" materialism exemplified in Weber's work,' then, he is reproducing Bourdieu's own Weber interpretation, which attends to only one of the dimensions of Weberian thought.

Bourdieu's field theory, furthermore, ultimately differs from the Weberian precisely in the fact that it does not carry the recognition of 'autonomization' all the way to an acknowledgment of 'closure.' To the contrary, at virtually every opportunity Bourdieu insists that each field must be seen as a microcosm – his preferred term is 'homology' (see pp. 139–41 above) – of a social system that is most decidedly capitalist in form. Even when he follows the post-Marxian path of field theory, then, Bourdieu remains committed to his general theory of 'practical action,' with all the systematic contradictions it entails. Practice is habitualized, habits are economized, and both practice and habitus give way to conceptions of unconscious strategizing oriented to structures of domination that almost always take on a class form.

Each social realm, for Bourdieu, can be allowed its own autonomy, and each can be seen as depending upon a specific habitus in turn. Each arena, however, must at the same time be understood as a venue for profit-making and calculation. For it is the objective material structure of each field that forms the actor's habitus and the telos of every field-specific social act. These structures, furthermore, are intimately related to – adumbrating, articulating, and recapitulating – the objective structures of capitalist society as a whole. In 1975, in one of his first applications of field theory to a specific institutional domain, Bourdieu already made this connection abundantly clear. After a lengthy presentation of the scientific field in terms of internally structured, asymmetrical struggles over the commodity of truth, he addressed 'the question of the field's degree of autonomy,' which he defined 'in relation, first, to the social demands of the dominant class and [second, to] the internal and external social conditions' (1975: 35). The apparent autonomy of the natural science field derives from the fact that 'the dominant class grants the natural sciences an autonomy corresponding to the interest it finds in the economic applications of scientific techniques' (ibid.: 36). The 'belated and precarious' autonomy of the social sciences, by contrast, can be explained because 'the dominant class has no reason to expect anything' except perhaps 'a particular valuable contribution to the legitimation of the established order and a strengthening of the arsenal of symbolic instruments of domination' (ibid.).

Indeed, in a retrospective discussion of the genesis of the field concept, Bourdieu claims that this stress on objective forces as structuring the field actually revises an earlier position which had stressed more autonomy for the field for agents.

> In order to truly construct the notion of the field, it was necessary to go beyond [my] first attempt to analyze the 'intellectual field' as a relatively autonomous universe of specific relationships: in fact the immediately visible relationships between the agents involved in intellectual life, especially the interactions among the authors or the authors and editors, had cancelled the objective relationships between the positions occupied by these agents, positions which determine the form of these interactions.
>
> (Bourdieu 1985: 17)

He suggests that this later, more deterministic position – which 'proposed a construct of the religious field as a *structure of objective relationships*' – displaced a more 'interactional view of the relationships between the religious agents' (ibid., italics in original).[30]

One should no more accept at face value this autobiographical narrative than Bourdieu's equally post hoc reconstruction of his field theory as Weberian in its intent. Yet, the theoretical point he is making here – his insistence on the objective and external structuring of field relationships as against a more emergentist, agentic, and internalist view – should be taken seriously indeed. Bourdieu's choice of 'homology' to conceptualize the relation between fields is a telling one. He might have chosen a concept like differentiation, autonomization, fragmentation, or even pluralization. Why did he not? Because ideas like these do not suggest the tight intertwining and determinate structuring that Bourdieu sees at the heart of contemporary life.

To be sure, the meaning Bourdieu attributes to homology is not entirely coherent. On the one hand, when responding to criticisms of his field theory as materialistic and reductionist, he insists on the fact that he is positing homology, *not* identity, between the field and its economic/class environment. On the other hand, when Bourdieu polemicizes against 'idealist' approaches to meaning which emphasize the relative independence of fields from other institutional environments, he insists that there is a homology between meanings, fields, and objective economic relations that assures their tight intertwining. This latter understanding reveals the equation in Bourdieu's theory between 'correspondence' and 'homology,' an equation that certainly confirms the traditional theoretical understanding of the term.

In neo-Marxist theory, Lucien Goldmann introduced 'homology' in *Toward a Sociology of the Novel* (1975), to emphasize the isomorphism he believed he had discovered between 'the literary form of the novel' and the 'everyday relationship of men with goods . . . in a society producing for the market' (ibid.: 127). Homology, for Goldmann, suggests a relationship of transformation between parallel lines, a movement from the more basic, economic plane of social life onto the superstructural level, where the imaginative forms of consciousness prevail. 'The novel form,' he writes, 'seems to be the transformation on the literary plane of everyday life in individualistic society born of production for the market' (ibid.). Homology implies such a 'rigorous' correspondence between levels, in other words, that it allowed Goldmann to see an identity undergirding apparent distinctions, 'a single structure manifest on two different levels.' It allowed him to speak, indeed, of a 'homologous history of the structures' involved (ibid.: 128).[31] Homology suggests an echoing process that reproduces essentially similar structures in interrelated entities while avoiding any suggestion of exact replication. It does not, then, suggest any real autonomy in a causal sense, in the sense in which structure B is conceived as feeding back to redirect and restructure the workings and direction of structure A. It was, in fact, precisely because of this merely echoing, iterative implication that Parsons and Shils (1951) criticized the notion of homology when they sought to define the relationship between culture, society, and personality as one of inter-penetration between relatively autonomous systems. Their polemical object was the 'culture and personality' school of interwar and post-war anthropology, as exemplified by Ruth Benedict.

Sympathetic interpreters of Bourdieu's field theory have failed to appreciate the importance of the difference between an analytical construction that involves real, if relative, autonomy for elements in various institutional fields and one that rests upon the notion of homology, which denies it. In speaking about the kinds of possible relationships between social realms, for example, Brubaker (1985: 748) describes only two alternatives – Bourdieu's theory of 'struc-turally homologous fields,' which is 'premised on the systematic unity of practical social life,' and Daniel Bell's notion of the 'disjunction of realms,' which argues that cultural, social, and psychological systems can run in directly contradictory directions within the same social formation. Surely, however, there is a third alternative between these two extremes, one which recognizes the disjunctive tensions yet simultaneous interdependencies between levels of organization and subsystems in societies that are differentiated to some degree.[32]

In virtually every systematic study of a field that he has made, and in virtually every casual discussion as well, Bourdieu carefully insists upon the imbeddedness of the field in a broader struggle between the social classes of late capitalist society. In a paper on the sociology of sport in the early 1980s, for example, Bourdieu begins by emphasizing closure and the internal, intra-systemic nature of the power struggles that, according to his field theory, mark sports off as a sociological domain: 'One has to notice the space of sporting practices as a system from which every element derives its distinctive value' (IOW: 156). He then turns immediately, however, to the underlying social categories of stratification and domination which he insists are associated with each distinctive sporting practice. 'The sociologist's work,' he writes, 'consists in establishing the socially pertinent properties that mean that a sport has an affinity with the interests, tastes and preferences of a determinate social category' (ibid.: 157). Indeed, Bourdieu insists that each sport 'is associated with a social position and an innate experience of the physical and social world' (ibid.), that is, with membership in a class fraction and position in an economic organiza-tion. In fact, in one of the more anomalous and revealing passages of his work, Bourdieu warns that 'we must beware of establishing a direct relation, as I have just done [sic], between a sport and a social position, between wrestling or football and workers, or between judo and the lower middle classes.' On theoretical grounds, however, he insists that just such an association is necessary, and he employs the concept of homology to make this point. There is a 'correspondence, which is a real homology . . . between the space of sporting practices, or, more precisely, the space of the different finely analyzed modalities of the practice of different sports, and the space of social positions' (ibid.: 158).

It is a pity that Bourdieu did not pay heed to his own advice. Instead, he continually stresses the intimate connection between internal position in a field and the external role played by the field in the reproduction of the capitalist economy. We will see, in fact, that in his theory of the particular reproductive demands of late capitalism Bourdieu discovers an empirical device for resolving the tension between the independent appearance of field-specific group struggles and their simultaneous subjection to the laws of capitalist life.

Research Program and Empirical Reduction: The 'Double Determinism' of the Empirical Studies

Bourdieu's empirical studies hardly confront the facts of the social world in an 'objective,' or unmediated, way, as he so often maintains (e.g. LOP: 1–21). These studies, rather, elaborate and specify the complex yet ultimately reductionistic presuppositions and models I have described above. They do so via a more empirically related, intermediate model of contemporary institutional life, one which draws substantially from the neo-Marxist tradition. The result is a series of empirical studies which, paradoxically, offer a densely 'empirical' account of contemporary society that is, at the same time, not only highly simplistic but highly contrived.[33]

The macro-theory that supplies the infrastructure – I use the term advisedly – for Bourdieu's empirical work on fields is a familiar amalgam of postscarcity Marxism and new class theory, cross-cut by residues from the conceptual labyrinth of structural Marxism. The evident importance in Bourdieu's model of structural Marxist categories may seem surprising in light of the striking animosity toward these theorists that Bourdieu has often expressed, for example in his (1975) shoot-up of Balibar's homage to the Althusserian reading of Marx. This animosity was not expressed, however, during the third and formative period of Bourdieu's work, the 1960s post-Sartrian development marked by the incorporation into his thinking of orthodox Marxist ideas (see Appendix). Nor did this animosity do anything to undermine the eagerness with which Bourdieu and his colleagues took up empirical investigations which demonstrated that education functioned, to use Althusser's term, as an ideological state apparatus that served merely to reproduce the class structure of capitalist societies.

The apparent conflict between such macro-structuralism and the 'praxis' language Bourdieu employs for the micro-level is mitigated not only by the reductionism of the habitus–strategy–field amalgam described above but also by the fact that Bourdieu employs them in different theoretical contexts. In the most generalized and discursive, that is, 'theoretical,' presentations of his perspective, Bourdieu makes heavy use of the praxis theory of the younger Marx (acknowledged in IOW: 13, denied in IOW: 20) and of the reverberations of this same Hegelian language in the works of Sartre, Wittgenstein, and phenomenology. In his empirical studies, by contrast, he makes equally strong use of the model of 'relative autonomy and determinism in the last instance' introduced by Althusser and his students. If Bourdieu cut his Marxist baby teeth on Sartre, he cut his Marxist wisdom teeth on Althusser.

The rough, ready, and vulgar metahistory that informs Bourdieu's empirical investigations posits three major historical phases. In the traditional-feudal period, economic underdevelopment allowed and even demanded that relations of domination be camouflaged by religion, producing symbolically mystified forms of cross-class solidarity. With the emergence of industrial capitalism, this camouflage became both unnecessary and impossible, for class domination assumed for the first time an effective and impersonal form.

> If it is true that symbolic violence is the gentle, disguised form which violence takes when overt violence is impossible, it is understandable that symbolic forms of domination should have progressively withered away as objective mechanisms came to be constituted which, in rendering the work of euphemization superfluous, tended to reproduce the 'disenchanted' dispositions that their development demanded.
>
> (LOP: 133)

In late capitalism, this disenchantment has given way, before both economic and political exigencies, to the re-enchantment of the world; in Bourdieu's terms, to a renewed emphasis on symbolic mystification.

> It is equally clear why the development of the capacity for subversion and critique that the most brutal forms of 'economic' exploitation have aroused, and the uncovering of the ideological and practical effects of the

mechanisms ensuring the reproduction of the relations of domination, should bring about a return to modes of accumulation based on the conversion of economic capital into symbolic capital, with all the forms of legitimizing redistribution, public ('social' policies) and private (financing of 'disinterested' foundations, donations to hospitals, academic and cultural institutions, etc.), through which the dominant groups secure a capital of 'credit' which seems to owe nothing to the logic of exploitation. . . . The denial of the economic and of economic interest which, in pre-capitalist societies, was exerted first in the very area of 'economic' transactions . . . thus finds its favoured refuge in the domain of art and 'culture', the site of pure consumption.

(ibid.: 133–4)

Bourdieu's class and institutional theory follows directly from these assertions about shifts in productive mode and attendant changes in legitimation. On the consumption side, there is a movement from producing material goods to producing taste and symbols. On the productive side, brute force is displaced by information-processing and the demand for technical skills that involve the manipulation of symbols. The fundamental struggle of this late capitalist period is between the 'old class' and the 'new.' The former, whose status is ascribed, includes the industrial owners and managers, bankers, the judiciary, and the old aristocratic families. The new class(es) include(s) scientists, advertisers, technicians, artists, professors, journalists, and writers whose status is relatively open and whose distinction must be asserted rather than assumed, achieved rather than inherited.

Emerging from 'a new field of struggle over the symbolic manipulation of the conduct of private life,' these agents fight over 'the principles of the construction of social reality' (Bourdieu 1987a: 119). In Poulantzian fashion, Bourdieu calls the first group the 'dominant fraction of the dominant class,' and he insists that it remains still in control. The second group ranges from the 'subordinate fraction of the dominant class' to all those who aspire to be included in it, which includes every other fraction of the urban middle and upper strata except the petty bourgeois. Below these two struggling 'dominant classes' are the peasants and the manual working class, with access neither to material nor to symbolic resources.[34]

When Bourdieu explores the structure of a social field, he analyzes it, first, as a site of intense struggle over field-specific goods. At the same time, however, he demonstrates that this struggle merely serves to reconfigure the broader conflict between the new and old class fractions of capitalist society. It is this double ambition that sets his work off from other efforts to develop a neo-Marxist research program, on the one hand, and from more Weberian sociological efforts, on the other.

Education and Science as Fields: Producing Habitus and Reproducing Stratification

Because in new class theory knowledge is the central commodity over which people fight, it is not surprising that in Bourdieu's society, as in Althusser's, schools become the central site of contention. Bourdieu, who has never written a word about factories or the production of material goods, has spent more time on the educational system than any other institutional domain. It might be said, of course, that such an emphasis on education seems to suggest a more 'voluntaristic' reading of habitus than I have inferred above. After all, Parsons, Mead, and Piaget are also distinguished by the importance they place on schooling as an arena for the formation of the socialized self. Bourdieu's treatment of schools, however, emphasizes exactly the opposite claim, reinforcing an antivoluntaristic reading of habitus in turn. As his well-known early studies with Passeron (1977, 1979) amply demonstrate, Bourdieu treats education primarily as an institution that reproduces existing class relations by providing 'the justificatory ideology which enables the privileged classes, the main users of the educational system, to see their success as the confirmation of natural, personal gifts' (Bourdieu and Passeron 1979: 71). Because schools 'practice an implicit pedagogic action' that requires an already existing 'initial familiarity with the dominant culture,' the information and training they offer can be competently acquired 'only by subjects [already] endowed with the system of predispositions that is the condition for [subsequent academic] success' (Bourdieu 1973: 80).

> The disposition to make use of the school and the predispositions to succeed in it depend, as we have seen, on the objective chances of using it and succeeding in it that are attached to the different social classes, these dispositions and predispositions in turn constituting one of the most important factors in the perpetuation of the structure of educational chances as an objectively graspable manifestation of the relationship between the educational system and the structure of class relations.
>
> (Bourdieu and Passeron 1977: 204)

What 'habitus' adds to this Marxist understanding of education-as-reproduction is to demonstrate that reproduction must be conceived in a more subtle, more psychologically and culturally centered way.[35] Given the conditions of late capitalist life, Bourdieu suggests, inherited wealth and class position more generally can be maintained across generations only if they are translated into mental structures that manifest themselves as personal and individualized qualities, as manifestations of talent and achievement.

> The most hidden and most specific function of the educational system consists in hiding its objective function, that is, masking the objective truth of its relationship to the structure of class relations.
>
> (Bourdieu and Passeron 1977: 208)

> By making social hierarchies and the reproduction of these hierarchies appear to be based upon the hierarchy of 'gifts', merits, or skills established and ratified by its sanctions . . . the educational system fulfills a function of legitimation which is more and more necessary to the perpetuation of the 'social order' as the evolution of the power relationship between classes tends more completely to exclude the imposition of a hierarchy based upon the crude and ruthless affirmation of the power relationship.
>
> (Bourdieu 1973: 84)

Insofar as class qualities become mystified in this way – as individual 'charisma' (cf. Bourdieu 1968) – education serves to camouflage the real structure of inherited domination.

> The official differences produced by academic classifications tend to produce (or reinforce) real differences by inducing in the classified individuals a collectively recognized and supported belief in the differences, thus producing behaviors that are intended to bring real being into line with official being.
>
> (D: 25)

> Among all the solutions put forward throughout history to the problem of the transmission of power privileges, there surely does not exist one that is better concealed, and therefore better adapted to societies which tend to refuse the most patent forms of the hereditary transmission of power privileges.
>
> (Bourdieu 1973: 72)

What is so extraordinarily effective about schooling, however, is that, simultaneously, it serves capitalism in exactly the opposite way. Because the medium it supplies for individual distinction is abstract, the achievements of every individual can easily be compared, ranked, and standardized. The social system thus becomes increasingly rationalized, not individualized, and a stronger cultural market results.[36]

The educational system minimizes the obstacles to the free circulation of cultural capital ... (without, however, destroying the profits associated with the charismatic ideology of the irreplaceable individual) ... thereby setting up a unified market for all cultural capacities.

(LOP: 132)

This linked attention to the field and its actors, on the one hand, and to the overarching and overdetermining structure of the capitalist system, on the other, also characterizes Bourdieu's work on scientific and intellectual life. He lays out the structure of the academic domain, the faculties, the training milieu, and the systems of budgetary control, insisting that these structures manifest themselves only through individual and group actions. The dynamics of the field are struggles within and between the faculties for power over resources and other academic media of domination. Law and medicine are on one side, liberal arts and sciences on the other. Group and individual action in the academic field are portrayed as thoroughly strategic and calculated; there is no attention – indeed, there is systematic inattention – to the actual content of disciplines or to the influence of ideas, much less to the rationality or truth of science as such.

Academic power presupposes the aptitude and propensity, themselves socially acquired, to exploit the opportunities offered by the field: the capacity to 'have pupils, to place them, to keep them in a relation of dependency' and thus to ensure the basis of a durable power, the fact of 'having well-placed pupils' implies perhaps above all the art of manipulating other people's [careers].

(HA: 88)

Since strategic calculation depends upon the quantity and quality of available resources, it is no wonder that Bourdieu dismisses not only the possibility of sincerely held academic values as motivating factors but the very notion of intellectual independence as such. It is structural constraints that determine the activities of academic persons.

All the declarations of the professors on the subject of the academic institution and the social world ... are motivated in the last analysis by their position within the field.

(ibid.: 128)

This microconstruction of the deterministic field is encapsulated inside a macro one. Bourdieu tries to link the field-specific dynamics of academic life directly to class struggles in the society at large.

Claiming homology between internal and external struggles, he points to 'the institutions of higher education (that is to say the whole set of the faculties and the *grandes écoles*) whose structure reproduces in specifically academic logic the structure of the field of power (or, in other words, the oppositions between the fractions of the dominant class) to which it gives access' (ibid.: 38).

The 'old faculties,' primarily law and medicine, are linked up with the old (dominant) segment of the capitalist, or dominant, class and produce knowledge and personnel that directly serve their interest. Bourdieu writes, for example, that 'the faculties which are dominant in the political order have the function of training executive agents able to put into practice without questioning or doubting, within the limits of a given social order, the techniques and recipes of a body of knowledge which they claim neither to produce nor to transform' (ibid.: 63). The more research-oriented, scientific and especially humanistic faculties, by contrast, provide more free-floating symbols which the 'new class' (the subordinate fraction of the dominant class) utilizes in its struggle for its own place in the sun. Yet, in writing about the creations of the human sciences, Bourdieu stresses that 'the specific effect of [their] constructions . . . resides precisely in the *illusion* of their rational genesis, free from any determination' (ibid.: 65, italics added). In fact, these constructions reflect – they are generalized from – a class-specific and class-derived habitus. They are 'rooted not only in a rational need for coherence and compatibility with facts, but in the social necessity of a system of objectively orchestrated dispositions and the more or less objectified and codified "arbitrary" culture values which express it' (ibid.: 64).

The result of this double determinism, both intra- and extra-field, is that the struggles in the academy are not really portrayed as agentic at all. The educated habitus is a mere mediator, not an activator of a self with relative autonomy or self-control. This degradation of the self is clear, first of all, in Bourdieu's understanding of the student.

> Differences in academic achievement . . . are so closely associated with social differences that they seem to be the retranslation into a specifically academic logic of initial differences of incorporated capital (the *habitus*) or of objectified capital which are associated with different social or geographical origins. They seem to be the result of a gradual transformation of inherited advantages into 'earned' advantages.
>
> (ibid.: 52)

It is clear also in Bourdieu's degradation of the educator: 'The structure of the university field reflects the structure of the field of power, while its own activity of selection and indoctrination contributes to the reproduction of that structure' (ibid.: 40–41).

These 'findings' on education can be challenged in different ways. In empirical terms, for example, they fly in the face of most empirical studies of status-attainment in industrial societies (e.g. Blau and Duncan 1967; Caillé 1992: 169–76). While at various times in his work Bourdieu dismisses these studies as the product merely of 'atomistic,' 'functionalist,' and 'American' theorizing, he never actually confronts their data.[37] Despite their theoretical limitations, these studies provide compelling evidence that educational attainment cannot be reduced to father's occupation but constitutes an independent achievement that has wide repercussions for social mobility.[38]

The approach to evaluating Bourdieu's work I have taken here, however, is not primarily an empirical one. My aim, rather, is to show how such studies are not, in fact, really empirical at all. Rather than efforts to confront the empirical world, they are efforts to specify and elaborate the broader, more discursive commitments that I have criticized above. It is not surprising, then, that the problems I have identified in Bourdieu's work more generally – the impoverished understanding of meaning, the caricature of motivation, the inability to conceptualize the interplay of sensible self and differentiated institution in contemporary society – should undermine these particular studies as well.

The full implications of Bourdieu's reduction of the intellectual domain become apparent in his studies of social theory itself. In Bourdieu's strikingly reductionist Heidegger study (Bourdieu 1991b), he applies his field theory of the academy to the ideas of a single thinker. In response to long-standing political criticisms of the existential phenomenologist who became a neo-Nazi, Bourdieu insists that his own sociological approach is superior to other explanations because it denies the German thinker autonomy as an active subject. Heidegger was produced by his place in society.

> As soon as one tries to understand, rather than to incriminate or excuse, one sees that the thinker [i.e. Heidegger] is less the subject than the object of his most fundamental rhetorical strategies, those which are activated when, led by the practical dispositions of his habitus, he becomes inhabited, like a medium so to speak, with the requirements of the social spaces (which are simultaneously mental spaces) which enter into relation through him.
> (ibid.: 105)

The language is familiar: social spaces produce 'requirements' which 'inhabit' the actor via the 'practical dispositions' of his habitus.

Heidegger's philosophy, Bourdieu insists, must not be seen as an individual creation but as a field-produced phenomenon, one which iterates, in a camouflaged way, the social structure outside of it. Once again, the concept of homology is central to his reductionist account.

> Imposing philosophical form entails observing political formalities, and the transformation implied by a transfer from one social space (which is inseparable from a mental space) to another tends to disguise the relation between the final product and the social determinants which hide behind it, since a philosophical stance is not more than a *homologue*, in a different system, of a 'naive' politico-moral stance.
>
> (ibid.: 42, italics added)

Or, more simply and directly put: The philosophical field becomes a venue for power struggles which merely translate the class fractions of the wider domain.

> The habitus of this 'professor ordinarius' whose origins were in the lesser rural bourgeoisie, and who was unable to think without using mental and verbal patterns borrowed from ontology . . . is in fact the enabling factor establishing homology between the philosophical and political fields . . . (in the social space it is that of the *Mittelstand* and the academic fraction of that class; in the structure of the academic field it is that of philosophy, etc.).
>
> (ibid.: 47)

It is worth noting that Bourdieu's disciples have carried this degradation of intellectual autonomy, and the elimination of intellectual responsibility it implies, into a full-fledged research program. Boschetti, for example, analyzes Sartre's career, and French existentialism more generally, as a desperate but ultimately rather unoriginal *méconnaisance* (false consciousness). Articulating a fantasy of escape, Sartre's theory of freedom is attributed to the evasive strategy common to middle-ranking bourgeois, who 'renounces the privileges [and limitations] of his class' (Boschetti 1992: 85). This class determination, according to Boschetti, is simply reinforced by the specific conditions of the French intellectual field, which must be seen as a reflection of macro-institutional life in turn.

> The illusion of escaping from social determination and being able to accede to an absolute view of the universe is a typical product of the situation intellectual work presupposes. Theory and contemplation imply a suspension of intellectual life and permit the removal of its conditioning.
>
> (ibid.: 86)

If Sartre's class habitus and the nature of the broad intellectual field explain his ideas, however, it was his strategic mastery of symbolic capital in two particular and different academic subfields, philosophy and literature, that explains his unique power.

> It was certainly to Sartre's advantage to be able to exploit his accumulated technical and symbolic capital in every sector. Literature and philosophy had long been separate and relatively autonomous fields. ... Sartre produced an extraordinary effect of legitimacy because his works fully conformed to the expectations of the production fields to which they belong. Perfectly at home among the Parisian intellectual elite, he intuitively mastered the rules of the game, producing a highly successful strategy.
>
> (ibid.: 82–3)

Neither does Boschetti ignore the social position of the audience for such highly strategic innovation. Locating Sartre's audience 'among the ranks of the new, less established intellectual public created by the expansion of secondary education,' she concludes that 'it is easy to understand Sartre's appeal for these somewhat marginal members of the intellectual field.' Why? Because 'the attractive image of intellectual greatness he proposed offered them a kind of compensation by proxy for their social irrelevance' (ibid.: 86). Even for the philosopher of freedom, intellectual choices boil down to strategies that are bound by the exegencies of field and class.

In the face of such colossal sociologism, one can only recall with wonder Bourdieu's oft-stated ambition to bring agency back into social thought: 'I wanted, so to speak, to reintroduce agents that Lévi-Strauss and the structuralists, among others Althusser, tended to abolish, making them simple epiphenomena of structure. And I mean agents, not subjects' (IOW: 9). In his studies of education and the intellectual field, he certainly has not found a way.

Taste, Strategy, and the Deformations of Class Habitus

In a post-accumulationist mode of production where needs are largely ideal, it makes sense that 'taste' would form the second principal arena of Bourdieu's empirical work. Formed by family and trained by school, the habitus becomes transformed into a consumer by taste. In Bourdieu's studies of high art and photography (Bourdieu et al., 1965; Bourdieu et al. 1991b [1966]) we find the doubleness of determinism once again at work. Because objects are not beautiful in themselves, interpretations of beauty rely upon established codes (cf. Bourdieu 1968). These codes are transferred from hegemonic culture to habitus via schools, the upper echelon of which provide access to the esoteric and valuable codes reserved for the dominant class – 'statistics show that access to "cultural works" is a privilege of the cultivated class' (Bourdieu et al. 1991b [1966]: 37).

In Bourdieu's early writings, this first level of reduction is baldly stated, couched in the terminology of Marx's theory of commodity fetishism: 'The sanctification of culture and art, this "currency of the absolute" which is worshipped by a society enslaved to the absolute of currency, fulfills a vital function by contributing to the conservation of the social order' (ibid.: 111). So broadly stated, however, such determinism misses what Bourdieu increasingly insists on calling the autonomy of the artistic field and the subtleties generated thereby. Because beauty is a specific, distinctive commodity that has become increasingly independent over historical time, it defines a field with its own 'laws' and players subject to its effects. The game of art, of course, can be no different than the games generated by every other field. It organizes a particular form of scarcity and it generates particular struggles thereby. Within the artistic field, artists and critics struggle with one another in an effort to monopolize aesthetic control. Rather than beauty, art buyers seek distinction, the superiority that possession of scarce yet highly valued symbols provides.

> Explicit aesthetic choices are in fact often constituted in opposition to the choices of the groups closest in social space, with whom the competition is most direct and most immediate, and . . . by the intention . . . of marking distinction vis-à-vis lower groups.
>
> (D: 60)

As for the players in this artistic field, they correspond to broader divisions between new class and old: abstraction is linked to the new, subordinate fraction of the dominant class and the avant-garde, Impressionism and the realism of the 'Great Masters' to the old, dominant fraction of the dominant class and to traditionalism.

Bourdieu's sociology of mass taste, which mixes high and popular culture, follows the same lines, both analytically and empirically. Once again, his field-specific analysis echoes the contradictions of his general model and presuppositions. While he begins with the suggestion that 'consumption is . . . a stage in a process of communication, that is, an act of deciphering, decoding, which presupposes practical or explicit mastery of a cipher or code' (D: 2), he makes it immediately evident that he views communication instrumentally, that is, as a means of domination. Consumption is strategically directed toward the acquisition of objects whose value is defined by codes that reflect the real division of social life.

To see what Bourdieu is really getting at in his studies of consumption, it is necessary to take this reflection theory very seriously. He is not merely providing a gloss on the old sociological saw that 'taste is social.' Rather, following the precise and explicit reduction of his habitus model, he is developing a reflection theory of consumption on a truly ambitious scale. Indeed, his approach replicates rather precisely the foundational theory of Marx. In the discussion of the commodity form in the famous first chapter of *Capital*, after all, Marx did a great deal more than speak vaguely about ideology and false consciousness. He defined the commodity as a fetishizing symbol that distorted conscious because its phenomenal appearance camouflaged the reality of the abstract, exploited labor upon which the production of commodities is based. Under capitalism, Marx believed, the wage relation turned labor into the ultimate commodity. Misrepresented as an exchange of money for human labor, what was being paid for actually was only labor power, the abstract and degraded capacity to produce surplus value. This is exactly the perspective – historicizing, reductive, and economic – that Bourdieu brings to his study of the objects that produce status distinction and taste.

> I contend that a power or capital becomes symbolic, and exerts a specific effect of domination, which I call symbolic power or symbolic violence ... only when it is *misrecognized* in its arbitrary truth as capital and *recognized* as legitimate. ... This act of (false) knowledge and recognition is an act of practical knowledge.
>
> (Bourdieu 1988b: 5, original italics)

Bourdieu's consumption theory easily can be misread, for in the specificity and ambition of its explanatory effort it draws heavily upon semiotics, a tradition that is internalist and purely symbolic in its orientation. Bourdieu makes use of such a structuralist approach, for example, when he describes the standards of popular taste in terms of binary oppositions, like high and low, hot and cold, shiny and dull, sharp and smooth, loud and quiet, harmonic and atonal, realistic and abstract. It is vital to see, however, that Bourdieu is actually turning semiotic structuralism upside down, for he insists that these oppositions are mere reflections of the 'real' oppositions of life, of differences in work experience, consumption practices, and more generally of the economic life of different classes and class fractions.

> Taste is the practical operator of the transmutation of things into distinct and distinctive signs, of continuous distributions into discontinuous oppositions; it raises the differences inscribed in the physical order of bodies to

the symbolic order of significant distinctions. It transforms objectively classified practices, in which a class condition signifies itself (through taste), into classifying practices, that is, into a symbolic expression of class position.

(D: 175)

Thus, the highly physical and intellectually restrictive qualities of working-class life demand, according to Bourdieu, a simplistic and realist aesthetic that cannot comprehend abstraction. Taste for the latter, by contrast, can be developed only among those classes for whom a more information-based labor process has produced distanciation from the concreteness of nature.

Bourdieu tries to demonstrate that the symbolic criteria which define every domain of fashion are reflections or inductions from reality, which are linked, in turn, with a particular work experience and the status it allows.

> Whereas the working classes, reduced to 'essential' goods and virtues, demand cleanness and practicality, the middle classes, relatively freer from necessity, look for a warm, 'cosy,' comfortable or neat interior, or a fashionable and original garment. These are values [in turn] which the privileged classes relegate to second rank because they have long been theirs and seem to go without saying.

(ibid.: 247)

Thus Bourdieu discovers 'the bourgeois predilection for the "Impressionists," whose simultaneously lyrical and naturalistic adherence to natural or human nature contrasts both with realist or critical representation of the social world ... and with all forms of abstraction' (ibid.: 20). Post-impressionist art, by contrast, 'is the product of an artistic intention which asserts the absolute primacy of form over function' (ibid.: 30). It is for this reason, Bourdieu confidently asserts, that Post-impressionism is appropriated by less secure, more intellectualized, more upwardly mobile groups, that is, by the so-called dominated factions of the dominant class. Even the most subtle distinctions of fashion have their objective correlate. Every quality has its place. Not only can the taste for composers and compositions be reduced to class habitus, but so even can contrasts in musical instruments – 'the sharp, rough timbre of plucked strings/the warm, bourgeois timbre of hammered strings' (ibid.: 19).

The consumption field, then, is defined by categories of popular taste that embody objective qualities and reflect actual differences in social experience. The struggles generated by such a field, in other words, are symbolic only in name. Relations are not about meaning but about acquiring capital in a symbolic form. In short, symbols are commodities in relation to which action is instrumental. Consumers aim to define themselves in terms of valued categories by acquiring the commodities thereof. Fashion in art, television, music, automobiles, and sports is simply class struggle by another name.

> The endless changes in fashion result from the objective orchestration between, on the one hand, the logic of struggles internal to the field of production, which are organized in terms of old/new, itself linked, through the oppositions expensive/(relatively) cheap and classical/practical (or rearguard/avant-garde), to the opposition old/young . . . and, on the other hand, the logic of the struggles internal to the field of the dominant and dominated fractions, or, more precisely, the established and the challengers.
>
> (ibid.: 233)

When class factions adopt a new style, or opt to maintain the old, they are making strategic decisions based on objective considerations of cost. Whether these calculations are conscious or not is, as we have seen, not an issue that is of any theoretical concern.

> The acquisition of culture competence is inseparable from insensible acquisition of a 'sense' for sound cultural investment. This investment sense, being the product of adjustment to the objective chances of turning competence to good account, facilitates forward adjustment to these chances, and is itself a dimension of a relation to culture – close or distant, off-hand or reverential, hedonistic or academic – which is the internalized form of the objective relationship between the site of acquisition and the 'center of cultural values.'
>
> (ibid.: 85)

Decisions to maintain styles are 'reproduction strategies,' referring to 'practices whereby individuals or families tend, unconsciously or consciously, to maintain or increase their assets and consequently to maintain or improve their position in the class structure' (ibid.: 125). The decision to adopt a new style, by contrast, is a 'reconversion strategy,' whereby capital is changed from 'one form to another' and made 'more accessible, more profitable or more legitimate' (ibid.: 131).

Once again, my interest here is to not provide an empirical response to this segment of Bourdieu's research program, but rather to demonstrate that, because these empirical studies are structured by his more general theory, they reveal problems that are not different in kind. It is difficult to leave unchallenged, however, the extremely distorted empirical image of the working class that permeates Bourdieu's studies, not only because such a caricature raises serious moral questions but because the very critical tradition within which Bourdieu works offers such a large body of countervailing material. Because of their oppressive working conditions and their proximity to nature, Bourdieu insists throughout his work, manual workers do not have the capacity to exercise taste in the sense of imposing an ideological sensibility on physical commodities, nor do they exhibit the capacity to exercise rationality in political life. Their sensibility is 'realist' by default, for the extremity of their social conditions forces their environment to be imprinted upon them. This patronizing perspective appears from the very beginning of Bourdieu's empirical studies of consumption. In his jointly authored text on photography (Bourdieu et al. 1965), for example, he and his co-authors not only reduce tastes and attitudes toward photography to class location but claim that the working class is more attached to photography than to other arts because it is realistic.

Because culture has been so crudely reduced to material circumstance, Bourdieu cannot recognize countercultures or popular culture. Such phenomena are independent or antagonistic to the centers of social power. They suggest that 'cultural tradition' can organize itself independently of power, a possibility that allows subordinated groups to maintain relatively independent, and often resistant, standards of judgment and taste. As one of his interviewers pointedly asked Bourdieu almost a decade ago:

> You have said that the dominated classes have only a passive role in strategies of distinction, that they are only a form of resistance. Is there not, in your view, a popular culture?
>
> (1980: 15)

Because it is British cultural Marxism, particularly in the historical form exemplified by E.P. Thompson, that represents an approach that is more sensitive to a popular culture approach, it seems fitting that it is a British sociologist, Craig Jenkins, who has been Bourdieu's most persistent critic in this regard. Although Jenkins's criticism is harsh, it speaks directly to the issue:

> The superficiality of Bourdieu's discussion of the working class is matched only by its arrogance and condescension. . . . Perhaps it is time Bourdieu took up the anthropologists's pith helmet again and actually went out and spent some time among the women and men about whom he writes.
>
> (Jenkins 1986: 104)

This statement touches on yet another element in the empirical evaluation of Bourdieu's studies which I have not been able to take up here. Paradoxically, his own recent insistence (1994: 9) on 'the universal validity of models constructed in relation to the particular case of France' points to the critical question: Is the validity of his models undermined because their avowedly universal propositions are based on what is, after all, specifically national data? While a comparative dimension could not, in itself, have 'invalidated' the more generalized elements in Bourdieu's theory, such consideration might well have forced him to elaborate these presuppositions in a different way. In his studies of art in American living-rooms, for example, Halle (1993) has demonstrated that realistic still-life paintings are preferred as living-room art in every social class. This finding starkly challenges one of the fundamental empirical propositions in Bourdieu's work on taste, for it suggests that such aesthetic judgments as the taste for abstraction over realism do not actually reflect differences in the labor process. Employing even more directly comparative data, Lamont (1992) has challenged Bourdieu's focus on aesthetic criteria *tout court*, demonstrating that, in status competition between American business managers, the exhibition of moral rectitude is more important than establishing aesthetic judgment.[39]

Epistemological Realism and Radical Truth: Reflexivity between Social Reduction and Disciplinary Conceit

When one reviews Bourdieu's research program one cannot help but be struck by the ample evidence it provides of interpretive brilliance. He possesses a fine sense for the texture of meaning, for symbolic relationships and psychological experience, for the oblique angles that reveal the color and nuance of language and mind. He would be a powerful interpreter of the meaning of contemporary life – in either a semiotic or a hermeneutic sense – if only he allowed himself the leave. He will not, however, and that is the point.

Bourdieu insists that interpretation is not his achievement. It is not the narration, the coding, the meaning-making, the solidarity, the spirituality of communicative interaction – or their inversions – which interest him. Rather, it is the status of such communicative processes as derivation or residue. Communicative acts and the culture that informs them are presented as reflections of the structured habitus rather than as refractions of cultural patterns that are in tension with, and often provide critical commentaries upon, social structure itself. They are presented as microcosms of the macrocosm, not as creations of selves which possess distinctive personhood. In the end, communicative interactions are not interpretive actions at all, but strategic interventions to gain profit from symbolic life. This is simply to say, of course, that the goals, methods, and findings of Bourdieu's research program are truncated and impoverished by the more generalized conceptions of action and order I have analyzed above.

In rejecting interpretation as his goal, however, Bourdieu is not only making an empirical and theoretical argument against the relative autonomy of culture and the authenticity of communication. He is making an epistemological point about the nature and possibilities of science, one which turns out to be rather orthodox in effect. At first glance, of course, Bourdieu's position on science is anything but an orthodox one. He argues (e.g. Bourdieu et al. 1991a [1968] and, more recently, Bourdieu in Bourdieu and Wacquant 1992: 224–60) that the social scientist must never base generalizations upon raw empirical facts, upon social processes as they appear in common sense. Social facts must be worked up, distanciated, theoretically reinterpreted, and put into a reflexive and historical frame. It is in this anti-empiricist vein that Bourdieu introduces the ideologically critical intent of his sociology, frequently referring to the unmasking and liberating implications that differentiate his method of 'socio-analysis' from a merely positivist sociology that has mere explanation as its principal goal. Thus, Bourdieu's empirical studies on education were not aimed simply at the empirical, but are intended also to be ideological – liberating and demystifying – in their effect. They are not only an explanation of how ideas serve class, but an 'unmasking of cultural privilege' that 'destroys the justificatory ideology which enables the privileged classes . . . to see their success as the confirmation of natural, personal gifts' (Bourdieu and Passeron 1979: 71). Similarly, in a recent retrospective look at his early *The Love of Art*, Bourdieu (1993: 265) warns that 'reading this book as a simple, self-contained description of the composition of the European museum-going public . . . is to reduce the real object of research . . . to the apparent object as [the positivist] tradition . . . defines it.' To the contrary, he attests (ibid.), 'this study had something more at stake, at the same time more important and more invisible.'[40]

This avowedly critical and supra-empirical ambition raises the problem of justification: on what grounds can the truth of normatively critical observations be sustained? The Frankfurt School argued that its critical thrust derived from an immanent historical reason, a Hegelian position that rejected objectivity in the empiricist sense. For his part, Habermas posits the normative counterfactual of free speech and the evolutionary development of moral reason. These resorts are not available to Bourdieu because, like Marx himself, he insists on defining his critical perspective as empirical science.

In fact, Bourdieu tries to establish the truth value of his critical evaluations in two different ways, vacillating between social reduction and disciplinary conceit (cf. Frow 1987: 72). In the first mode, which certainly squares with his theory of the social determination of ideas, Bourdieu falsifies social scientific ideas – typically, competing theories that are different from his own – by arguing that they have been warped by the material circumstances within which their authors were forced to write. In this mode Bourdieu continually points to the 'ideological' rather than 'scientific' dimensions of others' work. He even extends this method of truth-by-ascription to the work of Marxists thinkers with whom he disagrees, as when he lampoons Balibar and his structural-Marxist associates as 'prophets' or 'priests' (Bourdieu 1975b: 68).

But it is one thing to argue for the determination of thought by social structure when one studies the consumption behavior of status groups and quite another to apply this reductive and highly restrictive conception to the behavior of scientists, and ultimately, of course, to oneself. For such a sophisticated theorist, Bourdieu seems peculiarly unaware of the vulnerability of his position, which is undermined by the vicious circularity that confronts every radical exercise in the sociology of knowledge. If Bourdieu can dismiss structuralism as the 'professional ideology' (IOW: 31) of anthropologists, for example, how can he attribute to his alternative position any higher degree of interest-independent truth? Geertz (1973) called this self-contradictory epistemology 'Mannheim's paradox,' and it is certainly a dilemma from which this dimension of Bourdieu's theorizing has never been able to escape. Thus, while Bourdieu presents *Homo Academicus*, his most systematic and radical exercise in the sociology of scientific knowledge, as 'sociological-self-analysis ... which owes and concedes nothing to self-indulgent narcisssism,' one which will allow 'the scientific subject [to] gain a theoretical control over his own structures and inclinations' (HA: xii), he never does make an effort, here or elsewhere, systematically to apply such analysis either to the structures that, according to his own theories, must be producing his own work, or, much less, to his own scientific *habitus*, or inclinations. To the contrary, Bourdieu naively suggests that his application of this radical historicizing method to academic work actually allows him, as the practitioner, to escape from its historically relativising effects.[41]

By turning to study the historical conditions of his own production . . . the scientific subject can gain a theoretical control over his own structures and inclinations as well as over the determinants whose products they are, and can thereby gain the concrete means of reinforcing his capacity for objectification . . . In making a scientific analysis of the academic world . . . and appl[ying] it to sociological study itself [one] demonstrate[s] that sociology *can* escape from the vicious circle of historicism and sociologism, and that in pursuit of this end it need only make use of the knowledge which it provides of the social world in which science is produced.

(HA: xii–xiii, original italics)

It may be some sense of this conundrum that accounts for the fact that one also finds in Bourdieu's work the thoroughly conventional claim that validity rests upon a scientific objectivity rooted in disciplinary autonomy. 'Sociology claims an epistemological privilege,' he writes (HA: xiii), because it 'reinvest(s) in scientific practice its own scientific gains.'

Marx suggested that, every now and then, some individuals managed to liberate themselves so completely from the positions assigned to them in social space that they could comprehend that space as a whole, and transmit their vision to those who were still prisoners of the structure. In fact, the sociologist can affirm that the representation which he produces through his study transcends ordinary visions, without thereby laying claim to such absolute vision, able fully to grasp historical reality as such. Taken from an angle which is neither the partial and partisan viewpoint of agents engaged in the game, nor the absolute viewpoint of a divine spectator, the scientific vision represents the most systematic totalization which can be accomplished.

(HA: 31)

Because disciplinarity provides the analyst with distance from the conservative ideological pressures of the social environment, Bourdieu warns against interpretive methodologies that encourage a merely subjectivist slant. He insists that reconstructing meaning via interpretation is subordinate to establishing explanation via correlation and cause. Rejecting the postpositivist idea of a theory-laden, recursive, hermeneutic, and tradition-oriented social science, he denounces as 'theoreticism' and 'scholasticism' the notion that conceptualization and theory-building – much less verification or falsification – are carried out with any significant degree of independence from empirical work (Bourdieu in Bourdieu and Wacquant 1992: 161, 224).

In fact, Bourdieu has recently tried to defend the central concepts of his corpus by arguing that they are empirical rather than theoretical in intent. 'As I have said hundreds of times I have always been immersed in empirical research projects, and the theoretical instruments I was able to produce in the course of these endeavors were intended not for theoretical commentary and exegesis, but to be put to use in new research' (Bourdieu 1993: 271). Insisting that his 'theoretical elaborations' have been devoted exclusively to the task of developing a 'method' for empirical research, Bourdieu argues that they should be viewed not as 'theoretical treatises' but as practical guides for research that 'put forth so many programs for work, observation, and experimentation.' Rather than 'endlessly repeating commentaries and somewhat monotonous criticisms of habitus or some other concept of my making,' he would, in fact, prefer 'comprehension through use.' This preference, of course, is not surprising in itself. What theorist would not prefer to have his concepts used in empirical research rather than criticized in theoretical debates? What is surprising is that Bourdieu actually seems to believe that his concepts deserve to be treated in this way because they were not derived from abstracting ideas or traditions but from the investigation of empirical reality as such. A better indication of his ambivalent yet nonetheless deep commitment to an empiricist realism would be hard to find.

Indeed, despite his rejection of a scientistic sociology of brute facts, and his adherence to a strong program in the sociology of knowledge, Bourdieu's empirical studies are inspired by an empiricist belief that theories can be conceived as covering laws which can be validated or falsified by disciplined and continuous confrontation with empirical facts. Bourdieu sees his theories not as presuppositionally bound and interpretive in intent, but as abstractions that are objective and universal in scope. He describes himself as 'armed with a knowledge of the structures and mechanisms . . . common to all societies' and, therefore, as 'propos[ing] a constructed model that aims at universal validity' (Bourdieu 1993: 272, original italics; cf. Bourdieu 1994: 9 and HA: xii). These universal models establish correspondence rules between propositions and categories of facts, which in turn are tested by comparing them with causal relationships in reality itself.

Yet, just as the sociology-of-knowledge solution to the problem of critical objectivity led to Mannheim's paradox, this objectivist approach generates problems of authorial exceptionalism as well. For certainly Bourdieu would not argue that *most* practicing social scientists have achieved a critical distance from society. How, then, does one differentiate between sociology as a general discipline and the specific type of sociology – the socio-analysis – practiced by Bourdieu? Bourdieu can offer no explanation. Why is his own thought exempted from the vitiating pressures for irrational distinction and field-dependent strategization to which he routinely attributes the work of others, the conformist and conservative academics who form the subjects, or objects, of his empirical work? Why are the observations that emanate from his own sociological work more critical, and thus more true, than those of any other practitioner of social science?

Is it his sense of the failure of both these efforts to establish the objectivity of critical theory that leads Bourdieu to his periodic claims for a reflexive sociology (e.g. Bourdieu and Wacquant 1992, passim; Bourdieu 1993: 274), to the suggestion that he and his co-workers have somehow managed to separate themselves from the conservatizing social domination of knowledge, in both its social and academic forms? To be a reflexive and critical intellectual, Bourdieu acknowledges, means that one has succeeded in freeing one's habitus from its initial social moorings and from the binding distortions of the academic field. But how can Bourdieu explain this freedom, which runs so directly contrary to the entire thrust of his theoretical work? At certain points, in fact, he seems to acknowledge its residual status as an unmoved mover, talking simply about the unpredictable 'awakening[s] of consciousness' (Bourdieu 1988a: 6; cf. IOW: 145) that occasionally allow the formation of tiny but important groups of radical intellectuals. More typically, however, Bourdieu links reflexivity to a variation on the theme of disciplinary conceit. Once socio-analysis provides information about the coerciveness of social forces, knowledgable actors can free themselves from their effects. While 'it is not the sociologist who . . . invents the laws that human practices obey[,] this knowledge gives the sociologist the theoretical mastery of the social determinations of knowledge that can be the basis for the practical mastery of these determinations' (Bourdieu et al. 1991a [1968]: 24–5; cf. HA: xiii).

> It offers the sociologist (and to all others through him or her) the possibility of consciously grasping, so as to choose to accept or to reject . . . the probable stances assigned to him or her by virtue of the definite position he or she occupies in the game that he or she claims to analyze.
>
> (ibid.: 25)

But it is, of course, just such an ability – the ability of 'consciously grasping' in order to make an independent choice – that Bourdieu's theory of action, order, and field has so systematically denied. It is easy to understand how an ideological myth that ascribes ineluctable power to external forces can inspire heroic movements of reflexivity, resistance, and liberation. It is very difficult to understand how a scientific theory that posits a determinate relation between subjective dispositions and objective structures – holding that the former reproduce the latter – can explain the critical ability to choose or reject structural positions in anything but an ad hoc and thoroughly residual way. Indeed, in his more systematic writings about the scientific field, Bourdieu goes out of his way to deny the suggestion that critical social science is a product of a reflexivity vis-à-vis social structure. To the contrary, he insists that radical thinking, like all other kinds of thinking, must be seen as a strategic calculation for domination, one that is determined by, and linked to, the stratified structure of the scientific field.

> The strategies of [scientific] agents are in fact determined, in their leaning more either toward (scientific and social) subversion, or toward conservation, by the specific interests associated with possession of a more or less important volume of various kinds of specific capital, which are both engaged in and engendered by the game.
>
> (Bourdieu 1991c: 7)

At another point, Bourdieu (1975: 40) calls '"radical" ideology' simply 'a thinly euphemized expression of the interests of those dominated in the scientific field.' Far from indicating a distance from habitus and social structure, radical ideology actually represents compliance:

> I continue to believe that as much as, if not more than, conservatism, campus radicalism remains one of the main obstacles to the genuine breaks that social science must make . . . insofar as it allows certain intellectuals to give the appearance of radical critique to the most comfortable submission to intellectual conformity and, thereby, to a particularly well-hidden form of conservatism.
>
> (Bourdieu 1993: 270)

When Bourdieu attempts to explain his own work, he is caught between reduction, which would eliminate his very distinctiveness as a social thinker, and reflexivity, which, while acknowledging this distinctiveness, would fail to explain it in a 'Bourdieuian' way. In one recent autobiographical account, for example, he describes himself as a 'class defector' because, from the very beginning of his years at the prestigious Ecole Normale Supérieure, he was critical of the structures of the intellectual field that such prestigious *grandes écoles* legitimate and dominate. On the one hand, he attributes this class defection to his radical disposition, 'to a particularly sharpened and critical intuition' (ibid.: 269). On the other hand, he explains his radicalism by pointing to social structure, to the asymmetry between the demands of such

Parisian elite institutions and his own more humble social origins, which had formed his initial habitus in an entirely different way:

> If I was able, in a way which seems to me to be rather 'exact,' to objectivize the field that I had just entered, it was undoubtedly because [of] the highly improbably social trajectory that had led me from a remote village in a remote region of southwestern France to what was then the apex of the French educational system.
>
> (ibid.)

In the end, however, Bourdieu cannot allow himself to be explained in such a structural way. The highly improbable social trajectory did not, in fact, determine that his thinking would go in a certain direction; it merely 'predisposed me,' he says (ibid.). Disposition and predisposition, of course, are not at all the same things. One leads to action, the other to a consciousness about the possibility of doing so.

Bourdieu cannot explain his own reflexivity, much less that of others, because he can acknowledge neither the cognitive presuppositions that inform his writing nor the immanent, critical, often utopian strains that inform so much of modernist social science. These presuppositions and ideological strains simultaneously enhance and fundamentally alter the kind of decentering distance that disciplinarity provides. It is not only, or even primarily, disciplinary objectivity that provides sociologists with their critical stance, but rather moral judgments about the normative inadequacies of the empirical world, judgments that are in important ways independent of the structural positions these scientists hold. This capacity for critical judgment is rooted in a socially produced self that is not merely a habitus but actually provides an individualizing point of view, and it is informed by a cultural tradition that has made distanciation, dissatisfaction, and the search for justice some of its central themes. Bourdieu cannot thematize these foundations of critical science, despite the fact that his own presuppositional and ideological commitments are plain to see. Because he cannot do so, he fails to achieve the self-critical reflexivity that is so necessary if emancipatory social theories are to avoid, in their turn, either domination or deceit.

Politics without Civil Society: Domination and Fragmentation in a Society of Fields

In his empirical studies Bourdieu has written about a great many things, and in the short space of an essay I cannot pretend to have examined any of them in the detail they deserve. Yet, in trying to gain some overall perspective on his vision of contemporary society, what may be most important are those things about which Bourdieu has said hardly a word. What we do not find in Bourdieu is the acknowledgment of the empirical, much less the moral, significance of formal democracy, an idea of the meaning or significance of civil society, a conception of the public sphere. We have, instead, an image of a vertical society, of society equated with stratification, with struggles dictated by scarcity and regulated by the egoism of supply and demand. There is no horizontality, neither cross-class solidarities nor national identities which provide opportunities for inclusion, much less any conception of an institutionalized ideal of civility or universalism.[42] There is no conception that religious faith, even in its most devout or radical forms (e.g. Khosrokhavar 1993), is anything other than an instrument for using status in the metaphysical world to gain capital in the earthly one. There is scarcely any attention to how structures of ethnicity (e.g. Wieviorka 1993), gender (e.g. Bloch 1993) or region (e.g. Entrikin 1991; Friedland and Boden 1993) can establish communities and identities that can counter the manifest or hidden injuries of class.

Because there is no sense of a specifically political realm, much less a substantially moral one, in Bourdieu's conceptual armory there is no way to distinguish, in moral or political terms, an authoritarian from a democratic order, an inegalitarian democracy from a more socially just one, or even a fascist society that strives for distinction from a totalitarianism of a leftist kind. It is hardly surprising that, when Bourdieu recently tried formally to define 'the state,' he so intertwined symbolic and material violence that democracy in any substantial sense became impossible to conceive. Announcing that he had 'transformed' the 'famous formula of Max Weber,' Bourdieu (1994: 107, italics added) declared that the state monopolizes 'the legitimate useage of physical *and symbolic* violence.' Why did Weber, by contrast, deliberately conceptualize the state's monopoly of power in terms of physical violence alone? Because, in direct contrast with Bourdieu, he wanted to emphasize that, despite the extraordinary growth in power that the modern state represented, the mental structures of the dominated continue to occupy a separate space. According to Weber, the principles of legitimation are independent both of dominated and dominator alike. Whether states or leaders are understood as acting in a manner consistent with these principles is not something, Weber insisted, that can be determined in advance. The assumption that state power controls symbols and meanings is precisely what Weber tried to avoid when he declared political legitimacy – whether charismatic, traditional, or rational-legal – to be socially contingent. Legitimacy is something that may or may not be conferred on power by those subject to it. If it were otherwise, if power assumed the mantle of authority by definition, it would be impossible to define political opposition and democracy in a sociological way. But this, of course, is precisely the point of Bourdieu's work.

This work has spanned a period during which progressive intellectuals went from ignoring the repressive aspects of Soviet life to participating publicly in support of the dissent that played an increasingly important role in its demise, as the shifting attitudes and actions of an intellectual like Foucault clearly show (Eribon 1991). It is, therefore, not merely an ideological issue but a question of basic theoretical and empirical interest to ask why there is scarcely any reference in Bourdieu's theoretical or empirical studies to the sharply different form of repression that occurs in the Communist version of what Weber called the rational form of legitimate domination. On the few occasions when Bourdieu does refer to domination in Communist societies, indeed, he does so in order to relativize it, downplaying the differences in authority between what he calls 'formally democratic' and Communist regimes. He treats Communist party *apparatchiks*, for example, as no different from representative elites in democratic countries, such as priests, government officers, social movement leaders.

> When a [Communist] apparatchik wants to make a strong ideological point, he moves from I to we. . . . In the 'I' of the representative, the particular interest of the representative must be hidden behind the purported interest of the group. The representative must 'universalize its particular interest,' as Marx said, in order to pass it off as the interest of the group.

This, of course, is precisely the same kind of self-aggrandizing 'officializing strategy' that Bourdieu so consistently attributes to social groups in capitalist democratic societies, whether liberal or conservative, egoistical or seemingly altruistic. While this broad-brush insistence on the repressive elements in democratic capitalist societies is the common stuff of humanistic social criticism, the systematic, sweeping, and corrosive quality of the picture Bourdieu paints seems much more to reflect the kind of 'anti-humanism' that was so self-consciously championed by Althusser in his philosophical attacks on the 'humanistic Marxism' of thinkers like the early Lukács, Gramsci, Fromm, and Kolakowski.[43]

The most vivid illustration of Bourdieu's persistent relativising of the differences between dictatorship and democracy can be found in a lecture he delivered in East Berlin on October 25, 1989. This discussion, later reprinted as a brief essay (Bourdieu 1994: 31–5) in *Raisons pratiques*, represents his only systematic discussion of Soviet-style societies. In the midst of what was certainly one of the most dramatic periods of political emancipation in recent history, this theorist of practical action insisted that state Communist societies represent merely a variation on the domination that marks all developed societies. When Bourdieu gave this lecture it was only a few weeks after East Germany's religiously inspired 'New Forum' protest organization emerged out of nation-wide protests against the Communist government's efforts to celebrate its fortieth anniversary; only one week after protestors outside East Berlin's City Hall angrily shouted 'Give us free elections!' in the faces of the city's party leaders; and only two days after hundreds of thousands of East Germans marched through the streets of Leipzig demanding legalisation of opposition movements (Gwertzman and Kaufman 1990: 159–70). Yet, Bourdieu developed a sociological model of state communism that made no reference to such issues as free assembly or voting, much less to the suppression of critical public opinion or to social movements.

Confusing meta-methodological arguments about nomological versus interpretive science with political arguments about justice, Bourdieu begins by stressing his commitment to a 'universal model' of society that, while 'accounting for historical variation,' does not mistake such variation for a difference in type.* Social scientists must 'break with the propensity for substantialist and "naively realist" thought,' he asserts, for instead of distinguishing the fundamental 'relations' or 'structures' of societies, such a hermeneutical approach focuses only on 'the phenomenal realities in which they manifest themselves.' Despite the fact, in other words, that state communist and democratic capitalist societies seem different, when one looks beneath the surface at the fundamental relations of these societies one discovers that they are basically the same. In each, there is 'the same opposition between the dominant and dominated,' a relation that 'at different moments can be inscribed in phenomenologically different practices.' What determines these surface differences is, of course, the 'different kinds of capital' distributed in different societies. Whereas private, economic capital dominates the other forms in French society, in Soviet-style societies, 'where the other forms of capital are more or less completely controlled,' political capital becomes the dominant form.

---

* The following quotations are all from Bourdieu 1994: 31–5.

Who or what exercises this control over non-political capital is not Bourdieu's concern. This is a political question; he is concerned only with the broadly economic. Not politics and power but capital and its distribution are what interest him. To understand institutional processes in Soviet-style societies one need only develop an 'indicator of political capital' focusing on hierarchical position, social background, and political lineage. Yet, are there not fundamentally important institutions and processes other than various forms of capital, whether in its political, economic, or cultural shape? What about voting, public opinion, and the right to create social movements? Bourdieu goes so far, in fact, as to suggest that Scandinavian-style social democracy represents merely a less radical variation of Soviet societies. Because social democracies also centralize political capital, they too must be seen as 'patrimonial,' as based on a social form 'that assures to its owners a form of private appropriation of public goods and services.' In the Soviet 'variants,' this patrimonial form has simply been pushed to its 'limit.'

My point in this discussion must not be misunderstood. I am not at all suggesting that, either in his political or his personal *practice*, Bourdieu does not distinguish between social control in fascist, communist, and democratic regimes, much less that he is morally sympathetic to authoritarianism in any of its forms. To the contrary, in his personal and political life Bourdieu has offered moral witness against social degradations of many different kinds (e.g. Bourdieu et al. 1993); he has defended the rights of 'bourgeois' intellectuals like Salman Rushdie; he has participated in committees to defend 'elite' secular intellectuals in an Algeria threatened by fundamentalism; he has helped organize an international parliament of intellectuals to protect human rights. My point, in fact, is a very different one. While Bourdieu may embody universalism in his concrete practices, he cannot explain universalism in a theoretical way.

In the earliest work of his theoretical maturity (OTP: 167–8), Bourdieu insists on the importance of distinguishing between the Heideggerian 'doxa' and the liberal notion of 'opinion.' To have a doxic relation to the world is to be habituated to it, to respond to it in an automatic, unthinking, unreflective way. Opinion, by contrast, implies consciousness, deliberate reflection, ideology. Doxa suggests 'a perfectly closed world . . . which has no place for *opinion* as liberal ideology understands it' (OTP: 167, original italics). We have earlier seen how central this doxic conception of habitus is to every element of Bourdieu's work, how he insists that even strategization must assume an unconscious, unreflective form. What we can now understand is that this position also has political and normative force. Despite the ambiguities of his writings on a critical science, Bourdieu's project is, in fact, to negate the notion of reflexivity that lies at the center of the liberal democratic project. While occasionally acknowledging the heroic scientist or the rebellious free thinker, Bourdieu devotes himself primarily to demonstrating the very impossibility of critical thought. The category itself seems to defy the notion that action always derives from a practical base.

> As soon as he reflects on his practice, adopting a quasi-theoretical posture, the agent loses any chance of expressing the truth of his practice. . . . Simply because he is questioned, and questions himself, about the reasons and the raison d'être of his practice, he cannot communicate the essential point, which is that the very nature of practice is that it excludes this question.
>
> (LOP: 91)

Without supposing the capacity for exercising some independent, if historically conditioned, form of universalism or rationality, there can be no conception of the public realm, a notion which is certainly a prerequisite for any theory of democracy. An arena of discourse, responsiveness, narration, and interaction, the public is composed of institutions that center on opinion and that are to one degree or another independent vis-à-vis the demands of other spheres (Alexander and Smith 1993; Calhoun 1992; Cohen and Arato 1992). Bourdieu insists, by contrast, that it is 'the very notion of "personal opinion"' that 'needs to be questioned' (D: 398). Why? Precisely because this notion 'accepts a political philosophy which makes political choice a specifically political judgment [and] which credits everyone with not only the right but also the power to produce such a judgment.' The problem with 'public opinion' is that the notion 'is rooted in the rationalist belief that the faculty of "judging well" . . . of discerning good from bad . . . is a universal aptitude of universal application' (ibid.).

Bourdieu ferociously opposes the very idea of public opinion and the democratic possibilities it presents. He insists '*l'opinion publique n'existe pas*' (public opinion does not exist), at least 'under the form that is given to it by those who have an interest in affirming its existence' (Bourdieu 1980: 200; cf. Bourdieu and Champagne 1989). For Bourdieu, nineteenth-century salons were not, as many historians of civil society have suggested, milieux for public discussion and political debate, but circles of snobbery that functioned simply to allow the circulation and monopolization of market distinction (LOP: 137). Twentieth-century opinion polls do not take the measure of the public, exerting thereby a constraining political force, but are profit-making vehicles upon which 'market constraints' have had 'devastating effects' (IOW: 171; cf. Champagne 1993: 263–4). Newspapers neither narrate the social (Sherwood 1994) nor crystallize opinion; they are mere media for 'expressing' the struggle between dominant and dominated factions of the ruling elite (D: 451–2). Public-oriented statements are simply officializing strategies, according to which 'particular interests [are transmuted] into "disinterested", collective, publicly avowable, legitimate interests' (LOP: 109). Politics itself is nothing other than the 'authorized speech of status-generated competence' (ibid.: 413), speech that produces responses 'compatible with the practical premises of a practical relation to the world' (ibid.: 418). An interviewer once remarked to Bourdieu that 'in your work, you have no room for universal norms.' Bourdieu responded in a revealing way.

> Instead of wondering about the existence of 'universal interests', I will ask: who has an *interest* in the universal? Or rather: what are the social conditions that have to be fulfilled for certain agents to have an interest in the universal?
>
> (IOW: 31, italics added)[44]

Is it any wonder that Bourdieu dismisses public struggles on behalf of 'the people' as merely symbolic strategies designed only to profit social movement leaders themselves (ibid.: 150–55)? No doubt this disparaging position reflects the disillusionment experienced by so many on the French left with the orthodoxy of the French Communist Party. Nonetheless, theorizing social movement leaders, in principle, as egoistical symbolic strategists has fundamentally conservative, anti-political ideological implications. Would Bourdieu dismiss Gandhi or Martin Luther King in the same way? What about Jesus or, perhaps more to the point, Karl Marx himself?[45] Bourdieu devalues and degrades the achievements of those who succeed in gaining mobility, dismisses the working class as lacking developed taste and political rationality, mocks the efforts of social reformers, and is extraordinarily pessimistic about the possibility of creating a better, more just society.[46] One is justified in asking: What kind of critical theory is this?

Bourdieu's writing about the public is so impoverished that it makes one nostalgic for the utopian sincerity of Habermas, whose work (e.g. Habermas 1989 [1962]) underlines the fundamental importance of the public sphere despite its failure to conceptualize how one is actually constructed. Habermas has struggled against the cynical, instrumentalizing strain in Marxist action theory in order to open up a space for sincerity and authenticity in human relations,

qualities that he quite rightly understands as crucial in the conception
and institutionalization of a good society. Because of Bourdieu's
determination to reveal the pervasiveness of egoism, by contrast, his
theory is not only incapable of recognizing the nonstrategic elements
in modern societies,[47] but it is unable to provide the conceptual
resources for explaining how a good society could come about. His
political writing makes us wonder just how theorists like Parsons and
Durkheim, Tocqueville and Dewey, Weber and Simmel – or, in our
own time, thinkers, like Rawls, Walzer, and Boltanski and Thevenot
– could possibly be writing about the same world as he.

When Marxism emerged in the nineteenth century, it was theoretically inadequate, but its insight into the exclusions and inequalities of
early industrial capitalism made it much more empirically right than it
is today. A lot has happened in the hundred years since, as the middle
and working classes in the more developed countries have gained
not only civil but political and social rights. As central elements of
socialist reform became institutionalized inside of Western capitalist
countries, the Marxian version of anticapitalism began to lose its
power as a mass ideology. It has only been more recently, of course,
that the power of Marxism has also began to disappear in the East, as
the social and ethical implications of a theory that denied the very idea
of an independent public life became obvious to all.

History seems to be moving in a different direction than it did during
the years of the intellectual and political formation of Pierre Bourdieu.
His theory was crystallized by the sixties, by a New Left philosophy
and social science that sought to revive and transform Marxist social
theory and that negated bourgeois society in its democratic form.
Yet, while those days are over, the social theory produced by this generational social upheaval remains with us still. In English-speaking
countries, in fact, it has become hegemonic in the intellectual sphere
even as the social conditions that produced it, along with its popular
support and political significance, have all but disappeared.

This symbolic power cannot be explained by economic forces,
nor can it be understood as a strategy for distinction, no matter that it
so often and so effectively fulfills this very task. The influence of
Bourdieu's theory, rather, must be attributed to specifically theoretical
reasons. Neither Bourdieu nor many of his enthusiastic readers seem
to understand what a multidimensional social theory actually requires;
how individual action and its social environments can be interrelated
without reduction; how ideal and material dimensions can be brought
into play without sacrificing their autonomy and reducing one to
the other; how macro can be linked to micro without committing the

fallacy of assuming that the fit between them is entirely neat. Only a theory that is more analytically differentiated than Pierre Bourdieu's can come to grips with the empirical differentiation of the societies in which we live today, with the new possibilities for freedom and solidarity these societies offer, and with the gut-wrenching social conflicts and new forms of domination that so often are its result.

Appendix: A Note on Intellectual Chronology

In this discussion, I have emphasized the internal contradictions in Bourdieu's work and his theoretical strategies to resolve them. I have treated Bourdieu's œuvre, for the most part, as a whole larger than the sum of its parts, and I have interpreted the various parts as responses that Bourdieu has made to exigencies of theoretical logic, to pressures on his general theory that follow ineluctably from certain presuppositional commitments.

Yet, within the limits of such overarching cognitive constraints, theorists retain significant leeway. Faced with the strains imposed by a particular presuppositional position, one may struggle to maintain consistency or one may introduce contradictions by proposing supplemental lines of analysis that differ from this overarching position. Another alternative, of course, is to jettison the overarching position altogether. This choice is not at all uncommon in the biographies of major theorists, but it is rarely acknowledged by them as ever having occurred. One thinks here of what Althusser called the *coupure* between early and late Marx and of the striking shift in perspective that characterized Durkheim's later work.

As we have seen, Bourdieu actually engages in each of these strategies. Arguing for the consistency and strength of his overarching theoretical positions, he has continually presented his mature work as fundamentally 'materialist' and practical in scope. Yet there can be no doubt that he is also sensitive to the limitations of such an orienting position. He responds to these by formulating camouflaged 'normative correctives' orthogonal to his central tenets; at the same time, he undermines these suggestions by introducing complex concepts that circle back toward his 'materialism.' These conflicts in self-representation are exacerbated by the fact that Bourdieu (LOP: 1–22) sometimes describes himself as having undergone an epistemological break, as moving from a more cultural to a more materialistic and agentic structuralism during the early part of his career. Until as late as 1963, he asserts, he was a 'blissful structuralist' (ibid.: 9).

These claims and counterclaims in Bourdieu's own account of his *Bildung* are important to sort out, for they offer authoritative characterizations that contradict some of the interpretations I have made here. This sorting out is made all the more difficult because Bourdieu's insistence on the verisimilitude of his studies leads him to describe every change in his perspective as cumulative and inductive. He presents himself as having been compelled to give up on normative structuralism, for example, because he observed certain undeniable social facts

(LOP: Introduction; IOW: first interview). Thus, he argues that it was his empirical discovery that only a tiny percentage of marriages followed the normative rules which forced him to break with structuralist theory (LOP: 15–17; IOW: 20). In fact, his confrontation with anthropological structuralism developed over an extended period, and his changing relations with this approach were less reflections of his empirical findings than social and intellectual mediations of them.

Bourdieu's reconstruction of his intellectual biography, then, like virtually every other autobiographical account that intellectuals produce, represents a post hoc revision that serves his intellectual interests in contemporary time. Not only has he never been a purely empirical 'scientist' in the narrow sense in which he so often employs this term, but, in fact, he has never been a symbolic structuralist, blissful or otherwise. There have been four phases of Bourdieu's theoretical development, none of which is structuralist in form or content. It is the strikingly different character of these phases that one must keep in mind when efforts are made to substantiate this or that interpretive claim about Bourdieu's work.[48]

(1) Bourdieu's first book (1958) – which constitutes the first five chapters of The Algerians (1962c) – is an ethnography drawn from secondary sources that brought together decades of North African anthropology. Its interest derives primarily from the fact that it was written not from within a structuralist framework but from a structural-functionalist one that fit squarely within the tradition of British social anthropology. To my knowledge, this initial starting point has never been discussed either by Bourdieu or by his interpreters. Yet, it forms an extremely interesting counterpart to the work that follows, suggesting some remarkable shifts. For example, whereas in the later writings Bourdieu persistently identifies collective obligations as profit-taking strategies, in Sociologie de l'Algérie (1958) he stresses the importance and indivisibility of solidarity. In the following, for example, he sees profit-making pacts and solidarity as mutually supporting.

> [Because the economy and farming are harsh] there has been a wide development of pacts ... which are mutually profitable. [A]s if to counteract his powerlessness in regard to things, man had no other recourse than to develop association with other men in a luxuriant growth of human relationships.
>
> (1962c: 2)

Bourdieu also speaks in this early work of 'spontaneous solidarity' (ibid.: 12), insisting that it is mechanical solidarity motivated by altruism and collective obligation that creates adherence to Kabyle norms.

Adhesion to the injunctions of the group is assured by the sentiment of solidarity that is indissociable from the feeling of real fraternity, the sentiment of existing only in and through the group, of existing only as a member of the group and not as an individual in his own right.

(ibid.: 20)

(2) In what seems to have been an abrupt abandonment of the position that underlay his first book, Bourdieu entered into an important but highly compressed Sartrian phase between his originating orientation and the more orthodox, quasi-Althusserian Marxism of the decade that stretched between 1963 and 1972, the date when the run-up to *Outline of a Theory of Practice* (1976), *Esquisse d'une théorie de la pratique* (1972), was published and a new theoretical period initiated. This Sartrian phase emerges first in 'Révolution dans la révolution' (Bourdieu 1961), which was more or less republished as the final chapter in *The Algerians* (1962c), and is full-blown in 'Les Sous-prolétaires algériens' (Bourdieu 1962a) and 'Les Relations entre les sexes dans la société paysanne' (Bourdieu 1962b), both of which appeared in Sartre's journal, *Les Temps Modernes.*

Once again, to my knowledge, this second early phase of Bourdieu's development has never been mentioned, either by the French sociologist or by his interpreters. It left, however, a profound mark on Bourdieu's thought and seems to have been vital in providing a transition to the phenomenological and action theory elements that so marked his later work. Sometimes this influence can be seen in very specific ways. In *Travail et travailleurs en Algérie* (Bourdieu et al. 1963, drawing upon the findings in Bourdieu 1962c), for example, Bourdieu's discussion of the 'modern apartment' recalls the very terms Sartre employed in *Nausea* and *Being and Nothingness.*

As a tool, that is, a material object prepared for a certain use, it announces its future and the future use that one can (and must) make of it if one wants to conform to the 'intention' it contains. . . . It presents itself both as the site of demands to be satisfied and as an alien space to be cleared, humanized, in other words, possessed – and a space which resists.

(Bourdieu et al. 1963: 85)

This phase of Bourdieu's work is radically different from the first and third in that it reflects Sartre's phenomenological-Marxist attention to concepts like alienation, domination, consciousness, and liberation. It also differs from the third, much more traditionally Marxist phase of Bourdieu's writing by the relatively small roles played in it by the concepts of class and mode of production, and by the importance it places, instead, on the violent conflict between colonizer and colonized as the motor source of historical change and consciousness. It was the latter, much more Hegelian approach, of course, that also characterized the highly innovative studies of colonialism by Sartre's followers, Fanon and Memmi. One finds in Bourdieu's writings from this period the same left-existential emphasis on justice, inferiority, self-identity, and even solidarity. For example:

> The discovery that the dominant caste can be held in check and that the order over which it reigned can be shaken led the Algerian to set a higher value on his situation. He no longer felt ashamed of the inferiority of his own situation; he rather regarded as scandalous injustice all that he formerly endured. . . . The feeling of being engaged in a common adventure, of being subject to a common destiny, of confronting the same adversary, of sharing the same preoccupations, the same sufferings and the same aspirations, widened and deepened the sentiment of solidarity.
>
> (Bourdieu 1962c: 161–2)

It is important to recall, as well, that Bourdieu's later 'enemies' – structural anthropology and rationalistic behaviorism – are the very ones that Sartre placed himself against in his own neo-Marxist period, the phase which culminated with the *Critique of Dialectical Reason: Theory of Practical Ensembles* (1976, composed during the 1950s and 1960s). The confrontation between Sartre and Lévi-Strauss was certainly a dominant one in French thought during the 1950s and early 1960s, and Bourdieu closely follows Sartre in the language of his attacks on structural anthropology. Bourdieu's ambitions to restore intentionality to the actor and the meaningfulness of her world also recall Sartre's, although in my view, as I have suggested above, he was markedly less successful than his intellectual mentor in achieving these aims.

(3) The third phase of Bourdieu's work emerges as he incorporates, during the more politicized and intellectually revolutionary period of the 1960s, central categories of the more orthodox, structural-Marxist approach to capitalist society. With these writings, Bourdieu achieves a working theoretical perspective that in important respects does not change throughout the rest of his career. This perspective brought together elements from the praxis theory of Sartre and the early Marx, semiotic references to codes, structural-Marxist class and institutional ideas, and the idea of habitus as the embodiment of objective conditions. Despite what appears to be the eclecticism of this ingestion, and its clearly 'revisionist' ambition, Bourdieu's working theory during this phase was still much more traditionally

neo-Marxist than the body of work that began to appear later, in the early 1970s. This 'orthodoxy' is particularly clear when Bourdieu treats empirical topics to which he will return in his fourth stage, for example the work on education, photography (Bourdieu et al. 1965), and art (Bourdieu et al. 1991b [1969b]).

(4) The fourth phase began around 1970 and seems to have reached full clarity only with the English publication of *Outline of a Theory of Practice* in 1977. It is characterized by an increasingly explicit and polemical confrontation with Marxism (not Marx), attacks which did not appear in the third period; by an increasing emphasis on 'practice,' habitus, and the body; and, in general, by the concerted effort to produce an entirely new, highly generalized, theory of society. Whereas Bourdieu himself insists that his increasing emphasis on 'fields' represents a new and important departure in his work – a fifth phase, as it were – I have expressed my doubts about this claim above. 'Field' was a fairly pronounced emphasis throughout the fourth phase of Bourdieu's work. Indeed, as I have suggested in the body of this essay, despite its high originality Bourdieu's theorizing in this fourth and last phase remains a variant of neo-Marxist cultural theory rather than a genuine break. It is a reconstruction of the Marxist tradition, not the creation of a new one.

I indicated in the opening paragraphs of this essay, however, that such an interpretation has been steadfastly denied by Bourdieu's admirers, who point to the absence of Marxist political cant; the nonexistence of Marxian categories such as an economically driven developmental logic; and the criticisms Bourdieu himself continually makes of Marxism in its vulgar and reductionist forms. Bourdieu is supposed to have made a clean break with Marxism with the 1977 publication of OTP, the theoretical manifesto that, it is argued, actually had been published in French five years earlier, in 1972, and which, even then, had merely articulated the theory that had underlain Bourdieu's empirical studies for many years before. This retrospective claim for continuity lends support to the substantive briefs for the originality and independence of Bourdieu's later, reconstructed theory.

This claim does not sustain a comparison of the actual texts. While Bourdieu's 1977 OTP has a title that directly translates his 1972 *Esquisse d'une théorie de la pratique,* and while his close collaborators have stated that the second, English book with this title is, in fact, no more than a translation of the earlier one in French,[49] this is not the case. *Esquisse* is a transitional and very ambiguous work. On the one hand, there are indeed important continuities between this earlier

'Outline' and the one that appeared five years later; on the other, it differs from the later OTP in highly significant ways.

What *Esquisse* reveals is that Bourdieu's fourth theoretical phase emerged from within, and in its origins was thoroughly intertwined with, the more Althusserian framework of his third. While the chapter of the 1972 book which is actually entitled 'Esquisse d'une théorie de la pratique' does contain theorizing of the type that informs his later work, it is placed only at the end of that book, behind three ethnographic chapters. Much shorter than OTP and denuded of much of its empirical data, the chapter 'Esquisse' assumes here the modest character of a methodological and epistemological discourse rather than a new and original theory of society. In the earlier chapters of the book, moreover, Bourdieu is careful to explicitly indicate the continuities between his new thinking and the more Althusserian approach that he had employed up until that time. In his 'Foreword' to the book, for example, he provides an Althusserian gloss by speaking in language that evokes Althusser's (1970) theory of ideology. He suggests that *Esquisse* avoids the straw man of vulgar materialism by emphasizing that imaginary lived relations are essential to reproducing objective structures. One passage from this discussion is worth quoting in full.

> If the ultimate principle of the entire [Kabyle] system obviously resides in a mode of production which . . . by virtue of the more or less even distribution of land (in the form of small fragmented and dispersed properties) and the weak and stable instruments of production . . . excludes by its own logic the development of productive forces and the concentration of capital – almost the entirety of the agricultural produce enters directly into the consumption of its producer – it is no less true that *the ideological transfiguration of economic structures in the taxonomies of mythic discourse or ritual practice contributes to the reproduction of the structures* consecrated and sanctified in this way. [If] to account for the fact that a social formation is locked into a cycle of perfect reproduction one is content to invoke the negative explanations of an impoverished materialism, such as the precariousness or stability of the techniques of production, one forbids oneself from understanding *the determinate contribution that ethical and mythical representations can bring to the reproduction of the economic order of which they are the product*, through favoring the misrecognition of *the real basis of social existence*.
>
> (Bourdieu 1972: 12, italics added)

While Bourdieu's later analysis of Kabyle marriage strategies – the third of the ethnographic chapters – is conducted largely in the model of exchange theory, he frames its conclusions in a similarly neo-Althusserian mode.

Objectively oriented toward the conservation or augmentation of material and symbolic capital ... marriage strategies are part of a system of strategies of reproduction, understood as the ensemble of strategies through which individuals and groups tend to *objectively reproduce the relations of production associated with a determinate mode of production.*

(ibid.: 127, italics added)

Even the discussion in the 'Esquisse' chapter itself is concluded on a resoundingly materialist note.

Symbolic capital produces ... its own effects to the extent that ... it dissimulates the fact that *the material forms of capital are at its root and, in the final analysis, the origin of its effects.*

(ibid.: 243, italics added)

By the time of the publication of the English version of 'Outline' in 1977 these sorts of highly visible passages directly appealing to Marxist terminology – references to the 'last instance' primacy of the productive mode and equations of symbolic relations with the relations of production – were largely expunged, although by no means entirely eliminated. The 'survivals' that remain tend to be located in the depths of a text (e.g. Bourdieu 1977: 59–60, 188) rather than in key opening and closing statements.

In the preceding more or less historical discussion of the contingent sources of Bourdieu's work, I am not trying to explain the nature of his theorizing, much less evaluate it. To do so would be to repeat the very errors I have criticized Bourdieu himself for making. Rather, I am employing historical and contingent factors to describe shifts in the forms of his theorizing. Unless one distinguishes the forms of his theorizing from its more basic theoretical logic, one may mistake the trees for the forest. At the same time, one must not mistake the forest for the trees. There are significant shifts in Bourdieu's theorizing; yet, at least after the early 1960s, these should be seen as variations on the same chord structure rather than shifts in the theory's key, much less as the creation of theory in a fundamentally different – e.g. an atonal – mode. Whether or not he or his students realize it, even in his later works '*tout se passe comme si*' Pierre Bourdieu remains the leading neo-Marxist critical theorist of the day.

As this discussion suggests, rather than seeing Bourdieu's *Bildung* as having been induced by the accumulation of purely empirical discoveries, it would seem more plausible to link these shifts to theoretical discoveries and reconsiderations which were highly affected, although in no sense determined by, shifts in the social, theoretical, and ideological environments of French intellectuals: from the relatively quiescent mid-1950s; to the Algerian War period of the late 1950s and early 1960s, which brought Sartre particularly into a new political prominence; to the 'sixties,' a highly politicized, quasi-revolutionary period; to the later 1970s and beyond, a period marked by severe intellectual disappointment with the failure of the radical movements, by the rise of post-Marxist theorizing, particularly from Foucault, and by a growing neo-Weberian and neo-functionalist emphasis on the differentiation and pluralization of society. In thinking about the last two phases of Bourdieu's development, in other words, it seems likely that the intensification and subsequent diminution of revolutionary activities and aspirations, which corresponded to the rise and fall of the popularity of Marxist theorizing, had highly significant effects.

Finally, one must acknowledge that for English readers there are additional difficulties in essaying the discontinuities in Bourdieu's development, not only because of the lack of complete translations but also because of often very large discontinuities in publication dates between French original and English translation. One particularly striking example will have to suffice. *Algeria 1960* (Bourdieu et al. 1979), while being published some two years after OTP, during Bourdieu's later, fourth period, actually consists of three strikingly different essays that had been composed in different, earlier phases of his development: (1) 'The Disenchantment of the World' appeared first, in a longer form, in *Travail et travailleurs en Algérie* (Bourdieu et al. 1963), that is, at the height of Bourdieu's second, Sartrian period; (2) 'The Sense of Honour' is noted (Bourdieu et al. 1979: 95) as having first come out in 1966 in an 'earlier English version,' that is, during Bourdieu's third, Althusserian phase; (3) 'The Kabyle House' was initially written for a book of essays dedicated to Lévi-Strauss (Bourdieu 1970), appearing also in *Esquisse* in 1972, both dates belonging to the transitional period segueing into the final phase.

Notes

1. In the Anglophone world this influence is so obvious as to scarcely require documentation, viz. the rate of new translations, the growing number of theoretical commentaries, and the increasing use of Bourdieu's perspective in various kinds of empirical work. These Anglophone treatments have been largely positive and supportive of Bourdieu's own understanding, although there have been a number of critical treatments as well. The situation is more complicated in France, where Bourdieu seems at once omnipresent and *passé*. Leading theorists and researchers will suggest, in private, that Bourdieu is the 'last Marxist in France,' that his ideas are increasingly irrelevant to the very decided turn to interaction, agents, experience, and cultural communication

that has marked French social theory and sociology in the last fifteen years. While these opinions are very rarely exposed in print, Chazel's (1994: 152) remark that 'the principal concerns of the Bourdieu camp hardly seem in tune with the evolving trends' is in this regard emblematic. In public, however, Bourdieu's position is entirely different. He is a dominant intellectual both within the specialized domain of social science and outside it. This commanding position could not be better indicated than by quoting from the preface of a recent collective volume devoted to Bourdieu's work:

> The majority of sociologists questioned during a recent investigation – both researchers and university teachers – considered *Distinction* to be one of the 3 great books in their discipline, after Durkheim's *Suicide* and Weber's *The Protestant Ethic and the Spirit of Capitalism*. ... For those who are capable of expressing an opinion on the question, sociology is Bourdieu – in France in any case.
>
> (LASA 1992: 9–10)

Indeed, outside of a small number of neo-liberal critics in philosophy (e.g. Ferry and Renaud), there has been scarcely any critical commentary on Bourdieu in the French language – 'the oeuvre of Pierre Bourdieu, up until now, has scarcely been discussed' (ibid.: 9). In fact, if one excludes introductory material whose purpose is pedagogical, there exist less than a handful of articles, one ten-year-old book (the collective volume *L'Empire du sociologue*, Paris: La Découverte, 1984), and the 1992 LASA collection itself. By contrast, there has appeared, in French, a fair amount of sympathetic discussion, most of which has appeared in *Actes de la Recherche en Sciences Sociales*, the journal organized by Bourdieu and his associates which has also been a primary site for publishing applications of Bourdieu's theory.

2. In Bloom's (1973) study of poetic influence, he recognized that great poets 'cite' only figures whose effect on their work was relatively slight, typically ignoring the poets upon whose style their own work is most greatly in debt. In their critical study of Bourdieu, two French philosophers have argued, indeed, that 'one must not underestimate the role played by the strategy of constantly denying the model, which is among the conditions that made the survival of ... these [Marxist] currents possible' (Ferry and Renaut 1990: 75). Ferry and Renaut contend that the opposite is true and make a strong case for the epistemological relationship between Bourdieu and Althusserian structuralism.

> French Marxism continues to play a role in intellectual life [in France], despite the current state of crisis within Marxism. It maintains its vitality primarily through the work of Bourdieu. Althusser, and even the work of his disciples, seems very dated, irresistibly recalling a recent but evolved past, like the Beatles' music or the early films of Godard. ... It is the development of Bourdieu's work that undeniably represents the only really lively manifestation of the Marxist 'sensibility' [today].
>
> (ibid.)

3. The most important of these efforts, it must be stressed, have always depended upon establishing significant linkages between Marx's original ideas and competing, typically more contemporary approaches that have insisted on the integrity of moral or expressive action and/or on the relative autonomy of symbolic forms. Weber, Freud, Husserl, Heidegger, Saussure, Durkheim, and Parsons – the central ideas of each of these thinkers have been drawn very heavily into the complex and ambiguous strains of the neo-Marxist tradition (cf. Alexander 1982b). As we will see, Bourdieu's work is no exception.

4. While I very much agree, therefore, with Ferry and Renaut's argument that Bourdieu's theory must be linked to the neo-Marxism of the 1960s, I would suggest that they do not do justice to what is, after all, an authentically reconstructionist impulse in Bourdieu's work. It is just this impulse, as we will see, that creates the complexity and the contradictions of his thought.

5. No doubt it is this commitment to synthesis that has also earned for Bourdieu's efforts considerable sympathy from thinkers (e.g. Taylor 1993) whose interests are markedly outside his particular theoretical domain.

6. Despite the 'systematic' nature of this theoretical analysis of Bourdieu's work, it is important also to understand his theory as a historical project, as a *Bildung*. The following discussion refers occasionally to this developmental aspect. Bourdieu's first published work (Bourdieu 1958), for example, was framed in the structural-functional terms of British social anthropology, and in the years after he came under the influence of Sartre's historical anthropology. Such biographical facts may surprise readers, not only because they contrast with Bourdieu's own sharp criticisms of both tendencies – 'breaks,' after all, are not entirely unfamiliar to any student of social thought – but because they conflict with Bourdieu's understandable tendency to present the history of his own theoretical development in cumulative terms. In the Appendix, I make a brief effort to reconstruct the 'historical' dimension of Bourdieu's theorizing.

7. When referring to the works most frequently quoted in this essay, I employ initials rather than the traditional bibliographic citation. These are: *Outline of a Theory of Practice* (Bourdieu 1977) – OTP; *Distinction* (Bourdieu 1984) – D; *The Logic of Practice* (Bourdieu 1990a) – LOP; *Homo Academicus* (Bourdieu 1988a) – HA; *In Other Words* (Bourdieu 1990b) – IOW. All other references will be in the traditional bibliographic format. Unless otherwise indicated, I quote from the English translations of these works without retranslation.

8. This reference to communication calls to mind the obvious yet nonetheless extremely revealing contrasts between Bourdieu's reconstruction of neo-Marxism and Habermas's, which gives communicative action such pride of place (cf. pp. 192–3, below). Habermas conceptualizes symbolic language, and culture more generally, as opening up the possibility for a form of authentic communication aimed at establishing mutual respect. Yet, while Habermas has a normative framework for evaluating meaning, he has no sociological theory of culture at all. This Bourdieu certainly has, despite the debilitating problems I will discuss below. If Bourdieu has been extremely reluctant to associate himself directly with the Marxist tradition, Habermas – certainly the most important critical theorist in the philosophical world – has been much less so, despite the enormous critical oeuvre he has mounted against it. See, e.g. Habermas's recent remark 'I am the last Marxist' (1992: 469).

9. I say 'earlier' because it seems possible that Bourdieu's formulations of his objections to the structuralist suppression of reflexivity were inspired by Garfinkel's, despite the impression given by Bourdieu (e.g. OTP: 21). Garfinkel's book-length statement of ethnomethodology appeared in 1967, and several well-known essays had been published earlier. Bourdieu's book appeared in France in 1972. At the same time, it must be said that theorists throughout the social sciences were discovering the later Wittgenstein (1968) in the 1960s, encounters that surely could have inspired similar critiques of structuralism and briefs on behalf of 'practical action.' Garfinkel (personal communication) and Bourdieu (IOW: 9) both acknowledge the strong impact on their thinking of Wittgenstein's *Philosophical Investigations*.

10. *Parole*, generally translated as 'speech,' plays a role in structural linguistics that is the equivalent of 'contingency' in the theory of action. *Langue*, translated as 'language,' plays a role that in language theory is equivalent to 'structure.'

11. Contrary to the self-presentation quoted above, in which Bourdieu traces 'habitus' to his effort to carve out a role for agency in his battle with semiotic and Marxist structuralism in the late 1960s and early 1970s, the term seems actually to have appeared much earlier in his work (1962b: 322), where it already carried connotations of a decidedly deterministic kind. The notion that the self is merely an internalized reflection of economic circumstances also broadly informed a contemporaneous discussion (Bourdieu 1962c). Here, in an argument that is curiously parallel to the 'culture of poverty' writings that emerged earlier among American anthropologists committed to modernization theory, Bourdieu analyzes the social psychology of the Algerian subproletariat as a reflection of the uncertainty of their labor market and the powerlessness

of their social position more generally. This objective situation produced an 'apathy and fatalistic resignation' (ibid.: 327) that convinced them it was 'vain to struggle against an all powerful evil' (ibid.: 331), predispositions which spiralled back to reinforce the determinism of class position. This emphasis on passivity vis-à-vis external conditions is in tension with the existential Marxism that also played a strong role in Bourdieu's thinking during this period (see Appendix).

12. I will discuss the 'homology' concept at greater length below.

13. Given Bourdieu's own confusion about the differences between 'relative autonomy' and 'determinism in the last instance,' it is not surprising that his sympathizers, in their own attempts to defend his work, often simply repeat his mistakes. Wacquant (in Bourdieu and Wacquant 1992: 10–13), for example, argues that Bourdieu transcends 'dualities' by converting 'seemingly antagonistic paradigms into moments of a form of analysis designed to recapture the intrinsically double reality of the social world.' In the first moment of Bourdieuian analysis, Wacquant observes, 'we push aside mundane representations to construct the objective structures[,] the distribution of socially efficient resources that define the external constraints bearing on interactions and representations.' In the second moment, 'we reintroduce the immediate, lived experience of agents.' While claiming that the duality of structure/meaning has been abolished, in other words, Wacquant, like Bourdieu himself, actually insists on their hierarchical relationship: 'It should be stressed that, although the two moments of analysis are equally necessary, they are not equal: epistemological priority is granted to objectivist rupture over subjectivist understanding.'

Wacquant presents this reductionist model as a 'reformulation and generalization' of Durkheim and Mauss's argument in *Primitive Classification* (1963 [1903]) and, indeed (cf. Alexander 1982b), in that early effort to understand social representation a significant element of the mechanistic determinism of Durkheim's early and middle periods remains. As Durkheim's thinking about culture continued to develop he emphasized more clearly its relative autonomy, elaborating a theory of the internal dynamics of representations and of the role they played in stimulating rituals and structuring solidarity. Yet, even in Durkheim's later masterwork, *The Elementary Forms of Religious Life*, the relationship between morphology and representation remains a mechanistic one in the approach to the sociology of knowledge.

Wacquant is dissatisfied with *Primitive Classification*, not because it is too mechanistic, but because its theory of morphological determination is not as elaborated as the one developed by Bourdieu. He (Bourdieu and Wacquant 1992: 13) criticizes Durkheim and Mauss's analysis because, while embracing 'the social determination of classifications,' it 'lacked a sound causative mechanism' for actually explaining them. Wacquant believes that Bourdieu has done just this; he has shown that 'social divisions and mental schemata are structurally homologous because they are genetically linked: the latter are *nothing other* than the embodiment of the former' (ibid., italics added). Wacquant is right. In Bourdieu's work, the concept of homology (see below) indicates not relative autonomy but genetic linkage, a kind of mimetic overlapping, or molding, of superstructural dispositions and fields over the economic base.

14. Bourdieu has occasionally pointed to Panofsky's path-breaking art historical studies as a source for his habitus concept, yet Panofsky certainly himself did not dehumanize or strategize motivation in a similar way. To the contrary, despite his historical and sociological understanding of dispositions he stressed their moral and relational elements. 'The concept of *humanitas* as a value,' Panofsky (1955: 1–2) writes of antiquity, 'meant . . . the quality which distinguishes man, not only from animals, but also, and even more so, from him who belongs to the species *homo* without deserving the name of *homo humanus*, from the barbarian or vulgarian who lacks . . . respect for moral values [and] learning.' If we consider Bourdieu's (1985) suggestion that his habitus theory is derived in part from Thomist thought, we can observe the same kind of contrast. For Aquinas, the soul, the will, and the intellect possess a relative autonomy from the body (Anderson 1953). Is it any surprise, then, that the Thomist theory of education and childhood development – with its emphasis on the development of the personality

and moral sensibility – closely parallels that of Piaget? As one scholar puts it: 'To St Thomas Aquinas this power of man's detectability and plasticity is based on his power of abstraction. It is psychic, not neural' (Fitzpatrick cited in Joly 1965: 80).

15. Gramsci's theory of cultural hegemony is the only major neo-Marxist approach that largely escapes such reduction. Conceptualizing socialism as a counterhegemonic quasi-religious power that challenged the ability of capitalist ideology to motivate voluntary adherence to bourgeois society, Gramsci understood relative autonomy because he was nurtured on Crocean idealism and used the Catholic religion as his model for cultural power. This emphasis was one reason that Gramsci's work became such an important polemical target for Althusser, whose conception of relative autonomy always insisted that the economic structure was determinate 'in the last instance.' Althusserian ideas had a formative effect on the third stage of Bourdieu's work, from the early 1960s to the earlier 1970s, and their impact certainly remains visible in the very different, mature theory that has developed since.

16. The body theory of Foucault reveals the same welcome empirical emphasis and the same theoretical problems. The profound similarities between the social theories of Bourdieu and Foucault have not been emphasized in the critical literature, despite the fact that the friendship between them is well known (Eribon 1991: 298–308). If Foucault is the principal model for poststructuralism in history and social philosophy, Bourdieu is the model for the power/knowledge link in the social sciences more narrowly conceived. Bourdieu, of course, remains much more traditionally Marxist than Foucault, and he seems to possess neither the late Foucault's sensitivity to the oppressiveness of noncapitalist, totalitarian power, nor his late-flowering interest in anti-authoritarian counterdiscourses.

While Bourdieu does not often refer to Foucault (but see HA: 63), those who are associated with him clearly see in Foucault's emphasis on the destructive nature of internalized mental structures a kindred theoretical spirit. In Boschetti's praise for Foucault, for example, one sees clearly the link she is making between his ideas and the theory of Bourdieu.

> [Foucault] never ceased to struggle for the progress of truth and justice, practising and organizing a new kind of resistance to power which is conceived above all as a struggle against internalized power in the form of mental structures.
>
> (Boschetti 1992: 89)

17. In a penetrating critical evaluation of the subjective dimensions of Bourdieu's work, Axel Honneth writes in a similar vein:

> The concept of 'habitus' . . . depends on a reductionist model of representation. Because Bourdieu applies it only to the collective perceptual schemata and orientational models ensuring that the economic constraints and chances of a collective life situation are translated into the apparent freedom of an individual way of life, he cannot develop any theoretical sensitivity to *otherwise embedded everyday cultural meanings, nor to their expressive or identity confirming elements.*
>
> (Honneth 1986: 61, italics added)

The comparable observation by Schatzki (1987: 133–4), while simplistic in its equation of critical rationality with a theoretical emphasis on conscious thought, is also worth quoting:

> On Bourdieu's account, conscious thinking cannot produce action. Only subconscious processes, together with bodily dispositions, achieve this. . . . Thought, in other words, is a mere accessory to behavior. That it phenomenologically appears to people that they sometimes orchestrate their behavior according to what they think, is an illusion. . . . Human beings, therefore, are at the mercy of the habitus inhabiting them . . . and conscious reflection offers no avenue for escaping its embrace.

18. It might be remarked, in this context, that by exclusively emphasizing trust rather than differentiation in the ego's early socialization, Giddens's (1984) theory of the self distorts the Eriksonian approach upon which it ostensibly relies.

19. During this highly compressed Sartrian phase (see Appendix) – the same period when Bourdieu first introduced the notion of habitus – Bourdieu occasionally offered strong arguments for a more independent self which sustained a real reflexivity. Consider, for example, Bourdieu's discussion of the heavy bearing and clumsiness of the male peasant, which ill-equipped him to participate effectively in the dances that provided the opportunity for meeting potential wives in post-traditional societies. While Bourdieu insists, in the first place, that this heaviness results from the internalization of the peasant mode of production and social structure, he goes on to argue that it was not simply the clumsiness itself but the peasant's reflection on his clumsiness that really got in the way of marriage. 'He is embarrassed about his body and in his body', Bourdieu writes. It is 'because he knows [saisit]' himself in this way that the peasant has 'an unhappy consciousness [une conscience malheureuse]' (Bourdieu 1962b: 324). Bourdieu concludes, in fact, that the peasant's 'social and economic condition affects the marriage situation principally via the mediation of consciousness' (ibid.: 325). This phrase, 'unhappy consciousness,' comes from Hegel's discussion of the master–slave relationship in The Phenomenology of Mind, a discussion that Kojève injected so forcefully into the French reading of Marx in the 1930s and 1940s and which became central to Sartre's generation of neo-Marxist intellectuals.

20. 'While the mediation of the habitus can be effective in so far as it is self-modifying in response to practical reality, it is in fact illusory, at least as far as the actor is concerned, since he is credited with no real autonomy. Only the deficiency of these habituses, that is to say the extent to which they lag behind present reality, allows us to escape the dominant logic of reproduction, and it is only in this indirect way, and therefore to a very limited extent, that the habitus can be regarded, stricto sensu, as a "principle of invention"' (Chazel 1994: 152).

21. I discuss Bourdieu's field theory in a separate section, below.

22. The use of the phrase 'in the last analysis' in the founding theoretical work of Bourdieu's mature period (see Appendix) is telling, for it illustrates in a concrete and textual manner the strongly neo-Marxist dimension of his causal frame. In the neo-Marxist tradition the phrase derives from Engels's 1962 [1890] famous 'Letter to Bloch,' in which Marx's surviving co-author sought to defend the historical materialism that he and Marx had created against charges of monocausality. Engels did so by insisting that he and Marx had recognized that in any historical situation there were a plurality of different kinds of historical forces in play, that they had only insisted that economic and class factors were determinate 'in the last instance.'

23. In the following discussion I employ the terminology from Action and Its Environments (Alexander 1988b: 301–33), which suggests that action-processes can be seen as simultaneously involving strategization, typification, and invention. These processes articulate with the more structured 'environments' of action; the internal environments are personality and culture, the external are the actors and institutional domains of the social system (Cf. Alexander 1995b).

24. In this battle with Mauss's ghost, Bourdieu's situation parallels that of many other cultural materialists in anthropology, for whom Mauss's gift theory has also been the bogeyman. In his early, Marxist period, for example, Sahlins (1972: 149–85) devoted a seminal essay to providing a Marxian interpretation of the hau of the gift. In a manner that is similar to Bourdieu's, Sahlins condescendingly rebukes Mauss for mystifying what is, after all, merely an overtly instrumental act: 'The Maori [tribe] was trying to explain a religious concept by an economic principle, which Mauss promptly understood the other way around and thereupon proceeded to develop the economic principle by the religious concept' (ibid.: 157). In the most ambitious and sustained French criticism of Bourdieu, Caillé (1992) employs an anti-exchangist perspective inspired by Mauss.

25. Which is precisely the opposite move to the one Boudon has recently made in

his intriguing effort to escape from the contradictions of rational choice theory. Boudon (1993) insists that actors consciously conceive of themselves as rational – as having 'good reasons' – but he acknowledges that the unconscious motivations and inspirations of action are rooted in the moral order.

26. The reasoning in this paragraph draws from the arguments about theoretical logic developed in Alexander (1982a). I take the liberty here of quoting directly: 'Whether or not an element functions as condition is not determined by its corporeal nature, for an ideal element may function objectively if the sanctions that sustain it make it stand in relation to the actor as an unmovable force. In this case, the actor adopts toward it an instrumental motive, treating it as an [objective] condition rather than an end in itself' (ibid.: 189).

27. Elster (1990: 90) gets at this vulgar functionalism when he criticizes Bourdieu's 'incessant use of the phrase "*tout se passe comme si*"' (everything happens as if) in order to suggest that action consciously guided by a personal strategy seems virtually always to lead to an outcome that is functional for the powers that be. While Elster finds functionalism at work, Bourdieu himself insists that the reasons for this coincidence between action and systemic result can be found in the fact that actions are unconsciously strategic, permeated by a kind of omniscient rationality. Indeed, arguments that individual rationalities lead to appropriate system outcomes is a vice often exhibited by theories that employ ideas of rational choice. See, in this regard, Edles's (forthcoming) criticism of the plethora of rational choice approaches to democratic transitions in Latin America and Europe, which attribute the success of the transitions to the far-sighted cooperative pacts made by rational, forward-looking elites.

28. DiMaggio's (1979: 1468–9) sarcastic observation does not seem entirely misplaced: 'Capitals proliferate: in addition to economic, cultural, and symbolic capital, we have linguistic capital, social capital, academic capital, scholastic capital, credentialled cultural capital, capitals of authority and of consecration, university, scientific, and artistic capital. No doubt there are others.'

29. Van den Berg (1991: 14–15) has emphasized precisely this proximity to Weberian closure theory in Bourdieu's recent work, arguing from this proximity that his field theory signifies no real theoretical innovation.

> Bourdieu's depiction of kinship relations as outcomes of, and resources in, struggles between groups and individuals is in fact indistinguishable from accounts that neo-Weberian conflict theorists would give. . . . Oddly enough, Bourdieu seems less than fully conversant with this tradition even in the area of stratification theory which is, after all, his own principal speciality. . . . It is as though such rather standard fare of stratification theory as . . . 'labour aristocracy,' 'credentialism,' and '*occupational licensure*,' or (neo-)Weberian concepts like social closure, exclusion and usurpation . . . were entirely new to Bourdieu.

This conflation of Bourdieu's field theory with the closure approach overstates the case, however, as I indicate below.

30. Despite these clear signals from Bourdieu, and the fairly straightforward arguments for reductionism he makes in most of his texts, there are social scientists who continue to view field theory merely as describing a kind of indeterminate 'interdependence' between social spheres rather than a form of determinant dependence. For example, Ringer (1992) presents his work on the history of French intellectuals as being informed by Bourdieu's model of the intellectual field. Yet there is virtually nothing in his nuanced empirical account of the historical formation of the French academy that betrays the influence of field theory in its strong form. Indeed, there is much in Ringer's account that contradicts Bourdieu's field theory.

31. In his criticisms of Goldmann's use of homology, the neo-Marxist literary critic Fredric Jameson attacks the concept for implying 'structural parallelism.'

> What is unsatisfactory about this work of Goldmann's is not the establishment of a historical relationship among these three zones or sectors, but rather the simplistic and mechanical

model which is constructed in order to articulate that relationship, and in which it is affirmed that at some level of abstraction the 'structure' of the three quite different realities of social situation, philosophical or ideological position, and verbal and theatrical practice are 'the same.'

(Jameson 1980: 43–4)

32. Anne Kane's (1991) conception of analytic and concrete autonomy is the best recent discussion of the complex possibilities involved. She argues that it is necessary to recognize two kinds of autonomy in order to gain a thorough understanding of culture and society relations. The analytical autonomy of culture means that it possesses an internal structuration that is different and cannot be adduced or deduced from either social or psychological structures. Yet to recognize analytic autonomy in culture is not to specify what its relationship to social system institutions and process will be. This must be determined empirically for each specific historical relationship, although, given the analytic autonomy of culture, the causal relation can never be simply one-way. Cf. Alexander (1988b).

33. It should be added that these studies are also highly redundant, a major problem that has been somewhat obscured by the fact that, until recently at least, many French works were not translated. When the entirety of Bourdieu's corpus is examined, however, it is apparent that Bourdieu and his co-authors plow the same ground in a number of different books, often taking over entire chunks of text and manipulating the same, or very familar, samples of data, and coming up with what appear to be virtually similar results. Thus, there is not one book on mass education, on higher edcuation, on consumption, on aesthetics, but two or more on each of these empirical domains reiterating the same themes and findings. This puzzling redundancy is true for the two major theoretical works as well. *Logic of Practice*, published eight years after *Outline of a Theory of Practice*, is eerily similar to it. In Caillé's (1992: 187) words, '*Le Sens pratique* [LOP] en est la reprise directe.'

34. By emphasizing the role that the structuralist approach to class plays in Bourdieu's empirical analysis of fields, I am aware that this seems to contradict the author's own insistence that he has rejected the substantialist approach to class for a constructivist one. It is true that Bourdieu eschews the tendentious discussions of just what specific structural properties define class position and focuses more on processes involved in status and class consciousness. At the same time, as will become clear below, Bourdieu's class understanding is by no means antistructural. His analyses of class behavior extrapolate from arguments about the distribution of resources to different strata, and class actors can reconstruct the positon they are given by society only to the degree that shifts in their external material environments allow them to do so. If classes do not become 'actors' in his theory, it is not so much because Bourdieu has adopted a constructivist approach to class as it is because in his theory he allocates such small space to political and public life, as I will suggest in my concluding section, below.

35. As Ferry and Renaut emphasize, what Bourdieu objects to in the Marxist approach to ideas is that 'in the Marxist tradition class interest has too often been defined *without mediation, directly or brutally*' (1990: 77, italics in original). Their argument that Bourdieu's 'sociology is less a break with the Marxist practice of reducing behaviors to the class interests that they are supposed to explain than merely a more subtle variant of the same practice' (ibid.) is right on the mark.

36. The very distinctiveness of educational processes, in other words, the very difference in their feeling and texture from economic relationships, is precisely what allows this field to play its fundamentally reproductive role in capitalist society. What better example can one find of how Bourdieu emphasizes the autonomy of the field in order, paradoxically, to demonstrate the overarching control of the larger system?

37. 'It is curious,' Caillé writes (1992: 155), that 'Bourdieu never directly confronts . . . the classical question of social mobility':

> Everything in his analyses leads one to suppose that such mobility is either virtually zero, or else contrived and irrelevant. One is entitled to ask, indeed, what would remain of Bourdieu's sociology if upward mobility were not reduced to such a tiny stream.
>
> (ibid.)

38. While there have been penetrating critiques of Bourdieu's early work by specialists in education (e.g. Halsey et al. 1980), representatives of 'the American school' of stratification have not yet made an effort to evaluate systematically his quantitative findings or the empirical claims of his stratification theory more generally.

39. Lamont's criticism of Bourdieu's theory goes, in fact, well beyond this specific empirical point. Indeed, the broader conclusions she draws from her empirical findings on the status criteria employed by upper-middle-class managers in France and the United States – see particularly the section 'Differentiation, Hierarchy, and the Politics of Meaning' (Lamont 1992: 177–88) – are presented as falsifying some of the central tenets of Bourdieu's perspective on symbolic behavior and stratification, which in certain other respects Lamont makes use of herself. These conclusions confirm many of the criticisms which I have developed here on more theoretical grounds. Lamont shows, for example, that moral judgments about such things as honesty and altruism are employed almost as often by the French – and more often by the French outside Paris – as are aesthetic judgments that emphasize mastery over high culture. More generally, and more importantly, she shows that Bourdieu's perspective makes it impossible for him to explain why so many of the most important cultural judgments made even by high-status social actors are unrelated to their position in the stratification system. Rather than efforts to draw invidious distinctions or to legitimate domination, Lamont shows, cultural evaluations often are motivated by efforts to maintain individual integrity or even to extend solidarity across group lines. On these grounds, she concludes, Bourdieu's understanding of the 'field of power' as a zero-sum game is inadequate.

40. In terms of recent disputes in Anglo-American discussions in epistemology, Bourdieu is adopting a 'realist' position, which is typically presented as differentiated not only from a relativist position but also from a positivist one that is supposedly content with law-like descriptions of the visible surface of the social rather than seeking to explain deeper, less visible structures, in a supposedly more radical way. This distinction, typically advanced by the very authors who call themselves realists, is a fuzzy one, however; it conflates epistemological claims – generally valid ones – with ontological and moral issues about the particular nature of the social world. This conflation produces in much of the realist tradition the kinds of problems of justification I refer to below.

41. Is it an awareness of the contradictions of this position that later induced Bourdieu to suggest that in writing *Homo Academicus* he was, despite appearances to the contrary, actually applying his method to himself?

> The harshest and most brutally objectifying analyses [in HA] are written with an acute awareness of the fact that they apply to he who is writing them. And, moreover, with the knowledge that many of those concerned by them will not think for one moment that the author of this or that 'cruel' sentence bears it along with them. Consequently, they will denounce as gatuitous cruelty what is in fact . . . a socioanalysis. (I have in mind here several passages which separated me from some of my best friends. I have had . . . very dramatic clashes with colleagues who perceived very accurately the violence of the objectivation but who saw a contradiction in the fact that I could objectivize without thinking of myself, while of course I was doing it all the while.)
>
> (Bourdieu in Bourdieu and Wacquant 1992: 63)

It is one thing, however, to be '*thinking* of oneself' when one is objectifying others' work by reducing them to a positon in the academic field, and quite another to *write* about one's own work, publicly, that way. This is precisely Mannheim's paradox, the very revealing inconsistency in the situation of those who practice a strong program in the sociology of knowledge: no sensible person – one who wishes his or her work to be taken as cognitively valid – would present his or her own work in the same way.

42. 'What disappears completely [in Bourdieu's theory], and this is rather strange for one who appeals to the sociological tradition, is any represention of the social totality – even the least trace of it – in which fields and actors are necessarily joined. [It is] as if this totality were emptied of any capacity for transcendence vis-à-vis fields and actors, as if it merely had the status of a material reality [which was] reducible to the calculus of material interests by actors defined by their material practice alone. Nothing is more striking, in Bourdieu's work, than the abscence of any analysis of collective entities like "society," "nation," "democracy," etc. Entities like these must exist first in the mind and in the subtle layers of language – in symbolic form, in other words – before having the power to be crystallized in objects and practices' (Caillé 1992: 218).

43. That Bourdieu does not distinguish the specifically political, much less the democratic, was no doubt at the root of the intellectual enmity that the older Raymond Aron publicly expressed toward his former student. Although he never evokes Bourdieu's name, could Aron have been writing about anybody else in the despairing *cri de coeur* that marks the conclusions of his *Memoirs*?

> In an age dominated by ideas of liberty and equality, sociologists belong more than ever to the school of suspicion. They do not take at face value the language that social actors use about themselves. The boldest or most pessimistic, no longer possessing an image or a hope of the good society, consider their own with merciless severity.... Marxism no longer plays the role of crushing democratic-liberal regimes under the utopia of the classless society or the example of Soviet reality. [But] it may help to foster a kind of nihilism. By insisting on the arbitrary nature of values and the inequality of interpersonal relations in communities that are, in relative terms, the least tyrannical, one ends up by not recognizing the most obvious facts: although modern society reproduces itself – it would not be a society if it did not reproduce itself – it is changing more rapidly than all past societies. And the liberal order remains different from the tyrannical order offered to us by the Soviet Union. Whoever sees only a difference in degree between the ideology of the state in Moscow and 'symbolic violence' in Paris, blinded by 'sociologism,' finally obscures the fundamental questions of the century.
>
> (Aron 1990: 481–2)

44. There is actually one moment, in a discussion of what he calls 'the peculiar history of reason,' where Bourdieu acknowledges that univeralism exists. He insists on explaining it, however, as a functional effect, a by-product, of strategic behavior, not as an actually existing social fact.

> Under certain conditions, that is, in certain states of this field of struggles for symbolic power that indeed is the scientific field, these strategies produce their own transcendence, because they are subjected to the crisscrossing censorship that represents the constitutive reason of the field. [In this way,] the anarchic antagonism of particular interests is converted into a rational dialectic ... where the war of all against all transcends itself through a critical correction of all by all.... Reason realizes itself in history only to the degree that it inscribes itself in the objective mechanisms of a regulated competition capable of compelling interested claims to monopoly to convert themselves into mandatory contributions to the universal.
>
> (Bourdieu 1991c: 20–22)

Or, as he has recently put the issue in a succint way: 'The profit from universalisation is without doubt one of the historical motors in the progress of the universal' (Bourdieu 1994: 132).

45. It is revealing to contrast Bourdieu's work in this regard with that of the other French social theorist in his generation to whom he is most often compared – Alain Touraine. Because Touraine's attention to agency is much more substantial and explicitly humanistic (cf. Dubet 1994), it is natural that he would pay so much more attention

to the creative role and significance of social movements. It follows, as well, that he gives more theoretical respect, and empirical attention, to social resistance against authoritarian societies (e.g. Touraine et al. 1983), and to democracy itself (Touraine 1994). For a more recent discussion that highlights the positive and critical role of social movements and their leaders, and which does so specifically by emphasizing the role of culture rather than strategy, see Eyerman and Jamison (1991).

46. For example, speaking to East German intellectuals and students in the midst of the exhaltation of '89', Bourdieu tries to undermine the sense that the participants were heroes; he negates the possibility of idealism in principle and reduces their motives to base self-interest. 'Everything leads one to believe,' he argues (1994: 34–5), 'that the changes that have occurred recently in Russia and elsewhere find their principle in the rivalries between the owners of political capital ... and the owners of scholarly capital.' Bourdieu describes the latter group as 'the most inclined to impatience and to revolt against the privilege of the owners of political capital.' Those who own scholarly capital, moreover, have succeeded precisely because they were clever enough to turn against the Nomenklatura 'the [very] professions of faith, both egalitarian and meritocratic, which are fundamental to the legitimacy it claims.'

47. '[Habermas's] "ideal speech situation" becomes a reality when social mechanisms of communciation and of exchange are established, mechanisms that impose the unrelenting censorships of well-armed criticism, often through the quest for domination, and outside of any reference to moral norms' (Bourdieu 1991c: 21).

48. I should stress here that this account – which is preliminary and highly schematic – draws only from published papers and autobiographical accounts. I have had no access to Bourdieu's private ideas or interests insofar as these are not reflected in his published work. While it is perfectly possible that the public and private Bourdieus are, in fact, very different, it remains useful to reconstruct the public work, since it is this which forms the basis not only for Bourdieu's statements about his *Bildung* but for those of others.

49. In the first lines of his 'Translator's Foreword' to OTP, Bourdieu's long-time translator, Richard Nice, offers this highly ambiguous testimony:

> Outline of a Theory of Practice was first published in French in 1972 (*Esquisse d'une théorie de la pratique*). However, this English text incorporates most of the changes which Pierre Bourdieu has made since then ... [in addition] the order of exposition is recast, and partly for reasons of space, the ethnographic chapters with which the French edition opens have been curtailed.
>
> (OTP: vii)

In the 'Bibliography of the works of Pierre Bourdieu, 1958–1988, compiled by Yvette Delsaut' (IOW: 199–218), OTP is listed in the 1972 section (ibid.: 205) as one of the multiple translations of *Esquisse*.

References

Alexander J.C. (1982a) *Theoretical Logic in Sociology, Vol. 1: Positivism, Presuppositions, and Current Controversies*. Berkeley and Los Angeles: University of California Press.

Alexander J.C. (1982b) *Theoretical Logic in Sociology, Vol. II: The Antinomies of Classical Thought: Marx and Durkheim*. Berkeley and Los Angeles: University of California Press.

Alexander J.C. (1988a) 'The New Theoretical Movement,' pp. 77–101 in N.J. Smelser, ed., *Handbook of Sociology*. Los Angeles: Sage.

Alexander J.C. (1988b) *Action and Its Environments*. New York: Columbia University Press.

Alexander J.C. (1990) 'Introduction: Understanding the "Relative Autonomy" of Culture,' pp. 1–27 in Alexander and S. Seidman, eds, *Culture and Society: Contemporary Debates*. New York: Cambridge University Press.

Alexander J.C. (1995a) 'Reduction and Deceit in Social Theory,' in Alexander, *Neofunctionalism and After*. New York and Oxford: Blackwell.

Alexander J.C. (1995b) 'Beyond Neofunctionalism: Action, Culture, and Civil Society,' in Alexander, *Neofunctionalism and After*. New York and Oxford: Blackwell.

Alexander J.C. and P. Colomy, eds (1990) *Differentiation Theory and Social Change*. New York: Columbia University Press.

Alexander J.C., B. Giesen, N.J. Smelser, and R. Munch, eds (1987) *The Micro–Macro Link*. Berkeley and Los Angeles: University of California Press.

Althusser L. (1970) 'Ideology and Ideological State Apparatuses,' pp. 127–86 in Althusser, *Lenin and Philosphy and other Essays*. New York: Monthly Review Press.

Anderson, E. (1953) *The Human Body in the Philosophy of St. Thomas Acquinas*. Washington: Catholic University Press of America.

Aron, R. (1990) *Memoirs: Fifty Years of Political Reflection*. New York and London: Holmes & Meier.

Benveniste, E. (1985) 'The Semiology of Language,' pp. 226–46, in R. Innis, ed., *Semiotics*. Bloomington: Indiana University Press.

Blau, P., and O.D. Duncan (1967) *The American Occupational Structure*. New York: Free Press.

Bloch, R.H. (1993) 'A Culturalist Critique of Trends in Feminist Theory.' *Contention* 2 (Spring): 79–106.

Bloom, H. (1973) *The Anxiety of Influence*. London: Oxford University Press.

Boltanski, L., and L. Thevenot (1991) *De la Justification*. Paris: Gallimard.

Boschetti, A. (1992) 'Jean-Paul Sartre: A Paradigm Case of the Modern Intellectual,' pp. 81–9 in N. Kauppi and P. Sulkunen, eds, *Vanugards of Modernity: Society, Intellectuals, and the University*. Jyvaskyla, Finland: University of Jyvaskyla Press.

Boudon, R. (1993) *L'Art de se persuader*. Paris: Fayard.

Bourdieu, P. (1958) *Sociologie de l'Algérie*. Paris: Presses Universitaires de France.

Bourdieu, P. (1961) 'Révolutions dans la révolution.' *Esprit* 1: 27–40.

Bourdieu, P. (1962a) 'Les Sous-proletaires algériens.' *Les Temps Modernes* 199: 1030–51.

Bourdieu, P. (1962b) 'Les Relations entre les sexes dans la société paysanne.' *Les Temps Modernes* 195: 307–31.

Bourdieu, P. (1962c) *The Algerians*. Boston: Beacon.

Bourdieu, P. (1968) 'Outline of a Sociological Theory of Art Perception.' *International Social Science Journal* 10 (Winter): 589–612.

Bourdieu, P. (1970) 'La Maison Kabyle ou le monde renversé,' pp. 739–58 in J. Pouillon and P. Maranda, eds, *Echanges et communications: Mélanges offertes à Claude Lévi-Strauss*. Paris and the Hague: Mouton.

Bourdieu, P. (1972) *Esquisse d'une théorie de la pratique*. Geneva: Droz.

Bourdieu, P. (1973) 'Cultural Reproduction and Social Reproduction,' pp. 71–112 in R. Brown, ed., *Knowledge, Education, and Cultural Change*. London: Tavistock.

Bourdieu, P. (1975a) 'The Specificity of the Scientific Field and the Social Conditions of the Progress of Reason.' *Social Science Information* 14 (6): 19–47.

Bourdieu, P. (1975b) 'La lecture de Marx: quelques remarques critiques à propos de "Quelques remarques à propos de *Lire le Capital*".' *Actes de la recherche en science socials* 5/6: 65–79.

Bourdieu, P. (1977) *Outline of a Theory of Practice*. Cambridge: Cambridge University Press.

Bourdieu, P. (1980) 'L'Opinion publique n'existe pas,' pp. 222–35 in Bourdieu, *Questions de sociologie*. Paris: Editions de Minuit.

Bourdieu, P. (1984) *Distinction: A Social Critique of the Judgement of Taste*. Cambridge, Mass.: Harvard University Press.

Bourdieu, P. (1985) 'The Genesis of the Concepts of "Habitus" and "Field."' *Sociocriticism* 2 (2): 11–24.

Bourdieu, P. (1987a) 'La Dissolution du religieux,' pp. 117–23 in Bourdieu, Choses dites. Paris: Editions de Minuit.
Bourdieu, P. (1987b) 'La Délégation du fétichisme politique,' pp. 185–202 in Bourdieu, Choses dites. Paris: Editions de Minuit.
Bourdieu, P. (1988a) Homo Academicus. Cambridge: Polity Press.
Bourdieu, P. (1988b) 'On Interest and the Relative Autonomy of Symbolic Power.' Working Papers and Proceedings of the Center for Psychosocial Studies, no. 20. Chicago: Center for Psychosocial Studies.
Bourdieu, P. (1989) La Noblesse d'état: Grandes écoles et l'esprit de corps. Paris: Editions de Minuit.
Bourdieu, P. (1990a) The Logic of Practice. Cambridge: Polity Press.
Bourdieu, P. (1990b) In Other Words: Essays toward a Reflexive Sociology. Cambridge: Polity Press
Bourdieu, P. (1991a) Language and Symbolic Power. Cambridge: Polity Press.
Bourdieu, P. (1991b) The Political Ontology of Martin Heidegger. Cambridge: Polity Press.
Bourdieu, P. (1991c) 'The Peculiar History of Scientific Reason.' Sociological Forum 6 (1): 3–26.
Bourdieu, P. (1993) 'Concluding Remarks: For a Sociogenetic Understanding of Intellectual Works,' pp. 263–75 in C. Calhoun, E. Puma, and M. Postone, eds, Bourdieu: Critical Perspectives. Chicago: University of Chicago Press.
Bourdieu, P. (1994) Raisons pratiques: Sur la théorie de l'action. Paris: Seuil.
Bourdieu, P. et al., eds (1993) La Misère du monde. Paris: Seuil.
Bourdieu, P., and P. Champagne (1989) 'L'Opinion publique,' pp. 204–6 in Y. Afanassiev and M. Ferro, eds, 50 idées qui ébranlèrent le monde: Dictionnaire de la glasnost. Paris: Editions Payot.
Bourdieu, P., and J.-C. Passeron (1977) Reproduction in Education, Society and Culture. London: Sage.
Bourdieu, P., and J.-C. Passeron (1979) The Inheritors: French Students and Their Relation to Culture. Chicago: University of Chicago Press.
Bourdieu, P., and L.J.D. Wacquant (1992) An Invitation to Reflexive Sociology. Chicago: University of Chicago Press.
Bourdieu, P., A. Darbel, J.-P. Rivet, and C. Seibel (1963) Travail et travailleurs en Algérie. Paris: Mouton.
Bourdieu, P., L. Boltanski, R. Castel, and J.-P. Chamboredon (1965) Un Art moyen: Essai sur les usages sociaux de la photographie. Paris: Editions de Minuit.
Bourdieu, P., A. Darbel, J.-P. Rivet, and C. Seibel (1979) Algeria 1960. Cambridge: Cambridge University Press.
Bourdieu, P., J.-C. Chamboredon, and J.-C. Passeron (1991a [1968]) The Craft of Sociology: Epistemological Preliminaries. Berlin and New York: Walter de Gruyter.
Bourdieu, P., A. Darbel, and D. Schnapper (1991b [1966]) The Love of Art: European Art Museums and Their Publics. Cambridge: Polity Press.
Brubaker, R. (1985) 'Rethinking Classical Theory: The Sociological Vision of Pierre Bourdieu.' Theory and Society 14: 745–75.
Caillé, A. (1992) 'Esquisse d'une critique de l'économie générale de la pratique.' Cahiers du LASA/Lectures de Pierre Bourdieu 12–13: 109–220.
Calhoun, C, ed. (1992) Habermas and the Public Sphere. Boston: Beacon.
Champagne, P. (1993) 'La Vision d'état,' pp. 261–9 in Bourdieu et al., eds, La Misère du monde. Paris Seuil.
Chazel, F. (1994) 'Away from Structuralism and the Return of the Actor: Paradigmatic and Theoretical Orientation in Contemporary French Sociology,' pp. 143–63 in P. Sztompka, ed., Agency and Structure: Reorienting Social Theory. Amsterdam: Gordon and Breach.
Cohen, J. and A. Arato (1992) Civil Society and Political Theory. Boston: MIT Press.
Dahrendorf, R. (1968) 'Homo Sociologicus,' pp. 19–87 in Dahrendorf, Essays in the Theory of Society. Stanford: Stanford University Press.

DiMaggio, P. (1979) 'Review Essay: On Pierre Bourdieu.' *American Journal of Sociology* 84 (6): 1460–74.

Dubet, F. (1994) *La Sociologie de l'éxperience*. Paris: Seuil.

Durkheim, E. and M. Mauss (1963 [1903]) *Primitive Classification*. Chicago: University of Chicago Press.

Eco, U. (1985) 'The Semantics of Metaphor,' pp. 247–71 in R. Innis, ed., *Semiotics: An Introductory Anthology*. Bloomington: Indiana University Press.

Edles, L. (1995) 'Rethinking Democratic Transition: A Culturalist Critique and the Spanish Case.' *Theory and Society* 24.

Eisenstadt, S.N. (1981) 'The Axial Age: The Emergence of Transcendental Visions and the Rise of Clerics.' *European Journal of Sociology* 23: 293–313.

Elster, J. (1990) 'Marxism, Functionalism and Game Theory,' pp. 97–118 in S. Zukin and P. DiMaggio, eds, *Structures of Capital*. Cambridge: Cambridge University Press.

Engels, F. (1962 [1890]) 'Letter to Bloch,' pp. 448–90 in K. Marx and F. Engels, *Marx and Engels: Selected Writings II*. Moscow: International Publishers.

Entrikin, N. (1991) *The Betweenness of Place*. Baltimore: Johns Hopkins University Press.

Eribon, D. (1991) *Michel Foucault*. Cambridge, Mass.: Harvard University Press.

Erikson, E. (1950) *Childhood and Society*. New York. Norton.

Eyerman, R. and A. Jamison (1991) *Social Movements: A Cognitive Approach*. Cambridge: Polity Press.

Farr, R.M. and S. Moscovici, eds (1984) *Social Representation*. New York: Cambridge University Press; Paris: Editions de la Maison de Sciences de l'homme.

Ferry, L., and A. Renaut (1990) 'French Marxism.' *Society* 27 (5): 75–82.

Friedland, R., and D. Boden, eds (1993) *NowHere: Space, Time, and Modernity*. Berkeley and Los Angeles: University of California Press.

Frow, J. (1987) 'Accounting for Tastes: Some Problems in Bourdieu's Sociology of Culture.' *Cultural Studies* 1: 59–73.

Garfinkel, H. (1967) *Studies in Ethnomethodology*. Englewood Cliffs, New Jersey: Prentice Hall.

Garnham, N., and R. Williams (1980) 'Pierre Bourdieu and the Sociology of Culture: An Introduction.' *Media, Culture and Society* 2: 209–23.

Geertz, C. (1973) 'Ideology as a Cultural System,' pp. 193–233 in Geertz, *The Interpretation of Cultures*. New York: Basic Books.

Giddens, A. (1984) *The Constitution of Society*. London: Macmillan.

Goldmann, L. (1975 [1964]) *Toward a Sociology of the Novel*. London: Tavistock.

Goode, A. (1981) 'Prescription, Preference, and Practice: Marriage Patterns among the Kondaiyankottai Maravar of South India.' *Man* 16 (1): 108–29.

Gwertzman, B. and M.T. Kaufman, eds (1990) *The Collapse of Communism: By the Correspondents of 'The New York Times.'* New York: Random House.

Habermas, J. (1989 [1962]) *The Structural Transformation of the Public Sphere*. Boston: Beacon.

Habermas, J. (1992) 'Concluding Remarks,' pp. 462–79 in C. Calhoun, ed., *Habermas and the Public Sphere*. Boston: Beacon.

Hall, S. (1978) 'The Hinterland of Science: Ideology and the "Sociology of Science"'. pp. 9–32 in Hall, *On Ideology*. London: Hutchinson.

Halle, D. (1993) *Inside Culture: Art and Class in the American Home*. Chicago: University of Chicago Press.

Halsey, A.H., A.F. Heath, and J.M. Ridge (1980) *Origins and Destinations: Family, Class and Education in Modern Britain*. Oxford: Clarendon Press.

Honneth, A. (1986) 'The Fragmented World of Symbolic Forms. Reflections on Pierre Bourdieu's Sociology of Culture.' *Theory, Culture, and Society* 3: 55–66.

Hunt, L. (1984) *Politics, Culture, and Class in the French Revolution*. Berkeley and Los Angeles: University of California Press.

Jameson, F. (1980) *The Political Unconscious: Narrative as a Socially Symbolic Act*. Ithaca: Cornell University Press.

Jenkins, R. (1982) 'Pierre Bourdieu and the Reproduction of Determinism.' *Sociology* 16 (2): 271–81.
Jenkins, R. (1986) Review of Pierre Bourdieu, *Distinction. Sociology* 20 (1): 103–4.
Joly, R. (1965) *The Human Person in a Philosophy of Education.* Paris: Mouton.
Kane, A. (1991) 'Cultural Analysis in Historical Sociology: The Analytic and Concrete Forms of the Autonomy of Culture.' *Sociological Theory* 9 (1): 53–69.
Keniston, K. (1964) *The Uncommitted: Alienated Youth in American Society.* New York: Harcourt, Brace, and World.
Keniston, K. (1968) *Young Radicals: Notes on Uncommitted Youth.* New York: Harcourt, Brace, and World.
Keynes, J.M. (1965 [1936]) *General Theory of Employment, Interest, and Money.* London: Macmillan.
Klein, M. (1965) *Envy and Gratitude, and Other Works: 1946–63.* New York: Free Press.
Kohut, H. (1978) *The Search for the Self: Selected Writings of Heinz Kohut.* New York: International Universities Press.
Khosrokhavar, F. (1993) *L'Utopie sacrifiée: Sociologie de la révolution iranienne.* Paris: Presses de la Fondation Nationale des Sciences Politiques.
Lamont, M. (1992) *Money, Morals, and Manners: The Culture of the French and American Upper-Middle Class.* Chicago: University of Chicago Press.
LASA (Laboratoire de Sociologie anthropologique de l'université de Caen) (1992) 'Présentation.' *Cahiers du LASA/Lectures de Pierre Bourdieu* 12–13: 9–16.
Lévi-Strauss, C. (1969) *The Elementary Structures of Kinship.* London: Eyre & Spottiswoode.
Mauss, M. (1954 [1923–4]) *The Gift.* Glencoe, Ill.: Free Press.
Morris, C. (1946) *Signs, Language, and Behavior.* New York: Prentice Hall.
Moscovici, S. (1985) *The Age of the Crowd.* Cambridge: Cambridge University Press.
Moscovici, S., G. Mugny, and E. van Anermart, eds (1985) *Perspectives on Minority Influence.* Cambridge: Cambridge University Press.
Needham, R. (1972) 'Prescription.' *Oceania* 42: 166–81.
Panofsky, E. (1955) *Meaning in the Visual Arts.* New York: Doubleday.
Parsons, T., and E. Shils (1951) 'Values, Motives, and Systems of Action,' pp. 47–243 in Parsons and Shils, eds, *Towards a General Theory of Action.* Cambridge, Mass.: Harvard University Press.
Peirce, C. (1985) 'Logic as Semiotic: The Theory of Signs,' pp. 1–2 in R. Innis, ed., *Semiotics.* Bloomington: Indiana University Press.
Ringer, F. (1992) *Fields of Knowledge: French Academic Culture in Comparative Perspective.* Cambridge: Cambridge University Press.
Sahlins, M. (1972) *Stone Age Economics.* New York: Aldine.
Sahlins, M. (1976) *The Culture of Practical Reason.* Chicago: University of Chicago Press.
Sahlins, M. (1981) *Historical Metaphors and Mythical Realities: Structure in the Early History of the Sandwich Islands Kingdom.* Ann Arbor: University of Michigan Press.
Sartre, J.-P. (1963) *Search for a Method.* New York: Vintage.
Sartre, J.-P. (1976) *Critique of Dialectical Reason. Theory of Practial Ensembles.* London: New Left Books.
Schatzki, T.R. (1987) 'Overdue Analysis of Bourdieu's Theory of Practice.' *Inquiry* 30 (1–2): 113–26.
Schegloff, E.A. (1992) 'Repair After Next Turn: The Last Structurally Provided Defense of Intersubjectivity in Conversation.' *American Journal of Sociology* 97 (5): 1295–345.
Sewell, W. Jr. (1980) *Work and Revolution: The Language of Labor 1750–1848.* Cambridge and New York: Cambridge University Press.
Sherwood, S.J. (1994) 'Narrating the Social: Postmodernism and the Drama of Democracy,' *Journal of Narrative and Life History* 4(1/2): 69–88.
Taylor, C. (1989) *Sources of the Self: The Making of Modern Identity.* Cambridge, Mass.: Harvard University Press.

Taylor, C. (1993) 'To Follow a Rule . . . ,' pp. 35–44 in Calhoun et al., eds, *Bourdieu: Critical Perspectives*. Chicago: University of Chicago Press.

Terrail, J.-P. (1992) 'Les Vertus de la necessité: Sujet/objet en sociologie.' *Cahiers du LASA/Lectures de Pierre Bourdieu* 12–13: 221–62.

Touraine, A. (1994) *Qu'est-ce que la démocratie?* Paris: Fayard.

Touraine, A., F. Dubet and M. Wieviorka (1983) *Solidarity: The Analysis of a Social Movement, Poland 1980–81*. Cambridge: Cambridge University Press.

Turner, R. (1962) 'Role Taking: Process versus Conformity,' pp. 20–40 in A.M. Rose, ed., *Human Behavior and Social Processes*. Boston: Houghton Mifflin.

van den Berg, A. (1991) 'Review of Pierre Bourdieu, *The Logic of Practice*.' *Swedish Journal of Sociology*.

Walzer, M. (1983) *Spheres of Justice*. New York: Basic Books.

Weinstein, F., and G. Platt (1969) *The Wish to Be Free: Society, Psyche, and Value Change*. Berkeley: University of California Press.

Wieviorka, M. (1993) *La Démocratie à l'épreuve: Nationalisme, populisme, ethnicité*. Paris: Editions La Découverte.

Wittgenstein, L. (1969) *Philosophical Investigations*. New York: Macmillan. Third edition.

Index